First World War
and Army of Occupation
War Diary
France, Belgium and Germany

40 DIVISION
120 Infantry Brigade
Headquarters
13 April 1918 - 15 March 1919

WO95/2610/2

Published by

The Naval & Military Press Ltd

Unit 10 Ridgewood Industrial Park,

Uckfield, East Sussex,

TN22 5QE England

Tel: +44 (0) 1825 749494

www.naval-military-press.com

www.nmarchive.com

This diary has been reprinted in facsimile from the original. Any imperfections are inevitably reproduced and the quality may fall short of modern type and cartographic standards.

© **Crown Copyright**
Images reproduced by permission of The National Archives, London, England, 2015.

Contents

Document type	Place/Title	Date From	Date To
Heading	Signals June 1918-March 1919		
Heading	Subject. War Diary Of Head Quarters 120 Inf Bde For September 1918		
Miscellaneous	Headquarters, 120th Infantry Brigade	14/06/1918	14/06/1918
Miscellaneous	120th Inf. Bde. No. 120/415. 10th Garr. Bn. K.O.S.B.	15/06/1918	15/06/1918
Miscellaneous	Headquarters, 40th Division	21/06/1918	21/06/1918
Miscellaneous	120th Infantry Brigade	22/06/1918	22/06/1918
Miscellaneous	120th Infy Bde	22/06/1918	22/06/1918
Miscellaneous	120th Infy. Bde. No. 120/438. 10th. Gar. Bn. K.O. Sco. Bordrs.	18/06/1918	18/06/1918
Miscellaneous	Light Trench Mortar Batteries.	15/06/1918	15/06/1918
Miscellaneous	120th Infantry Brigade Warning Order No. 199	22/06/1918	22/06/1918
Miscellaneous	120th Infantry Brigade Order No. 200	22/06/1918	22/06/1918
Miscellaneous	Table To Accompany 120th Infantry Brigade Order No. 200		
Miscellaneous	Administrative Instructions-Move 23rd June 1918.	22/06/1918	22/06/1918
Miscellaneous	120th Inf. Bde. No. 120/415. 10th Garr. Bn. K.O.S.B.	01/07/1918	01/07/1918
Map			
Miscellaneous	40th Division	07/07/1918	07/07/1918
Miscellaneous	120th Inf. Bde. No. 120/415/1. 10th Garr. Bn. K.O.S.B.	10/07/1918	10/07/1918
Miscellaneous	A A 25 of 13.4.18		
Miscellaneous	120th Inf. Bde. No. 120/401. 10th Garr. Bn. K.O.S.B.	12/07/1918	12/07/1918
Miscellaneous	Orders Regarding Firing At Aircraft From The Ground At Night.	13/04/1918	13/04/1918
Miscellaneous	40th Division. Orders Regarding Firing At Aircraft From The Ground At Night.	31/07/1918	31/07/1918
Miscellaneous	Second Army G. T. 991. XV Corps. No. 593/18 G.	15/07/1918	15/07/1918
Miscellaneous	O.C. 11th Com. Hus. For Information	17/07/1918	17/07/1918
Operation(al) Order(s)	120th Infantry Brigade Order No. 206	18/07/1918	18/07/1918
Operation(al) Order(s)	120th Infantry Brigade No. 120/423. 10th K.O.S.B.	06/08/1918	06/08/1918
Miscellaneous	120th Infantry Brigade No. 120/406. 10th K.O.S.B.	10/08/1918	10/08/1918
Miscellaneous	1st Australian Division.	05/08/1918	05/08/1918
Miscellaneous	120th Inf. Bde. No. 120/401. 10th K.O.S.B.	06/08/1918	06/08/1918
Miscellaneous	Noted Returned	07/08/1918	07/08/1918
Miscellaneous	2nd Li Lyon	07/08/1918	07/08/1918
Miscellaneous	120th Inf. Bde. No. 120/415. 10th Bn. K.O.S.B.	29/07/1918	29/07/1918
Miscellaneous	XV Corps Anti-Gas Instructions.	23/07/1918	23/07/1918
Miscellaneous	Amendment To XV Corps Anti-Gas Instructions.	21/08/1918	21/08/1918
Miscellaneous	120th Infantry Brigade No. 120/477. 10th K.O.S.B.	10/08/1918	10/08/1918
Miscellaneous	92 Bd Buzo	19/08/1918	19/08/1918
Miscellaneous	40th Div. No. 53/44 G. Station Code Calls, 40th Division (6th Series).		
Operation(al) Order(s)	120th Infantry Brigade Order No. 207.	10/08/1918	10/08/1918
Miscellaneous	March Table To Accompany 120th Inf. Brigade Order No. 207.		
Miscellaneous	120th Infantry Brigade Administrative Order No. 207	10/08/1918	10/08/1918
Operation(al) Order(s)	121st Infantry Brigade Order No. 37	12/08/1918	12/08/1918
Miscellaneous	Headquarters, 120th Infantry Brigade.	10/08/1918	10/08/1918
Operation(al) Order(s)	120th Infantry Brigade Order No. 208	10/08/1918	10/08/1918

Type	Description	Date	Date
Miscellaneous	Relief Table To Accompany 120th Inf. Bde. Order No. 208		
Miscellaneous	120th Inf. Bde. No. 120/416 10th Bn. K.O.S.B.	13/08/1918	13/08/1918
Miscellaneous	120th Infantry Brigade No. 120/406. 15th K.O.Y.L.I.	13/08/1918	13/08/1918
Miscellaneous	120th Inf. Bde. No. 120/415. 120th Infantry Brigade Defence Orders	13/08/1918	13/08/1918
Miscellaneous	Anti-Aircraft Defence. Appendix II.		
Miscellaneous	120th Infantry Brigade Defence Orders.	14/08/1918	14/08/1918
Miscellaneous	31st Division.	14/08/1918	14/08/1918
Miscellaneous	120th Infantry Brigade No. 120/427. 10th K.O.S.B.	14/08/1918	14/08/1918
Miscellaneous	120th Infantry Brigade No. 120/429. 15th K.O.Y.L.I.	14/08/1918	14/08/1918
Miscellaneous	120th Infy Bde No. 120/400. 10th K.O.S.B.	13/08/1918	13/08/1918
Miscellaneous	40th Div. No. 136/2 G. 119th Infantry Brigade.	11/08/1918	11/08/1918
Miscellaneous	Training Of Officers For The Staff.		
Miscellaneous	120th Infantry Brigade	15/08/1918	15/08/1918
Operation(al) Order(s)	120th Infantry Brigade Order No. 209	15/08/1918	15/08/1918
Miscellaneous	Administrative Instructions For La Motte Area	15/08/1918	15/08/1918
Miscellaneous	120th Inf. Bde.	15/08/1918	15/08/1918
Miscellaneous	120th Infy. Bde. No. 120/400. 10th K.O.S.B.	14/08/1918	14/08/1918
Miscellaneous	120th Inf. Bde. No. 120/406. 11th Cameron Hrs.	17/08/1918	17/08/1918
Miscellaneous	120th Infantry Brigade No. 120/406. 11th Cameron Hrs.	17/08/1918	17/08/1918
Miscellaneous	120th Inf. Bde.	15/08/1918	15/08/1918
Miscellaneous	120th Inf. Bde.	18/08/1918	18/08/1918
Miscellaneous	120th Infantry Brigade No. 120/426. 10th K.O.S.B.	20/08/1918	20/08/1918
Operation(al) Order(s)	120th Infantry Brigade Order No. 210	20/08/1918	20/08/1918
Operation(al) Order(s)	120th Infantry Brigade Order No. 212	21/08/1918	21/08/1918
Miscellaneous	Administrative Instructions No. 213. Right Brigade.	23/08/1918	23/08/1918
Miscellaneous	O.C., 10 K.O.S.B.	21/08/1918	21/08/1918
Operation(al) Order(s)	120th Infantry Brigade Order No. 214	22/08/1918	22/08/1918
Miscellaneous	120th Infy. Bde. No. 120/474. 10th K.O.S.B.	23/08/1918	23/08/1918
Miscellaneous	40th Division No. C/136/Q.	23/08/1918	23/08/1918
Miscellaneous	O.C. 11th Cam. Ingh	24/08/1918	24/08/1918
Miscellaneous	Headquarters, XV Corps. "Q".	19/08/1918	19/08/1918
Miscellaneous			
Miscellaneous	Winter Accommodation-1918-1919.		
Miscellaneous	Transport Lines.		
Operation(al) Order(s)	120th Infantry Brigade Order No. 215	23/08/1918	23/08/1918
Miscellaneous	40th Division.	23/08/1918	23/08/1918
Miscellaneous	31st Division, etc. etc.	05/08/1918	05/08/1918
Miscellaneous	120th Infantry Brigade No. 120/426. 15th K.O.Y.L.I.	27/08/1918	27/08/1918
Miscellaneous	120th Infantry Brigade Administrative Instructions.	29/08/1918	29/08/1918
Miscellaneous			
Miscellaneous	40th Division.	29/08/1918	29/08/1918
Miscellaneous	120th Inf. Bde. No. 120/474 11th Bn. Cam. Highrs.	04/09/1918	04/09/1918
Miscellaneous	XV Corps.	05/09/1918	05/09/1918
Miscellaneous	40th Div. No. 137/4 (G). 120th Inf. Bde.	05/09/1918	05/09/1918
Miscellaneous	Armies.	09/09/1918	09/09/1918
Miscellaneous	Infantry Battalion.		
Miscellaneous	Headquarters, XV Corps.	07/09/1918	07/09/1918
Miscellaneous	120th Inf. Bde. No. 120/477. 10th K.O.S.B.	09/09/1918	09/09/1918
Miscellaneous	10 Inf. Bde. No 120/ 10th K.O.S.B.	18/09/1918	18/09/1918
Miscellaneous	New Years Honours Despatch-1919.	17/09/1918	17/09/1918
Miscellaneous	Appendix "A" to 40th Division No. C/117/A. dated 17-9-18. Extract From Letter To War Office.	10/09/1918	10/09/1918
Miscellaneous	New Year's Honours Despatch-1919. Addendum No. 1 to Instructions dated 17th September, 1918.	18/09/1918	18/09/1918

Type	Description	Date	Date
Miscellaneous	120th Inf. Bde. No. 120/420. 10th Bn. K.O.S.B.	19/09/1918	19/09/1918
Miscellaneous	New Year's Honours Despatch-1919. Addendum No. 2 to Instructions dated 17th September, 1918.	18/09/1918	18/09/1918
Miscellaneous	120th Inf. Bde. No. 120/420/1. 10th Bn. K.O.S.B.	19/09/1918	19/09/1918
Miscellaneous	New Year's Honours Despatch-1919. Addendum No. 4 to Instructions dated 17th September, 1918.	20/09/1918	20/09/1918
Miscellaneous	120 Inf. Bde. No. 120/420. 10th K.O.S.B.	20/09/1918	20/09/1918
Miscellaneous	New Year's Honours Despatch-1919. Addendum No. 4 to Instructions dated 17th September, 1918.	23/09/1918	23/09/1918
Miscellaneous	120th Inf. Bde. No. 120/438/1. 10th K.O.S.B.	14/09/1918	14/09/1918
Miscellaneous	120th Inf. Bde. No. 120/420. O.C., 11th Bn. Cam. Highrs.	30/09/1918	30/09/1918
Operation(al) Order(s)	120th Infantry Brigade Order No. 224	30/09/1918	30/09/1918
Miscellaneous	Second Army.	11/09/1918	11/09/1918
Miscellaneous	Relief Table To Accompany 120th Infantry Brigade Order No. 224		
Miscellaneous	120th Infantry Brigade Instructions No. 1.	05/10/1918	05/10/1918
Operation(al) Order(s)	120th Infantry Brigade Order No. 225.	05/10/1918	05/10/1918
Miscellaneous	Relief Table To Accompany 120th Infantry Brigade Order No. 225 dated 5-10-18.	05/10/1918	05/10/1918
Operation(al) Order(s)	120th Infantry Brigade Order No. 227	11/10/1918	11/10/1918
Miscellaneous	120th Inf. Bde. No. 120/426/1. O.C., 11th Bn. Cam. Highrs.	11/10/1918	11/10/1918
Miscellaneous	C Form. Messages And Signals.	07/10/1918	07/10/1918
Miscellaneous	C Form. Messages And Signals.	06/10/1918	06/10/1918
Miscellaneous	C Form. Messages And Signals.	05/10/1918	05/10/1918
Miscellaneous	120th Inf. Bde. No. 120/426. 10th Bn. K.O.S.B.	11/10/1918	11/10/1918
Miscellaneous	120th Inf. Bde. No. 120/406. 11th Bn. Cam. Highrs.	10/10/1918	10/10/1918
Miscellaneous	Headquarters, 120th Infantry Brigade.	08/10/1918	08/10/1918
Miscellaneous	Second Army	28/09/1918	28/09/1918
Miscellaneous	120th Infantry Brigade Instructions No. 2	07/10/1918	07/10/1918
Miscellaneous	120th Inf. Bde. No. 120/418. 10th K.O.S.B.	29/10/1918	29/10/1918
Miscellaneous	XV Corps Anti-Gas Instructions	26/10/1918	26/10/1918
Miscellaneous	120th Inf. Bde. No. 120/426 10th K.O.S.B.	31/10/1918	31/10/1918
Miscellaneous	40th Division No. 169 (Q)	24/10/1918	24/10/1918
Miscellaneous	Second Army.	19/10/1918	19/10/1918
Miscellaneous	Administrative Instructions For Relief Of 120th Infantry Brigade by 121st Infantry Brigade.		
Operation(al) Order(s)	120th Infantry Brigade Order No. 228	12/10/1918	12/10/1918
Miscellaneous	Relief Table To Accompany 120th Infantry Brigade Order No 228 dated 12-10-18.	12/10/1918	12/10/1918
Operation(al) Order(s)	120th Infantry Brigade Order No. 226	08/10/1918	08/10/1918
Miscellaneous	Headquarters, 120th Infantry Brigade.	29/01/1919	29/01/1919
Miscellaneous	120th Inf. Bde. No. 120/407. O.C. 11th. Cameron Highrs.	08/03/1919	08/03/1919
Miscellaneous	XV Corps School. Report on officers attending Infantry Course 10/2/19 to 3/3/19.		
Miscellaneous	120th Infantry Brigade.	31/01/1919	31/01/1919
Miscellaneous	120th Inf. Bde. No. 120/401. 10th Bn. K.O.S.B.	06/02/1919	06/02/1919
Miscellaneous	Not To Be Taken In Front Of Brigade Headquarters.		
Miscellaneous	Scale Of Issue.		
Miscellaneous	120th Inf. Bde. No. 120/429. 10th Bn. K.O.S.B.	08/03/1919	08/03/1919
Miscellaneous	Not To Be Taken In Front Of Brigade Headquarters.		
Miscellaneous	Scale Of Issue.		
Miscellaneous	Bde. 1919 Div		
Miscellaneous	O.B./1831/A	02/07/1918	02/07/1918

Miscellaneous	120th Infantry Brigade Warning Order.	08/07/1918	08/07/1918
Miscellaneous	40th Division.	05/07/1918	05/07/1918
Miscellaneous	Headquarters, "G" 31st Division.	01/07/1918	01/07/1918
Miscellaneous	Notes On Conference.	29/06/1918	29/06/1918
Miscellaneous	O.C. 11th G.Bn Cam. Hrs	30/06/1918	30/06/1918
Miscellaneous	Hd. Qrs. 40th. Divn. No. 858 (A).	27/06/1918	27/06/1918
Miscellaneous	40th Division No. 835 (A)	22/06/1918	22/06/1918
Miscellaneous	11th Gar. Bn. Cameron Highrs	22/06/1918	22/06/1918
Miscellaneous	40th Division. Prevention Of Trench Foot	20/06/1918	20/06/1918
Miscellaneous	40th Div. No. 19/12 (G). H.Q., 119th Inf. Bde.	21/06/1918	21/06/1918
Miscellaneous	40th Division No. 843 (A).	18/06/1918	18/06/1918
Miscellaneous	11th Gar. Bn. Cameron Highrs For information	19/06/1918	19/06/1918
Miscellaneous	H.Q., 40th Division No. 835/A/21.	18/06/1918	18/06/1918
Miscellaneous	11th Gar. Bn. Cameron Highrs	19/06/1918	19/06/1918
Miscellaneous	40th Div. No. 19/9 (G). Second Army.	13/06/1918	13/06/1918
Miscellaneous	119th Infantry Brigade.	15/06/1918	15/06/1918
Miscellaneous	40th Division No. 835/10 (Q)	15/06/1918	15/06/1918
Miscellaneous	11th Garr. Bn. Cameron Highrs	15/06/1918	15/06/1918
Miscellaneous	40th Division No. 835 (A).	11/06/1918	11/06/1918
Miscellaneous	O.C. No. 6 Garr. Battn.	11/06/1918	11/06/1918
Miscellaneous	40th Division No. 835/15 (A).	15/06/1918	15/06/1918
Miscellaneous	11th Garr. Bn. Cameron Highrs	15/06/1918	15/06/1918
Miscellaneous	VII Corps.	11/06/1918	11/06/1918
Miscellaneous	34th Division.	12/06/1918	12/06/1918
Miscellaneous	Headquarters, 40th Division.	28/06/1918	28/06/1918
Miscellaneous	40th Division.	01/07/1918	01/07/1918
Miscellaneous	40th Division.	07/07/1918	07/07/1918
Miscellaneous	Headquarters, Second Army.	03/07/1918	03/07/1918
Miscellaneous	Second Army No. G.T. 887, dated 10th July, 1918. XVCorps No. 593/15 G. dated 11/7/1918.	12/07/1918	12/07/1918
Miscellaneous	40th Div. No. 10/32/1 G. 119th Inf.Bde. Div. Sig. Co.	07/08/1918	07/08/1918
Miscellaneous	40th Division.	02/08/1918	02/08/1918
Miscellaneous	Ref. Map Sheet 36 A.	02/08/1918	02/08/1918
Miscellaneous	11th Carr. Hrs.	02/08/1918	02/08/1918
Miscellaneous	40th Division No. 844 (Q)	29/07/1918	29/07/1918
Miscellaneous	11th Bn. Cam. Highrs	30/07/1918	30/07/1918
Miscellaneous	XV Corps.	21/07/1918	21/07/1918
Miscellaneous	XV Corps.	13/07/1918	13/07/1918
Miscellaneous	40th Division.	08/08/1918	08/08/1918
Miscellaneous	Second Army	12/05/1918	12/05/1918
Miscellaneous	Second Army	08/08/1918	08/08/1918
Miscellaneous	To O.C. A. Coy.		
Miscellaneous	M.Q., 48th Division No. G/144/A	12/08/1918	12/08/1918
Miscellaneous	Anti-Gas Instructions. Appendix III.		
Miscellaneous	Administrative Arrangements-40th Division in connection with XV Corps Defence Scheme-Administrative Arrangements.	14/08/1918	14/08/1918
Miscellaneous	40th Division No. G/18/A.	01/08/1918	01/08/1918
Miscellaneous	40th Division No. 169 (Q)	23/08/1918	23/08/1918
Miscellaneous	Winter Accommodation.	20/08/1918	20/08/1918
Miscellaneous	XV Corps Anti-Gas Instructions.	21/07/1918	21/07/1918
Miscellaneous	40th Div. No. 10/51. (G). 119th Inf. Bde.	03/09/1918	03/09/1918
Miscellaneous	120th Inf. Bde. No. 120/418. 10th K.O.S.B.		
Miscellaneous	40th Div. No. 10/34 (G). 119th Inf. Bde.	08/09/1918	08/09/1918
Miscellaneous	120th Inf Bde. No 120/418	09/09/1918	09/09/1918
Miscellaneous	Amendments To XV Corps Anti-Gas Instructions.	21/09/1918	21/09/1918

Miscellaneous	120th Infantry Brigade No. 120/418. 10th K.O.S.B.	22/09/1918	22/09/1918
Miscellaneous	40th Division No. 23 (A).	06/09/1918	06/09/1918
Miscellaneous	All Divisions.	19/04/1918	19/04/1918
Miscellaneous	29th Division.	06/09/1918	06/09/1918
Miscellaneous	Amendment No. 1 To 40th Division Administrative Instructions No. 1, Dated 8th September, 1918.	10/09/1918	10/09/1918
Miscellaneous	40th Div. No. 10/61 (G). 119th Inf. Bde. C.R.E.	18/09/1918	18/09/1918
Miscellaneous	XV Corps.	13/09/1918	13/09/1918
Miscellaneous	120th Infantry Bde. No. 120/418. 10th K.O.S.B.	15/09/1918	15/09/1918
Miscellaneous	120th Inf. Bde. No. 120/400. 10th Bn. K.O.S.B.	16/09/1918	16/09/1918
Miscellaneous	40th Division No. 483 (A).	15/09/1918	15/09/1918
Miscellaneous	119th Inf. Bde.	03/10/1918	03/10/1918
Miscellaneous	Second Army	29/09/1918	29/09/1918
Miscellaneous	119th Infantry Bde.	01/10/1918	01/10/1918
Miscellaneous	XV Corps.	24/08/1918	24/08/1918
Miscellaneous	Second Army	01/08/1918	01/08/1918
Miscellaneous	Administrative Instructions.	01/10/1918	01/10/1918
Miscellaneous	O/C 11th Bn Cameron Highlanders	02/10/1918	02/10/1918
Miscellaneous	Gas Zones.	03/10/1918	03/10/1918
Miscellaneous	Second Army	23/10/1918	23/10/1918
Miscellaneous	40th Division. Administrative Instructions, No. 6.	21/10/1918	21/10/1918
Miscellaneous	40th Division No. S/136/Q/5	12/10/1918	12/10/1918
Miscellaneous	O/C 11th Bn Cameron Highlanders	12/10/1918	12/10/1918
Miscellaneous	Reference 40th Divn 'G' Instructions No. 6 dated 5.10.18.	05/10/1918	05/10/1918
Miscellaneous	O/C 11th Bn Cameron Highlanders		
Miscellaneous	Hd. Qrs 40th Divn. No. S/146/Q/5	10/10/1918	10/10/1918
Miscellaneous	O/C. 11th Bn Cameron Highlanders	10/10/1918	10/10/1918
Miscellaneous	40th Division. Amendment No. 1 to Administrative Instructions No. 6. dated 21/10/1918.	23/10/1918	23/10/1918
Miscellaneous	O/C 11th Bn Cameron. Highrs	23/10/1918	23/10/1918
Miscellaneous	40th Division.	20/10/1918	20/10/1918
Miscellaneous	O.C. 11th Cam. Hrs.	21/10/1918	21/10/1918
Miscellaneous	40th Division.	18/01/1919	18/01/1919
Miscellaneous	40th Division No. D/30/A	15/01/1919	15/01/1919
Miscellaneous	40th Division No. 1001 (A)	12/01/1919	12/01/1919
Miscellaneous	120th Inf. Bde. No. 120/474. 10th K.O.S.B.	13/01/1919	13/01/1919
Miscellaneous	40th Division No. D. 10/A	28/01/1919	28/01/1919
Miscellaneous	To O/C A Coy.	22/01/1919	22/01/1919
Miscellaneous	Headquarters XV Corps. Summary "Q" Branch. (442)	28/02/1919	28/02/1919
Miscellaneous	XV Corps No. A.C. 47/159	04/02/1919	04/02/1919
Miscellaneous	40th Division No. 84 (A)	15/03/1919	15/03/1919
Miscellaneous	B & D Co.		
Miscellaneous	40th Division No. 84 (A)	15/03/1919	15/03/1919
Miscellaneous	Order Of Battle O.C. II Com High	27/01/1919	27/01/1919
Miscellaneous	Divisional Artillery		
Miscellaneous	Order Of Battle 40th Divisional Headquarters.		
Miscellaneous	121st Infantry Brigade.		
Miscellaneous	Units-119th Infantry Brigade.		
Miscellaneous	Medical Units		

SIGNALS   JUNE 1918 - MARCH 1919.

SUBJECT.

War Diary
of
Head Quarters
120 Inf Bde
for
September 1918

CONFIDENTIAL. 40th Division No. 835.Q. 75
              120th Infy. Bde. No. 120/412.

Headquarters,
    120th Infantry Brigade.
    ----

1.   It is most important that Garrison Battalions
should not retain any unauthorised equipment or
stores. It is requested therefore that you will take
energetic measures to cause all surplus personal
equipment and Battalion Stores to be returned at once
to D.A.D.O.S., 40th Division for disposal.

2.   Pending a ruling being received from higher
authority the blankets now in possession of Garrison
Battalions will be retained.

                        (Sgd) A.L.COWTAN, Major,

13th June 1918.   for D.A.Q.M.G., 40th Division.

                    * 2 *.
    11th Garr. Bn. Cameron Highrs.
    13th Garr. Bn. R. Innis Fusrs.
    13th Garr. Bn. E. Lancs Regt.
    10th Barr. Bn. K.O. Sco. Bordrs.
    15th Garr. Bn. K.O.Y.L.I.
    12th Garr. Bn. N. Staffs Regt.

        Forwarded in continuation of this office No.
    120/475 dated 12th June.

                                        Captain,
                                    Staff Captain,
                              120th Infantry Brigade.

14th June 1918.

120th Inf. Bde. No. 120/415.   SECRET.

10th Garr. Bn. K.O.S.B.
15th Garr. Bn. K.O.Y.L.I.
11th Garr. Bn. Cameron Hdrs.
****

With reference to 120th Inf. Bde. Order No. 197: Battalions will be prepared to act on this order at short notice.

Reconnaissances of the line will be carried out to-morrow, 16th inst. Two busses will be at Brigade Headquarters at 8 a.m. to convey 8 officers and 8 N.C.Os. per battalion to the vicinity of the trench system to make the reconnaissance.
After picking up Officers and N.C.Os. of 11th Camerons at Bde. H.Q., busses will proceed to BUYSCHEURE to pick up representatives of the other two battalions.

Battalions will make a general reconnaissance of the whole Brigade Front, as well as a more detailed one of their own particular section.

15:6:18.

Captain,
Brigade Major,
120th Infantry Brigade.

CONFIDENTIAL.

A.G., G.H.Q. No. A.G.833(M).
40th Divn. No. 850(A).
120th Infy. Bde. No. 120/475.

Headquarters,
    40th Division.
----

1.   Will you please submit in duplicate statement by Battalions shewing the present shortage in detail of the various specialists, both officers and other ranks.

2.   As it is possible that certain of the personnel of the following battalions may be unfit for the duties which they may be called upon to perform, arrangements will be made to have them inspected by the Medical Officer of Drafts.
        Orders will be issued from this office as regards the disposal of such as are found unfit.

            X   X   X   X   X
                11th Garrison Battalion Cmeron Highlanders.
                15th Garrison Battalion K.O.Y.L.I.
                10th Garrison Battalion K.O. Sco Bordrs.
            X   X   X   X   X

G.H.Q.,   (Sd) J.WHITEHEAD, Lt.Col.,
1st Echelon,   A.A.G. for
18/6/18.   Adjutant General.

                            * 2 *

Headquarters,
10th Gar. Bn. K.O. Sco. Bordrs.
15th Gar. Bn. K.O.Y.L.I.
11th Gra Bn. Cameron Highrs.
    ----

1.   Forwarded.

        The statement required by para. 1 of Minute 1 will be forwarded to these Headquarters in detail on 23rd June by 10 am.
        Single copy only required.

2.   Further instructions will be issued regarding the visit of the Medical Inspector of Drafts.

                                            Lieut.,
                                        A/Staff Captain,
                                    120th Infantry Brigade.

21.6.1918.

120th Infantry Brigade.

Reference your No 120/475
I have to report that this unit
is short of the following specialists

Signallers
1 officer   18 other ranks

Armourers
1 NCO

Pioneers
1 Saddler

Pipers
1 Sgt Piper 5 pipers

Drummers
15.

11th Garr. Bn Cameron High Lt Col.

22/6/18

120th Infy Bde

Your Order No 200
has been received

Lt Col.
11th Cameron Highrs

22/6/18

120th Infy. Bde. No. 120/436.

10th Gar. Bn. K.O. Sco. Bordrs.
15th Gar. Bn. K.O.Y.L.I.
11th Gar. Bn. Cameron Highrs. ✓

Reference attached.

1. A Light Trench Mortar Battery will be formed at once.

2. As it appears that there are very few officers and other ranks trained in the handling of the Stokes Mortars it will be necessary to obtain untrained personnel to complete the establishment.

3. Each battalion will therefore forward to this office by 19th June the following nominal rolls. In the case of the officers and qualifications or experience should be stated.
   (a) One officer not above the rank of Captain recommended for command of the Battery.
   (b) One subaltern recommended for duty with the battery.
   (c) One sergeant, three corporals and twelve o.rs.

4. All trained personnel are to be included in these rolls and their names are to be starred.

5. In selecting the remaining personnel care must be taken that the officers and other ranks are keen, intelligent and have good hearing. As far as possible volunteers, provided they have these qualifications, should be taken.

                                          Lieut.,
                                     A/Staff Captain,
18th June 1918.   120th Infantry Brigade.

SECRET

40th Division No. 835/14/A.

LIGHT TRENCH MORTAR BATTERIES.

1. Each Brigade will form a Light Trench Mortar Battery from the personnel of the Garrison Battalions now forming each Brigade.

2. Establishment of each Battery :-

   1 Captain,
   3 Subalterns,
   2 Sergeants,   2 bicycles.
   8 Corporals,
   32 Privates,
   4 Servants,
   ___
   50
   ===

3. Suitable personnel will be selected as early as possible and Headquarters, 40th Division will be informed of the date upon which each Battery comes into existence as a Unit.

4. "G" Branch 40th Division are notifying Brigades of the arrangements being made to train the personnel of these Light Trench Mortar Batteries.

5. Officers employed with these batteries will be struck off the strength of their Battalions from the date of the formation of the Battery. Their names will be reported to Divisional Head Quarters for transmission to A.G., G.H.Q., and will be reported to D.A.G., 3rd Echelon, in the Army Form B.213 of the Unit concerned.

6. N.C.O's and men will be held in excess of the authorized establishment of their Battalions and personnel to replace will be demanded in the normal way on Army Form B.213. Full particulars of N.C.O's and men detached to Light Trench Mortar Batteries will be reported to the D.A.G., 3rd Echelon, in the Army Form B.213 of the Unit concerned.

7. D.A.D.O.S., 40th Division, will indent for complete Mobilization equipment for these Batteries.

8. Light Trench Mortar Batteries will bear the number of their Infantry Brigade e.g., the Light Trench Mortar Battery of 119th Infantry Brigade will be called 119th Trench Mortar Battery.

A. L. Crotan.
Major,
D.A.A.G., 40th Division.

15th June, 1916.

(JM)

Distribution :- 119th, 120th, 121st Infantry Brigades.
40th Divisional Train,
D.A.D.O.S., 40th Division.
All branches 40th Divisional Headquarters,

D.A.G., 3rd Echelon,)
H.Q., Second Army "A")   for information.
H.Q., VII Corps,   )

SECRET.   Copy.No....

120TH INFANTRY BRIGADE WARNING ORDER No.199.
****

Map
Hazebrouck 1/100,000
Sheet 27/ 1/40,000   22-6-18.

    The 120th Infantry Brigade, less transport, will move on 23rd instant by Busses or Lorries from LEDERZEELE Cross Roads G.28.a.0.3. to LA BELLE HOTESSE. *(sh 36ᵃ NW. C 22)*

    Brigade Headquarters will be established at C.22.c.4.4.

    Units of the Brigade will be accommodated under canvas in C.14, 21 and 22.

    Transport will move by road to the Camp.

ACKNOWLEDGE.

                                                        Captain,
Issued through Signals   A/Brigade Major,
   at 10-30 a.m.   120th Infantry Brigade.

10th Garr. Bn. K.O.S.Bs.
15th Garr. Bn. K.O.Y.L.I.
11th Garr. Bn. Cam. Highrs.
120th T. M. Battery.
Bde. Supply Officer.

SECRET.   COPY NO. 8
               120TH INFANTRY BRIGADE ORDER NO. 200.
               ✳✳✳✳✳✳✳✳✳✳✳✳✳✳✳✳✳✳✳✳✳✳✳✳✳✳✳✳✳

Maps. HAZEBROUCK.
                                                                       22-6-18.
Sheet 27   1/40,000
  "   36A 1/40,000
  ----

1.   120th Infantry Brigade Group will move by bus in
     accordance with attached table from LEDERZEELE AREA
     to Area WEST of LA BELLE HOTESSE to-morrow, 23rd inst.

2.   1st Line Transport will be Brigaded under Captain
     TRITTON, Transport Officer, 14th Garr. Bn. K.O.S.Bs.,
     and will move to new area in following order :-

          120th Brigade Headquarters (including Signal Section)
          10th Garr. Bn. K.O.S.Bs.
          15th Garr. Bn. K.O.Y.L.I.
          11th Garr. Bn. Cameron Highlanders.
          12th Yorks Regt. (Pnrs)

     ROUTE.   OOST HOUCK - M.12. - COIN BERGU - Cross Roads
              N.33.b. - T.11.a. - EBBLINGHAM - LYNDE.
     Roads to be reconnoitred by Brigade Transport Officer
     Head of column to pass starting point (OOST HOUCK
     CHURCH) at 9-30 a.m.   Battalions will arrange to have
     guides for transport at LYNDE CHURCH.

3.   No. 3 Coy. 40th Divnl. Train will move by march route
     to new Area under their own arrangements.

4.   Brigade Headquarters will close at LEDERZEELE at
     9-30 a.m. and will re-open at LA BELLE HOTESSE,
     C.22.c.6.1. on arrival.

5.   ACKNOWLEDGE.

                                             H B K___
                                                   Captain,
                                               A/Brigade Major,
Issued through Signals   120th Infantry Brigade.
     at 10 p.m.

          Copy No. 1 ... G.O.C.
                   2 ... Brigade Major,
                   3 ... Staff Captain,
                   4 ... War Diary.
                   5 ... File.
                   6 ... 10th Garr. Bn. K.O.S.Bs.
                   7 ... 15th Garr. Bn. K.O.Y.L.I.
                   8 ... 11th Garr. Bn. Cam. Highrs.
                   9 ... 12th Yorks Rgt. (Pnrs)
                  10 ... 120th T. M. Bty.
                  11 ... No. 3 Coy. Div. Train.
                  12 ... Bde. Supply Officer
                  13 ... 40th Divn. "G"
                  14 ... 40th Divn. "Q"
                  15 ... 119th Inf. Bde.
                  16 ... 121st Inf. Bde.
                  17 ... A.P.M., 40th Divn.
                  18 ... Bde. Signals.
                  19 ... Captn. TRITTON, K.O.S.Bs.

TABLE TO ACCOMPANY 120TH INFANTRY BRIGADE ORDER No.200.

Serial No.	UNIT.	LOCATION.	ROUTE TO EMBUSSING POINT.	BUSSES ALLOTTED.	REMARKS.
1.	120th Bde. Hd.Qrs.	LEDERZEELE.	LEDERZEELE - ST MOMELIN ROAD.	Two Busses of First Group.	
2.	10th G.Bn. K.O.S.Bs.	BUSSYCHEURE.	G.35. G.34. G.33.	CENTRAL Group.	
3.	15th G.Bn. K.O.Y.L.I.	- do -	- - do - -	FIRST Group less 4 Busses.	To follow Serial No. 2 from BUSSYCHEURE.
4.	120th T. M. Battery.	- do -	- - do - -	Two Busses of FIRST Group.	To follow serial No. 3 from BUSSYCHEURE.
5.	11th G.Bn. Cam. Highrs.	CROMB STRAETE - LEDERZEELE ROAD.	CROME STRAETE - LEDERZEELE CROSS ROADS.	LAST Group less two Busses.	
6.	12th Yorks Rgt. (Pnrs)	LES CINQ RUES (E.25.c.)	LEDERZEELE - ERKELSBRUGGE ROAD.	Two Busses of LAST Group.	

A. EMBUSSING POINT. ... ST MOMELIN - LEDERZEELE ROAD, Head of Column facing S.W. at G.33.c.

B. TIME OF EMBUSSING. ... 8 a.m.

C. ROUTE FOR LORRIES. ... ST MOMELIN - OWERSTEL - SERQUES - TILQUES - X.4. - X.10. - ARQUES - CAMPAGNE - B.23.d. - BLARINGHEM.

D. DEBUSSING POINT. ... EAST of BLARINGHEM from E.23.b. to C.13.d.

E. One Officer per Unit will report to Brigade Headquarters at 7-30 a.m. to-morrow for instructions regarding the embussing of his Unit. Units will not enter main LEDERZEELE - ST MOMELIN ROAD until Embussing Officer has reported to Commanding Officers concerned.

Administrative Instructions - Dove 23rd June 1918.

To accompany 120th Brigade Order No.199.

1.   Accommodation.   Units of the Brigade will be accommodated in tented camps and available billets as follows :-

    Brigade Headquarters   .....   Billet No.5. C.22.c.4.4.
    10th K.O. Sco. Bordrs.   .....   C.21.a.2.0.
    15th K.O.Y.L.I.   .....   C.14.d.5.0.
    11th Cam. Highrs.   .....   C.14.d.0.8.
    12th Yorks (P) Regt.   .....   (With Cam. Highrs) C.14.d.0.8.
    120th T.M.Batty. (with 15th K.O.Y.L.I). .. C.14.d.5.0.
    No.5 Coy., A.S.C. Train.   .....   C.14.c.4.7.

A number of tents and shelters will be dumped at C.13.b.8.8 at 11 am. on 23rd June 1918.

Units will arrange to have a representative at the dump at 11 am. to meet the Staff Captain and take over the canvas which will be pitched under unit arrangements. Lorries conveying baggage will be used to take canvas from dumps to camp sites.

The exact map reference of all fields in which camps are pitched will be forwarded to Brigade Headquarters as early as possible so that notification may be sent to the Rents Officer concerned. Claims for damages will thus be diminished.

2.   Lorries are reporting to Brigade Headquarters at 7 am. on 23rd June and will be allotted to units as under. A guide from each unit will report to Staff Captain by 7 am.

Unit.	No. of lorries.	To be used for
10th K.O.Sco. Bordrs.	3.	)
15th K.O.Y.L.I.	3.	) To carry stores,
11th Cam. Highrs.	3.	) blankets, (packs)
12th Yorks (P) Regt.	1.	) and D.A.A.
Bde. Hd. Quarters.	2.	)

120th T.M.Batty. half lorry from Brigade Headquarters will be detailed to carry stores, baggage, etc. of battery.

N O T E :- Packs to be carried on the man in motor omnibus.

3.   All tents now in possession will be handed in to Area Commandant and receipts obtained. Receipts to be forwarded to Brigade Headquarters by 24th instant.

4.   Advance parties will proceed on the lorries allowed for stores etc. Such parties to be cut down to a minimum.

5.   Baggage wagons should be used for Officers kits, etc. L.G.S. Wagons for Lewis Guns and ammunition. Remainder of ammunition on lorries.

6.   Surplus Kit. Any surplus kit which is not likely to be required in the HAZEBROUCK Area will be dumped by Battalions in Battalion Stores and a guard of 1 N.C.O. and 3 o.rs. left in charge. The guard to have two days rations and instructions to report at once to Area Commandant so that he may arrange for their rations in the future. Site of any dumps so formed to be reported to Area Commandant and these Headquarters as early as possible.

7.   D.A.D.O.S., 40th Division will remain at EBBLINGHEM.

s/-

8. Supply Railhead will be EBBLINGHEM from and including 23rd June, 1918.

9. Personnel Railhead remains at WATTEN for the present.

10. 51st Mobile Veterinary Section will be located near LYNDE.

11. **Medical.** 137th Field Ambulance will be located at SERCUS.

12. Water Supply. The BORRE BECQUE from U.21.d. to the HAZEBROUCK - ST.SYLVESTRE CAPPEL Road is an important source of water supply and must be protected from pollution. The following precautions will be taken:-
    (a) No washing or bathing will be allowed in the stream.
    (b) No camp or horse lines will be permitted within 200 yards of the stream.
    (c) No baths or ablution places are to be allowed to drain into the stream.

A.P.M., 40th Division, will arrange for Military Police to assist Regimental Police in enforcing this order.

13. Full advantage will be taken of the cover from view afforded by hedges and trees when pitching camps.
Tents and shelters must be coloured. If kutch is not obtainable mud is to be used.

Lieut.,
A/Staff Captain,
120th Infantry Brigade.

22nd June 1918.

120th Inf. Bde. No. 129/415.   S 57   SECRET.

10th Garr. Bn. K.O.S.B.
15th Garr. Bn. K.O.Y.L.I.
11th Garr. Bn. Cam. Highrs.

H.Q. "G" 40th Division (for information).

> HEADQUARTERS,
> 120TH
> INFANTRY BRIGADE.
> No.............
> Date............

1. Each Battalion in the Brigade will in turn occupy its own sub-section of the WEST HAZEBROUCK LINE for a period of 4 days, beginning as follows :-

    10th Garr. Bn. K.O.S.B.   ...   July, 3rd.
    15th Garr. Bn. K.O.Y.L.I. ...   July, 7th.
    11th Garr. Bn. Cam. Hrs. ...   July, 11th.

2. Battalions will be disposed as if in the front system of defence and will be trained in all trench duties, sentry duties, reliefs etc.

3. In addition they will be employed on the construction of the EAST HAZEBROUCK LINE under the direction of C.E., XV Corps and orders of C.R.E., Corps Troops.
    Units of this Brigade will be affiliated for purposes of work to 145 A.T. Coy. R.E.

4. A tracing is attached showing location of work to be done. Details will be forwarded later.

5. To assist Battalions in training their men in Trench Routine, a number of Officers and Warrant Officers or N.C.Os. will be attached by 31st Division to Battalions while in occupation of WEST HAZEBROUCK LINE.
    Details will be forwarded later.

6. Transport Lines and Quartermasters stores will remain in present location.
    Location of Battalion Headquarters chosen will be forwarded to Brigade Headquarters.

7. The above arrangements in no way alter instructions already issued that in case of necessity the 120th Infantry Brigade will man the WEST HAZEBROUCK LINE (vide 120th Infantry Brigade Order No. 201 dated 25-6-18).

8. ACKNOWLEDGE.

H.B.Kerr
Captain,
A/Brigade Major,
120th Infantry Brigade.

1-7-18.

SECRET

D 1	2	3 HAZEBROUCK Canal 4	5	6 D
7	8	9 Trocadero le Grand Hasard	10	11	12
13	14	15			
19 Morbecque	20	21			

— Red - incomplete
— Green - complete

Tracing taken from Sheet ....
of the 1/.............. map of ....

Signature .... Date ....

NOTE.—(1). These traces are intended to facilitate the communication of information as to the position of targets, which have been located on a squared map.
(2). The squares on this trace are 500 yards in length on the 1/40,000 scale, 1,000 yards in length on the 1/20,000 scale, and 2,000 yards in length on the 1/10,000 scale.
(3). The squares on the trace are fitted to the squares of the map showing the targets, which are then drawn on the trace. Sufficient letters and numbers must also be added to enable the recipient to place the trace in the correct position on his own map. A little detail may also be traced, but this is not essential. The name and scale of the map to which the trace refers must be always given. The trace can be used for the 1/10,000, 1/20,000, or 1/40,000 scale.

G.S.G.S. 3025.

URGENT.   XV Corps No. Q.C. 271/6.
40th Divn. No. 844 (Q).

40th Division.

In the event of an enemy attack, it may be considered desirable to evacuate all superfluous transport from the forward area to points further in rear.
It is suggested that all baggage wagons could move off at once and a certain amount of the 1st Line Transport of Units.
Will you please consider the question of what you could send away without impairing the fighting efficiency.
A conference will ne held at Corps Headquarters at an early date on which occasion proposals connected with this will be considered.
All superfluous stores now in your possession should be sent back to your Divisional Store at LONGUENESSE.

(Sgd) N. BUXTON, Lieut.-Colonel,
A.Q.M.G., XV Corps.

4-7-18.

- 2 -

PRESSING.

Headquarters, 120th Inf. Bde.

Reference above, will you notify your proposals as to :-

(a) Evacuation of Stores etc., by use of Baggage Wagons.
(b) What 1st Line Transport of Units could also be utilized if required for this purpose.
(c) Sites for Brigade Dumps.
(d) Amount of baggage etc.(by G.S.Wagon loads) which is to be collected at once at Brigade Dumps for conveyance to Divisional Dump.
(e) Amount of baggage etc., which will still remain and which will be evacuated on emergency.

(f) The Pioneer Battalion will form a Battalion Dump and act as above.

(Sgd) G. T. MOORES, Lt. ZCol.
A.A.&Q.M.G.
40th Division.

3-7-18.

- 3 -

120th Inf. Bde. No. 120/478.
10th Garr. Bn. K.O.S.B.
15th Garr. Bn. K.O.Y.L.I.
11th Garr. Bn. Cam. Highrs.

URGENT

SECRET

Please forward as early as possible any proposals you may have on above minutes.
Reference para (d). The amount of Stores left with battalions should not be more than can be carried on the baggage wagons.
Reference para (e). Blankets would be withdrawn from the men and evacuated on emergency.

Lieut.
A/Staff Captain,
120th Infantry Brigade.

7-7-18.

120th Inf. Bde. No. 120/415/1.   S E C R E T.

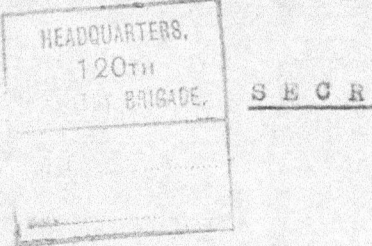

10th Garr. Bn. K.O.S.B.
15th Garr. Bn. K.O.Y.L.I.
11th Garr. Bn. Cam. Highrs.

        Reference practice manning of WEST HAZEBROUCK LINE 10-7-18.

1.   Southern Sub-section.
     The Divisional Commander does not approve of the dispositions of troops in the Southern Sub-section.
     O.C., 10th Garr. Bn. K.O.S.B. will arrange to hold this sub-section with three companies in the front system, each with two platoons in the front line and two in close support.
     The fourth company will occupy the GREEN LINE from Southern boundary C.30.c.3.8. to The STEENBECQUE and No.3 Labour Company will occupy from the STEENBECQUE to Northern boundary at C.24.b.0.5.

2.   CENTRE SUB-SECTION.
     Map is attached showing in RED the line which is to be held as the MAIN LINE OF RESISTANCE (This alteration affects Centre Sub-jection only) This line is the one which is heavily wired and marked with boards "FRONT LINE".
     Each of the three companies in the front system will occupy part of MAIN LINE of Resistance and of the OUTPOST LINE (shown in BLUE) with observation posts pushed out in front of latter.

3.   Battalions will return by last D.R. 12th inst. the attached maps showing the dispositions of all troops in each Sub-section (by Platoons in the case of battalions, by Companies in the case of Labour Units).

                                    Captain,
                              A/Brigade Major,
10-7-18.   120th Infantry Brigade.

AA 25 of 13.4.18

To pass for information
of O i/c Cos + Bn L.G. Officer

Initial + pass last named
to return to this Office please

Odo Vivian
Lt Col

O/c A   R.W.E.
   B   [signature]
   C   [signature]
   D   [signature]
L.G. Officer   AHL

SECRET.

FRENCH 6.   The French Regulations, copies of which have been
AIRCRAFT.   issued will probably be followed by French Aircraft flying
             over British Areas, and must be known to all concerned, so
             that any visiting French aircraft may be recognised.

===================================

120th Inf. Bde. No. 120/401.

10th Garr. Bn. K.O.S.B.
15th Garr. Bn. K.O.Y.L.I.
18th Garr. Bn. Cam. Highrs.
120th T. M. Battery.

For information.

12-7-18.

M B Kew
Captain,
A/Brigade Major,
120th Infantry Brigade.

S E C R E T.   A.A.25. dated 13-4-18.

S 50

HEADQUARTERS,
120TH INFANTRY BRIGADE.
No..........
Date.........

ORDERS REGARDING FIRING AT AIRCRAFT FROM THE GROUND AT NIGHT.

Classification of Areas.

see attached

1. Areas are classified as follows :-
   (i) **Defended Areas**.
       The whole area occupied by the British Armies, except the area lying East of the line joining the Headquarters of Divisions in the line.

   (ii) **Unprotected Area**.
        The area lying East of a line joining the Headquarters of Divisions in the line.

Notification of Night Flights.

2. No notification of night flights by aeroplanes will be given in future.

Opening of Fire against Aeroplanes by Night.

3. (a) RIFLE AND MACHINE GUN FIRE.

   In ~~"The Defended Area"~~ *Intermediate & Back area*
   (i) Rifle and Machine Gun fire will be opened on any aeroplanes located in this area by night, which does not either sound its Klaxon horn or show its navigation lights, or which is unmistakably identified as hostile in the beam of a searchlight.

   N.B. - The navigation lights are four in number, one on the top of the outer edge of each of the bottom planes, one on the tail, and one underneath the machine shining vertically downwards. The port and starboard lights on the plane are red and green respectively. The lights on the tail and underneath are white. The fact that the machine is not showing navigation lights is not to be taken as proof that it is an enemy machine, providing it is sounding its Klaxon horn.

   (ii) As the successful action of our defences at night depends very largely on locating the enemy aircraft by means of listening instruments and thus being able to direct the searchlights in the right direction with a reasonable prospect of picking them up, indiscriminate firing or barrage either by guns or small arms is likely to do more harm than good.
   Moreover, when they know that searchlights are in the vicinity, enemy aircraft seldom fly at heights below 7,000 feet at which height small arms fire is useless. As a general rule it may be taken that an aeroplane is within range of small arms fire (a) if the plane can be seen against the sky, (b) if the struts can be seen when the plane is in the beam of a searchlight.
   It is important, therefore, that the fire of units in the vicinity of A.A. Defences should be efficiently controlled in order that the efficacy of these defences may not be impaired

   In ~~"The Unprotected Area"~~. *The forward area*
   No rifle or machine gun fire will be opened on aeroplanes by night unless they disclose their hostile identity unmistakably✗ revealed in the beam of a searchlight.

   ✗ *by dropping bombs or opening fire or their identity is unmistakably)*

(b) ARTILLERY FIRE.

In the "Defended" and "Unprotected" Areas.

(i) Fire will not be opened on any aeroplane sounding its Klaxon horn or showing its navigation lights unless it proves itself to be hostile by dropping bombs or opening fire.

(ii) Fire will be opened on any aeroplanes which is unmistakably recognised as an enemy aeroplane in the beam of a searchlight or which proves itself to be hostile by dropping bombs or opening fire.

(iii) When an aeroplane is heard which has not sounded its Klaxon horn or shown its navigation lights and which has not proved itself hostile by dropping bombs or opening fire, the beam of the searchlight will be flashed in the direction of the sound of the motor. On seeing this the aeroplane will immediately fire the signal of the day. If this is not fired within half a minute of the first flash, fire will be opened.

(iv) Anti-Aircraft Sections not in possession of searchlights will not open fire unless the aeroplane has proved itself to be hostile by dropping bombs or opening fire.

4. (a) RIFLE AND MACHINE GUN FIRE.

In the "Defended" and "Unprotected" Areas.

Opening of fire against Airships by night.

Rifle and Machine Gun fire against any airship is prohibited unless the airship has revealed its hostile character unmistakably by dropping bombs.

(b) ARTILLERY FIRE.

In the "Defended" and "Unprotected" Areas.

(i) Intimation will be given by General Headquarters from time to time to Armies for communication to all concerned as to the area through which the Allied Airships are likely to pass during specified periods. All troops occupying that area will be warned by the Army concerned that during the period specified no firing against airships will take place.

(ii) It will not always be possible to define the exact route to be followed. In order, therefore, to afford airships a means of disclosing their identity they will be provided with coloured lights or signals rockets. The colouring of the lights and rockets will be changed from time to time under instructions to be issued by General Headquarters. Until further orders the colour of the lights will be the colour of the day as given in the French daily table of colours forwarded to Armies from time to time.

(iii) Except in the areas and during the periods referred to in para 4 (b) (i) above, the artillery will regard all airships as hostile, unless they make the special signal referred to in para. 4 (b) (ii).

SEARCH-LIGHTS. 5. Searchlights must carefully avoid holding in their beam aeroplanes which are clearly distinguished as friendly, or have given the correct signal.

S E C R E T   XV Corps No. 83/23.G.

40th Division.

ORDERS REGARDING FIRING AT AIRCRAFT FROM THE GROUND AT NIGHT.

The following amendments will be made to G.H.Q. letter No. A.A.25 dated 13:4:18 issued with XV Corps No.83/18/2 G. dated 8:7:18:-

1. Cancel para. 1 and substitute :-

    Classification of Areas.

    1. Areas are classified as follows :-

        (i) Forward Area. The area between the British Front line and a line joining the Headquarters of Divisions in front line.

        (ii) Intermediate and Back Area. The whole Area occupied by the British Armies except the area lying East of a line joining Headquarters of Divisions in the line.

2. Paragraphs 3 and 4 amend sub-headings as follows :-

    For "The Unprotected Area" read "The Forward Area".

    For "The Defended Area" read "Intermediate and Back Area".

                                      (Sd.) D. CORRIGALL. Major for
                                                     Brigadier-General,
                                                       General Staff.

XV Corps,
26:7:18.

-ii-

40th Div. No. 9/6/1 G.
120th Infantry Brigade No. 120/401.

10th K.O.S.B.
15th K.O.Y.L.I.
11th Cameron H'rs.
120th T. M. Battery.

     For information.
     Copy of G.H.Q. letter No. A.A.25 dated 13th April 1918 was forwarded under these H.Q. No. 120/401 dated 12:7:18.

                                                   Captain,
                                            Brigade Major,
                               120th Infantry Brigade.

31:7:18.

SECRET.

Second Army G.T.991.
XV Corps No. 593/18 G.

In continuation of G.T. 887 of 10th July, 1918, the following is the result of further experiments carried out on the 15th July, at the Second Army School of Musketry, with a view to testing the effects of rifle and Lewis Gun fire through belts of standing corn.

A. RIFLE FIRE.

Conditions under which the experiments were carried out :-

(a) Fired by 29 N.C.O. Students, just arrived at the School.

(b) Normal conditions, i,e., no auxiliary aiming marks or tracer bullets, but Instructors standing up ensured that the line of each rifle was correct for direction.

(c) Targets. Screen 60-feet, by 4-feet high, placed so that the top was just visible to Instructors standing.

(d) Firers about 4-yards from corn, which was average green wheat.

(e) Carried out after 3 or 4 days rain.

EXPERIMENTS AND RESULTS.

	Rounds fired.	Percentage of direct hits.	Percentage of turned hits.
1. At 50 yards.	435.	2.	39.
2. At 100 yards.	435.	1.3	15.
3. At 150 yards.	435.	nil	5.7

B. LEWIS GUN FIRE.

One gun used, fired by an Instructor under conditions similar to above, except that some tracer bullets were used and that the target was 30-feet, by 4-feet high.

RESULTS.

	Rounds fired.	Percentage of direct hits.	Percentage of turned hits.
1. At 50 yards. (traversing).	230.	22.	44.
2. At 100 yards. (traversing).	280.	6.	34.
3. At 100 yards. (not traversing).	140.	1.4	18.
4. At 150 yards. (traversing).	280.	1.	6.

No. 3 with the Lewis Gun, was fired with the view of ascertaining what number of rounds concentrated, would cut a lane in the corn. After 140 rounds it was not apparent to the firer that any lane was cut. Standing up behind him, it could be seen that a lane about 1-foot wide started some 10 yards in the corn, where the bullets began to disperse slightly, and continued for some 50 yards. Neither the lane nor the percentage of hits was as satisfactory as when traversing.

The fact alluded to in G.T.887, that the majority of bullets from rifle or Lewis Gun emerge from the corn at about 60 to 70 yards was confirmed. At about that distance from the firer, tracer bullets from the Lewis Gun were seen to richochet in all directions.

15th July, 1918.

(sgd) F.C. TANNER. Lt.-Col.
for M.G.G.S., Second Army.

SECRET

O/C 11th Cam'lrs

For information

HEADQUARTERS
120TH
INFANTRY BRIGADE
No. 120/4/2
Date 17/7/18

17/7/18

A B Kent
CAPTAIN
BRIGADE MAJOR,
120TH INFANTRY BRIGADE

SECRET.   S 63.   COPY NO. 8

120TH INFANTRY BRIGADE ORDER NO. 208.

Ref. Maps.
36a N.W. 1/20,000
36a N.E. 1/20,000
MECKHOUT CASTEEL
sheet 1/20,000.
                                              18-7-18.

1. The following moves will take place to-morrow, 19th instant.

   120th Inf. Bde. Headquarters to Headquarters vacated by 121st Inf. Bde. at C.3.c.5.3.

   11th Bn. Cam. Highrs. to Camp which is being vacated by 8th R. Irish Regt. at C.3.a. by 11 a.m.

2. Tents and Shelters at present occupied by 11th Cam. Highrs. will be moved by them under regimental arrangements. O.C., 11th Cam. Highrs. will also take over tents and shelters from 8th Irish Regt. at new Camp site. Numbers to be reported to this office.

3. Camp sites to be left thoroughly clean and certificates from Area Commandant or Billot Warden to be forwarded to Brigade Headquarters.

4. Brigade Headquarters will close at C.21.d.6.3. at 2 p.m. and will re-open at C.3.c.5.3. at the same hour.

5. ACKNOWLEDGE.

                                    J.B. Kerr
                                    Captain,
Issued through Signals at   A/Brigade Major,
         p.m.   120th Infantry Brigade.

DISTRIBUTION:-

Copy No. 1 . G.O.C.
        2 . Brigade Major.   12 . 40th Division "G"
        3 . Staff Captain.   13 . 40th Division "Q"
        4 . War Diary.   14 . 40th Divnl. Train.
        5 . File.   15 . O.C. 26th Lab. Group.
        6 . 10th Bn. K.O.S.B.   16 . O.C., 33rd Lab. Group.
        7 . 13th K.O.Y.L.I.   17 . O.C. 64th Lab. Group.
        8 . 11th Bn. Cam.Hrs.   18 . Lt-Col. BUTLER, BLARINGHEM
        9 . 120th T.M. Bty.   19 . Bde. Supply Officer.
       10 . 119th Inf. Bde.   20 . Brigade Signals.
       11 . 121st Inf. Bde.   21 . A.P.M. 40th Division.
                                 22 . Bde. Q.M. Sergt.
                                 23 . 135th Field Ambulance.

S 91.

120th Infantry Brigade No. 120/423. S E C R E T

10th K.O.S.B.
15th K.O.Y.L.I.
11th Cameron Hrs.
****

The attached copy of XVth Corps letter No. 656/13 (G) dated 8th August, 1918, is forwarded for information and guidance of all concerned.

Captain,
Brigade Major,
120th Infantry Brigade.

6th Aug. 1918.

S.94

120th Infantry Brigade No. 120/406.   S E C R E T

10th K.O.S.B.
15th K.O.Y.L.I.
11th Cameron Hrs.
120th T.M.Bty.
****

    All orders and instructions as to S.O.S., Gas, and A.A. firing will be taken over from units of 121st Inf. Bde. being relieved, and will remain in force in the 120th Inf. Bde. until further orders.

10th Aug. 1918.

Captain,
Brigade Major,
120th Infantry Brigade.

S E C R E T.

1st Australian Division.
9th (Scottish) Division.
29th Division.
31st Division.
40th Division.
G.O.C.R.A.
XV Corps Cyclist Battalion.
Comandant, XV Corps Troops.

XV Corps No. 656/13 (G).
5th August 1918.

---

1.   The practice of machine gunners shooting at our own aeroplanes is becoming more and more prevalent and in one case quite recently the results were fatal.

2.   The Corps Commander directs that immediate steps be taken to prevent a recurrence of such regrettable incidents. Attention is directed to S.S. 142, Appendix, para. 5 (iii).
    Orders should be issued to the effect that no firing is permissible by day unless the "Iron Crosses are visible to the naked eye".
    Aeroplanes are not to be fired on at night unless their identity as enemy planes has been clearly established.

H. Knox
Brigadier General,
General Staff.

XV Corps,
5th August 1918.

120th Inf. Bde. No. 120/402.

10th K. O. S. B.
15th H. L. I.
11th Cameron H'rs.
120th T. M. Battery.

Special attention is called to 119th Brigade No. 119/401
dated 21.7.18 about Lewis guns opening fire on aeroplanes.

The greatest precautions must be taken to ensure that fire is not opened on our aeroplanes, especially at night time when very often, both our own and hostile planes are in the air together.

Battalion Commanders will be responsible for ensuring that all teams of A.A. guns fully understand that fire is not to be opened unless the aeroplane is actually dropping bombs or the black cross can be seen.

G.S.18.

Captain,
Brigade Major,
120th Infantry Brigade.

[handwritten top: I & Major please note & initial SS]

Noted & Returned
as requested.

a/f Lyon 2/16
o/c Lewis Gunner

7/8/16

2nd Lt: Lyon

For information
necessary action
and return, please.
Neilson.
  Capt + Adj.t

11th Camerons

7/8/18

120th Inf. Bde. No. 120/415.

10th Bn. K.O.S.B.
15th Bn. K.O.Y.L.I.
11th Bn. Cam. Highrs.
33rd Labour Group.)
64th Labour Group.)   for information.
26th Labour Group.)

40th Division "G"

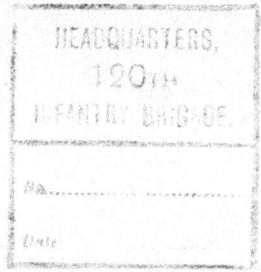

    Reference 120th Infantry Brigade Order No. 205, it is probable now that only 100 rifles per Labour Company will be available for defensive purposes, but no definite orders, except with regard to Nos. 4 and 35 Companies, have yet been received.

    Changes in locations of Companies and transfers from Group to Group are becoming so frequent that the even distribution to Battalions is impossible. As long as Labour Companies remain at the disposal of the 120th Infantry Brigade, they will be attached to Battalions as laid down in Appendix 'A' of 120th Infantry Brigade Order No. 205, irrespective of the Labour Group by which they are being administrated. Local transfers of Labour Companies for defensive purposes may possibly be carried out after arrival in the defensive area, if considered advisable by these Headquarters.

29-7-18.

Captain,
Brigade Major,
120th Infantry Brigade.

S.82

SECRET.

XV Corps No. 89/126 G.
dated 24-7-18.

XV CORPS ANTI-GAS INSTRUCTIONS.

(The Instructions contained in XV Corps No.
89/109 G. dated 23/4/18 are cancelled)

---

1. **STANDING ORDERS.**

   Standing Orders for Defence against Gas are contained in Appendix IV, S.S. 534, dated March, 1918.

2. **GAS ZONES.** (S.S. 534 Appendix IV, paragraph 1).

   (a) The boundaries of the "ALERT" and "PRECAUTIONARY" Zones are as follows :-

   "ALERT" ZONE. The country East of the following line :-

   MORBECQUE - HAZEBROUCK - CAESTRE Railway within the Corps Area.

   "PRECAUTIONARY" ZONE. The country between the Western limits of the "ALERT" ZONE and the following line :-

   MONT DUPIL, B.26.b. (exclusive) - BLARINGHEM - EBBLINGHEM - CASSEL (all inclusive).

   (b) The Divisions in the forward area will be responsible, within their respective areas, for the erection and maintenance of the necessary Notice Boards on all roads to mark the limits of the "ALERT" Zone.   C E XV Corps

   The Reserve Division in the BLARINGHEM Area will arrange for the erection and maintenance of Notice Boards to mark on all roads the limits of the "PRECAUTIONARY" Zone.
   READY

   (c) Reference S.S.534, Appendix IV, paragraph 3, sub-paragraph A (ix) and B.(ii).

   In order to ensure that all Units pay attention to the direction of the wind, at all Headquarters, and at such other places as Divisional Commanders may direct within the "ALERT" Zone, Notice boards will be placed stating when the wind is "DANGEROUS"

   "WIND SAFE" Boards will not be put up, and any already erected will be removed.

3. **GAS SHELL BOMBARDMENT.**

   (a) Attention is called to paragraph 4 (vi) of S.S. 534, Appendix IV.

   Units occupying positions in Woods, Valleys and Villages, within range of a gas shell bombardment, will be warned of the persistent effect of the gas which is liable to be dangerous even after several days have elapsed.

   (b) Enemy gas shell bombardments should invariably be reported, and it is important that any new gas or projectile should be investigated at once.

   (c) All ranks should be warned that the recognition of gas shell by the degree of detonation is not to be relied upon

   P.T.O.

4. GAS SHELLING AND GAS BOMBING OF BACK AREAS.

In view of the fact that the enemy has gas shelled villages up to eight or ten miles behind the line, and that there is a possibility of gas bombs being dropped by hostile aeroplanes, Anti-gas precautions must not be neglected in the back areas.

A Reserve of 28 lbs. of Chloride of Lime will be kept at Area Commandants' Offices and at Labour Group Headquarters.

5. INSTRUCTIONS FOR WARNING IN EVENT OF HOSTILE CLOUD GAS ATTACK. (S.S. 534 Appendix IV, Paragraph 5).

(a) Divisions are responsible for warning all troops in their areas.

Divisions will also warn the necessary civil authorities in their respective areas to ensure the warning and protection of all civilians. Arrangements to be made with French Mission.

(b) WARDRECQUES and BLARINGHEM Areas.

Area Commandants will be responsible for warning all troops in their respective areas. They will also warn the necessary civil authorities responsible for warning all civilians in their Areas. Arrangements to be made with French Mission.

(c) WARNING MESSAGES.

Reference S.S. 534, Appendix IV, paragraph 5 (ix).

Messages conveying the warning of gas cloud attack will take the form of the letters "G.A.S.", followed by the map reference of the trench opposite to which the gas is being liberated and the sheet number of the map reference. If, for any reason, the map reference cannot be given, the name of trench or sector may be sent, but local or unauthorised names of trenches and sectors must not be used.

To minimise delay, messages which are to be telegraphed or sent by Despatch Rider or Orderly, will be kept ready filled in, with the names of the recipients and the letters "G.A.S." The message to be completed before despatch.

XV Corps. (Sgd) W.P.LIPSCOMBE, Captain,
21=7=18. for B.G., G.S.

120th Inf. Bde. No. 120/418. SECRET.
*****

10th Bn. K.O.S.B.
15th Bn. K.O.Y.L.I.
11th Bn. Cam. Highrs.
120th T.M. Battery.

The above "XV Corps Anti-Gas Instructions" dated 21st July, 1918 should be substituted for Instructions dated the 23rd April, 1918, copy of which was forwarded under this office No. 120/418 dated 26th June, 1918.

23-7-18.

Captain,
Brigade Major,
120th Infantry Brigade.

S 130

SECRET
****

XV Corps No.80/120/1 G.
20th August 1918.

AMENDMENTS TO XV CORPS ANTI-GAS INSTRUCTIONS.

(XV Corps No. 89/126 G. dated 21/7/18.)

1. Para. 2 is cancelled and the following substituted :-

   "2. **Gas Zones.** (S.S.534 - Appendix IV, Para. 1.)

   (a) The rear boundaries of the ALERT and READY Zones are as follows :-

   ALERT ZONE.

   Corps Southern Boundary (D.28.b.7.3.) along N.W. edge of BOIS CLEBERT - D.23.d.0.6. - D.16.d.2.2. - along road to D.6.d.0.8. to D.6.a.5.8. - W.19.c.7.8. - West of COQ de PAILLE.

   READY ZONE.

   OXELAERE - THIENNES Road to Road Junction U.5.a. - East of ST. MARIE CAPEL.

2. In Para. 2 (b) for "Reserve Division in the BLARINGHEM Area" read "C.E. XV Corps" and for "Precautionary Zone" read "Ready Zone".

sd. W.P.LIPSCOMB, Capt.,
for Brigadier-General,
General Staff.

XV Corps
20/8/18.

-ii-

40th Div. No. 10/40 G.
120th Infantry Bde. No. 120/418.

10th K.O.S.B.
15th K.O.Y.L.I.
11th Cameron Hrs.
120th T. M. Bty.
*****

Forwarded with reference to "XV Corps Anti-Gas Instructions" dated 21st July 1918 (120th Bde. No. 120/418 dated 23:7:18).

Captain,
Brigade Major,
120th Infantry Brigade.

21:8:18.

[Stamp: HEADQUARTERS, 120TH INFANTRY BRIGADE.]

120th Infantry Brigade No. 120/477.   S E C R E T

10th K.O.S.B.
15th K.O.Y.L.I.
11th Cameron Hrs.
120th T.M.Bty.
****

    Attention of all units is called to 120th Inf.Bde. No. 120/477 dated 7:8:18.

    These Code Calls will be taken into use directly units are in the area in front of Divisional Headquarters in the line.

Captain,
Brigade Major,
120th Infantry Brigade.

10th Aug. 1918.

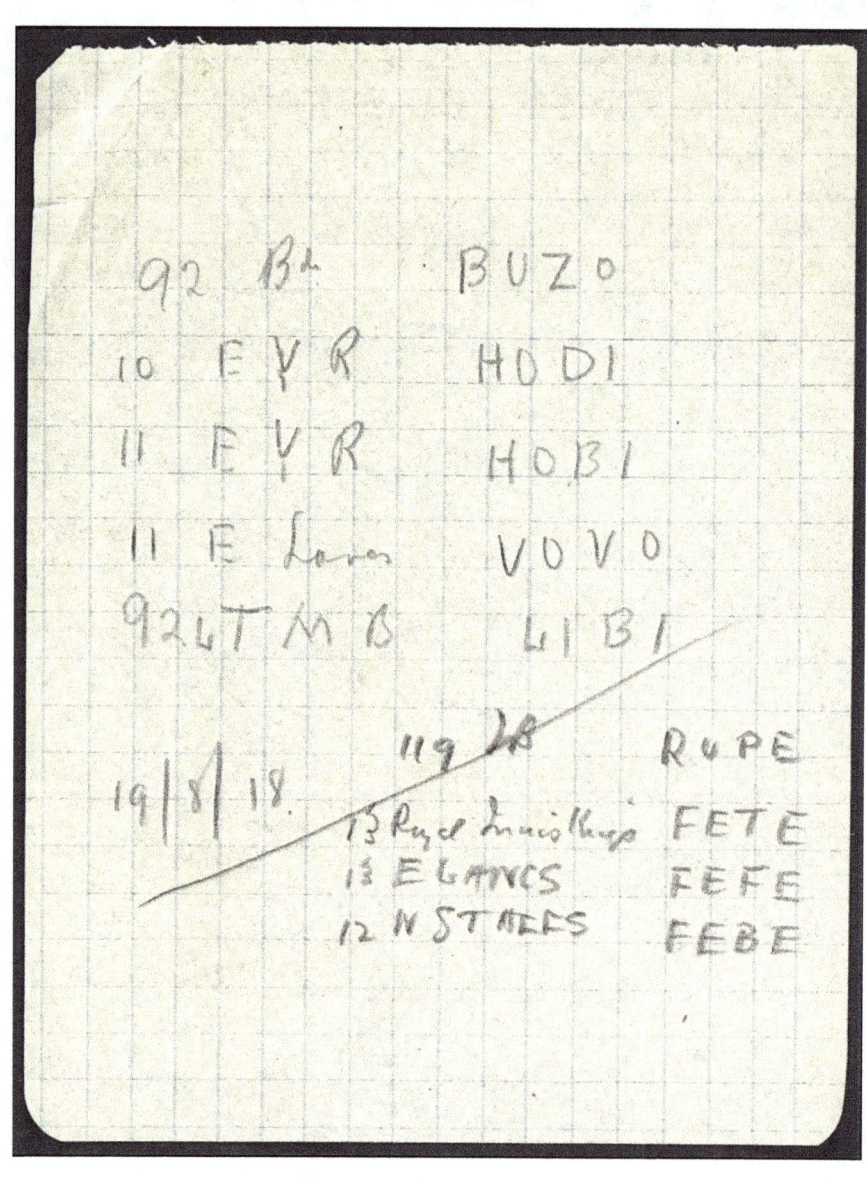

40th Div. No. 53/44 G.   SECRET.   Copy No......

STATION CODE CALLS, 40th DIVISION (6th Series).

(These calls will be taken into use after midnight 7/8th Aug.)

Name of unit.	Code call.	Name of unit.	Code Call
40th Div. H.Q. "G"	MEVI	120th Infantry Bde H.Q.	RUQE
,, "Q"	MEJI	10th K.O.Sco.Bord.	FEQE
,, C.R.E.	MEZI	15th K.O.Y.L.I.	FEPE
,, A.D.M.S.	MENI	11th Cameron Hrs.	FEDE
,, D.A.D.O.S.	MEKI		
		120th T.M.Battery.	GADO
H.Q. 40th Div. Artillery.	WUZO	121st Infantry Bde H.Q.	RUDE
		8th Royal Ir. Regt.	NELI
178th Bde R.F.A.,H.Q.	LUFU	23rd Lan. Fusiliers.	FERE
"A" Battery	LUTU	23rd Cheshire Regt.	NEFE
"B" Battery	LUGU		
"C" Battery	LULA	121st T.M.Battery.	GABO
"D" Battery	LUHA		
		17th Worc. Regt.(Pnrs).	FEWE
181st Bde R.F.A.,H.Q.	LUQA		
"A" Battery	LUDA	Div.Train H.Q. & No.1 Coy.	RAGU
"B" Battery	LUBA	,, No.2 Coy.	RALA
"C" Battery	LUFA	,, No.3 Coy.	RAHA
"D" Battery	LUTA	,, No.4 Coy.	RAVA
		40th Div. M.T.Coy.A.S.C.	WASI
Div.Ammunition Col.	DIME		
		135th Field Ambulance.	VARA
224th Field Coy. R.E.	GIVU	136th ,,	VAPA
229th ,,	GISU	137th ,,	VAQA
231st ,,	GIMU		
		51st Mobile Vet. Sect.	HAHO
40th Div. Signal Coy.	ROKA		
		237th Div. Employt Coy.	ZADO
119th Infantry Bde H.Q.	RUPE		
13th R.Innis. Fus.	FETE	
13th E.Lancs. Regt.	FEFE	
12th N.Staffs. Regt.	FEBE	
119th T.M.Battery	GAQO	

NOTE The call for 40th Div."Q" preceded by the branch letters will be used for all departments of Divisional Headquarters, e.g. A.P.M. MEJI.

1. The above are intended to replace existing Station Code Calls and code names and will be taken into force after midnight 7/8th Aug. They will not, however, be used by units and formations occupying back areas in rear of Divisional Headquarters in the line.

2. In the event of a copy of this code being lost, a short report on the circumstances should be forwarded to Divisional Headquarters immediately.

3. Copies will be destroyed when a new list is issued and a certificate rendered to these Headquarters to that effect.

4. No copies or extracts from this list are to be made.

****

SECRET   COPY NO. 8

120TH INFANTRY BRIGADE ORDER NO. 207.

Ref.Map
attached   10:8:18.
(only to Battns.)

1. The 120th Infantry Brigade will relieve the 121st Infantry Brigade in the Sector West of VIEUX BERQUIN on the night 12/13th instant.

2. All movement will be in accordance with attached March Table.
   Battalion Transports will move to Transport Lines on the same day as the Battalions, in accordance with Administrative Instructions already issued.

3. Details of reliefs and advanced parties will be arranged by Battalions concerned, and Battalions of the 120th Infantry Brigade will assume similar dispositions to those adopted by the Battalions which they relieve.

4. All secret maps, aeroplane photographs, defence schemes, etc. will be taken over from units relieved, receipts given, and duplicates forwarded to this office by 6 p.m. 15th instant.

5. Completion of relief will be wired to both 120th and 121st Inf. Bde. Headquarters, using the following code words :-

15th K.O.Y.L.I.	...	SPRING
10th K.O.S.B.	...	SUMMER.
11th Cameron Hrs.	...	AUTUMN.
120th T.M.Bty.	...	WINTER.

6. Brigade Headquarters will close at its present location at 10 a.m., 13th inst., and re-open at the same hour at D.17.a.7.3. at which hour G.O.C. 120th Infantry Brigade will assume command of the sector.

7.   A C K N O W L E D G E.

                                    Captain,
Issued through   Brigade Major,
   Signals   120th Infantry Brigade.
at 7.30 p.m.

Distribution :-

Copy No.					
1	...	G.O.C.	12	...	119th Inf. Bde.
2	...	Bde.Major.	13	...	121st Inf. Bde.
3	...	Staff Captain.	14	...	31st Div. "G".
4	...	War Diary.	15	...	31st Div. "Q".
5	...	File.	16	...	135 Field Ambce.
6	...	10th K.O.S.B.	17	...	40th Div. Train.
7	...	15th K.O.Y.L.I.	18	...	Area Commandant,
8	...	11th Camerons.			BLARINGHEM.
9	...	120th T.M.Bty.	19	...	Bde.Supply Officer.
10	...	40th Div. "G".	20	...	Bde. Signals.
11	...	40th Div. "Q".	21	...	229 Field Coy.R.E.
11a	...	173 Tunng.Coy.	22 to 25		Labour Groups Nos.
					26, 31, 33 & 64.

MARCH TABLE TO ACCOMPANY 120TH INF. BRIGADE ORDER NO. 207.

Date	Unit.	From	To	Route	In relief of	Remarks & route
11th	15th K.O.Y.L.I.	MILL FONTAINE	Reserve Area about D.12.a. & c. and D.17.	March Route.	23rd Lancs. Fusiliers.	Hour of start/to be notified later.
-Do-	120th T.M.Bty.	MILL FONTAINE	Reserve Area.	To march with 15th K.O.Y.L.I.		To be accommodated by 15th K.O.Y.L.I Reconnaissance of T.M.positions occupied by 121 T.M.Bty. to be carried out night 11/12th and day of 12th.
-Do-	23rd Lancs.Fsrs.	Reserve Area.	SERCUS Area.			
12th	10th K.O.S.B.	LUMBRES.	Camp at LE NOIR TROU.	By bus.		To ombuss at LUMBRES at 12 noon in busses, bringing Battalion of 119th Bde. to LUMBRES.
-Do-	11th Camerons.	SERCUS Area.	Support Area.	By bus.	23rd Cheshire Regt.	To ombuss at 10 a.m. at C.1.d.6.2. To debuss at D.3.central. Busses will return with 23rd Cheshire Regt.
-Do-	23rd Cheshire Rgt.	Support Area.	SERCUS Area.	-Do-		
Night 12/13	15th K.O.Y.L.I.	Reserve Area.	Line.		8th R.I.R.	
-Do-	120th T.M.Bty.	-Do-	-Do-		121 T.M.Bty.	
-Do-	8th R.I.R.	Line.	Reserve Area.			
-Do-	121 T.M.Bty.	Line.	Reserve Area.			
13th	10th K.O.S.B.	LE NOIR TROU	Reserve Area.	March Route.	8th R.I.R.	Hour of start 9 a.m.
-Do-	8th R.I.R.	Reserve Area.	SERCUS Area.			
-Do-	121 T.M.Bty.	-Do-	-Do-			

SECRET.

~~120th Infantry Brigade Administrative Order No. 9.~~
120th Infantry Brigade Administrative Order No. 207.

Ref. Sheets :
27 & 36.a. (1/40,000).
36.a. N.E. (1/20,000).

10th August 1918.

1. **Location of Units.**

Brigade Headquarters	D.17.a.7.3.
Front Line Bn. H.Qrs.	E.14.d.5.3.
Support Bn. H.Qrs.	D.11.d.7.3.
Reserve Bn. H.Qrs.	D.12.a.3.2.
120th T. M. Battery.	D.18.c.8.4.
210 Fd. Coy., R.E.	D.5.c.9.1.

See attached S.112 of 15/8/18

Transport Lines and Q.M. Stores.

Brigade Hd.Qrs and T.M. Battery.	D.8.d.3.0.
10th K.O.S.B. (from 8th R.Irish).	D.8.c.1.2.
15th K.O.Y.L.I. from 23rd Lancs Fus).	C.12.b.9.9.
11th Cam. Hrs. (from 23rd Cheshires).	C.12.b.9.9.
No.3 Coy. Train and Brigade Post Office.	C.14.c.2.8.
Refilling Point.	C.14.d.5.5.

2. **Railhead.**

   (a) Railhead remains at EBBLINGHEM.
   (b) All reinforcements arriving will be sent to Battalion Transport Lines.

3. **Rations.**

   (a) Rations will be delivered to Transport Lines by No.3 Coy., Train.
   (b) For the Front line battalion rations are taken by limber to Battalion Headquarters and COBLEY HOUSE.
   Rations for the two companies in the line to be taken to Company Headquarters by pack animals.
   (c) For the battalions in Support and Reserve rations can be taken to all companies by limber, to Reserve by day, Support by night.
   (d) Limbers proceeding to the Company of the Support Battalion in "Z" Line via SANITAS CORNER must do so singly.
   (e) Transport and pack animals are to be pushed as far forward as possible to save man-handling.
   Carrying parties are not to be used for rations or water behind the Company Headquarters of the Companies in the line.
   (f) **Water.** As the supply of petrol tins for water is very limited, steps **must** be taken to ensure that the same number of **empty** tins are returned each day as the numbers brought up full of water.
   Unless this routine is rigidly enforced units in the line will not get sufficient water.
   (g) **Cookery.** (1) For the front Line Battalion the bulk of the cooking should be done at the transport Lines.
   (2) At present only 15 hot food Containers are available. Care must be taken to have these thoroughly scalded out each day, otherwise the food inside quickly gets tainted.

(3) For the /-

See attached S.112 of 15/8/18

* 2 *.

(3) ~~For the~~ *While in* Support and Reserve ~~Battalions~~ cooking can be done forward, provided every precaution to avoid smoke is taken.
(4) Cookers can in some cases be taken forward.

5. Ammunition.

(a) The Divisional Dump is situated in the S.A.A. Section 31st D.A.C. Lines - U.21.b.6.5.
(b) The Brigade Dump is established at - E.7.d.9.3. Units draw direct, notifying Brigade Headquarters of amounts drawn.
(c) Where not already in existence water proof recesses are to be constructed. Owing to the danger of ignition, sandbags are not to be employed, corrugated iron sheets being used instead.
(d) A careful check is to be kept of all S.A.A.. The promiscuous tearing open of the tin linings of S.A.A. Boxes is forbidden. Except in the cases of emergency, S.A.A. Boxes will be opened only on the order of an Officer.

The wooden lids must be worked frequently to prevent jamming.

Future ammunition returns and receipts will shew separately the number of open and the number of unopened boxes.
(e) Loose bandoliers and clips of ammunition will not be left lying about the trenches but kept in the boxes.
(f) O.C., 120th T.M. Battery will arrange for the detonating of T.M.C. in the Brigade Dump as required.

6. R.E. DUMPS.

(a) The Main Divisional R.E. Dump is established at V.19.c.8.7 ... near CINQ RUES.
(b) A forward dump is located at BRICKSTACKS DUMP. E.20.b.7.0.
(c) All indents for R.E. Material should be submitted to this Headquarters. *by 9 am*

7. Medical.

(a) The 31st Division evacuates all cases from the ~~Brigade Sector~~.
(b) R.A.P.   E.14.d.5.3.

Relay Posts.   E.8.c.5.6.
               E.19.b.8.3.

A.D.S.   D.18.a.5.3.   (Reserve A.D.S. D.9.d.1.8)

M.D.S.   C.5.a.6.9.

Divisional Rest Station. ... T.18.a.9.9.

8. Cemeteries.
                       E.20.c.8.8.
           GRAND HAZARD.   D.8.c.9.6.
           HAZEBROUCK.   D.3.a.8.4.
Burials in other than authorised cemeteries are strictly forbidden.

9. Receipts.

At all inter-Unit reliefs, whenever trench stores, ammunition, rations, etc., are taken over or handed over, receipts must be exchanged and duplicate copies sent to ~~Brigade~~ Headquarters. It is pointed out that once a receipt has been given the recipient is responsible for the Stores, and any shortage subsequently discovered must be accounted for by him.

10. Trench Foot.

* 3 *.

10. Trench Foot.

(a) In the event of continued wet weather, trench foot preventative measures will be carried out.
(b) Whale oil is available on application at Refilling Point.
(c) Clean socks can be obtained from 40th Divisional Clothing Store, RENESCURE.

11. Baths.

A Bath (capacity 100 men per hour) is being erected at FETTLE FARM D.24.c.7.6. for the use of Reserve Battalion.
Soyer stoves are available in billets of Reserve Battalion for heating water. Battalions can improvise baths by use Tarpaulin Sheets.

12. Clean Clothing Store.

Brigade Clean Clothing Store is located at Brigade Q.M. Stores, ~~D.8.a.3.0.~~ D8 d 30.
(b) 31st Division Clean Clothing Store is at WALLON CAPPEL.

13. Gassed Clothing.

A stock of 500 S.D. Jackets and trousers together with underclothing is held as a Divisional Reserve for Gas Cases and is distributed between the Main Dressing Station and the 31st Divisional Clean Clothing Store, WALLON CAPPEL.
Such men as have been affected by Yellow Cross Gas will be sent to the main Dressing Station with a certificate signed by an Officer, stating that their clothing has been affected, when fresh clothing will be issued.

14. Salvage.

(a) The 31st Divisional Salvage Dump is located at WALLON CAPPEL.
(b) Salved stores of all sorts are to be conveyed there by returning ration limbers.
(c) It is to be impressed upon all men that it is their duty to collect and send back to the rear by ration parties etc., steel helmets, rifles, pieces of equipment, etc., however muddy or apparently useless..
(d) No man moving away from the line for any distance however short, on any duty whatsoever, should do so empty-handed.
(e) All empty Preserved Meat tins should be collected and sent to the 31st Divisional Solder kiln at WALLON CAPPEL.

15. Economy.

Waste paper, Jam cartons, dripping; tea, biscuit and other large tins, etc., will be returned to the Base through 40th Division.

16. Sanitation.

1. (a) Latrines of the bucket type only. Systematic burial of excreta is essential.
(b) On no account are food refuse and tins to be left lying about.
(c) Disciplinary action is to be taken against any man found throwing food refuse or tins over the parapet or parados.

2. (a) No.49 Sanitary Section located at B.22.d.6.5 ~~administers~~ the area.
(b) Indents /-

* 4 *.

(b) Indents for requirements to be sent to this Office for transmission, through the Area Commandant, WALLON CAPPEL to 49 Sanitary Section.

(c) Approval of the indents will be notified to units by wire, when pioneers with tools must be sent to 49 Sanitary Section.

17. Ordnance.

The Brigade will continue to be administered by D.A.D.O.S 40th Division, located at T.18.c.2.8., EBBLINGHEM.

19. 18. Canteens.

WALLON CAPPEL U.23.c.20.25.
LE GRAND HAZARD. D.13.b.5.8.
There is a Y.M.C.A. at D.13.a.3.8.

19. Transport.

1. On the day of reliefs, Baggage wagons of the two units concerned may be retained after delivering supplies, in order to take up packs and blankets of the unit coming into reserve and remove those of the unit moving into the line.

2. Baggage wagons must be returned to No.3 Coy's Lines on completion.

20. Armourer Sergeant.

(a) The Armourer Staff Sergeant of 10th K.O.S.B. will report to the battalion in Reserve at 12 noon on the day following relief under arrangements to be made by O.C., 10th K.O.S.B. He will remain with the Reserve Battalion until all work required is completed.

(b) O.C., 120th T.M. Battery will apply to Brigade Headquarters if the services of Armourer Staff Sergeant are required.

21. Communication.

(a) A central telephone station will be established in the Transport Lines of 10th Bn. K.O.S.B.
The Battalion in Brigade Reserve will find the personnel (3 men) for the station, who will be attached to the 10th Bn. K.O.S.B. for rations and accommodation.

(b) The 15th Bn. K.O.Y.L.I. and 11th Bn. Cameron Highrs. will send a cyclist to be attached to the 10th Bn. K.O.S.B for rations and accommodation at the Transport Lines.

(c) A D.R.L.S. Service will be established as follows :-

LEAVE BDE. H.Qrs. D.17.a.7.3.	LEAVE 10th K.O.S.B. TRANSPORT LINES.
10 a.m.	10-45 a.m.
6 p.m.	5-45 p.m.

22. Baggage Wagons.

Baggage Wagons will be sent to Units on the night prior to the move.
After baggage has been cleared on the day of the move of units, all baggage wagons will be returned to No. 3 Coy. Train the same day as they will be required for supply services.

T Knox-Shaw
Captain,
Staff Captain,
120th Infantry Brigade.

SECRET   Copy No....

121st INFANTRY BRIGADE ORDER No. 37.

                                                12th August 1918.

Ref. Sheet 27)
        36.a.) 1/40,000

1. (a). 15th K.O.Y.L.I. will relieve 10th E. Yorks. Regt. in the
        Reserve Area, 92nd Infantry Brigade, to-day, 12th August.
   (b). Relief to be completed by 9 p.m.
   (c). 15th K.O.Y.L.I. will move by platoons with distances of
        200 yards between platoons.
   (d). 15th K.O.Y.L.I. will come under the orders of G.O.C. 92nd
        Infantry Brigade on entering 92nd Infantry Brigade Area.
   (e). Completion of this relief will be reported to H.Q. 92nd
        Infantry Brigade.

2. (a). On completion of the above relief, 8th R. Irish Regt. will
        be relieved by the 10th E. Yorks. Regt. in the front line
        of the Centre Brigade Sector.
   (b). On completion of relief, 8th R. Irish Regt. will withdraw to
        Brigade Reserve Area, Centre Sector, as already ordered.
   (c). Troops of the 10th E. Yorks. Regt. will not move East of Z
        line before 9 p.m.
   (d). Troops of the 10th E. Yorks. Regt. will come under the orders
        of G.O.C. 121st Infantry Brigade, on entering 121st
        Infantry Brigade Area.
   (e). Completion of relief will be reported to Brigade Headquarters
        as already ordered.

3.   All details of relief will be arranged direct between
Commanders concerned.

4.   All defence schemes, trench stores, aeroplane photographs
and T.S. maps will be handed over and receipts exchanged.

5.   121st Trench Mortar Battery will remain in the line until
further orders and will not be relieved by 120th Trench Mortar
Battery on night 12th/13th August.
        120th Trench Mortar Battery will remain in present position.

6.   Serial numbers 3 and 4 of Table issued with 121st Infantry
Brigade Order No. 36 are cancelled.

7.   Acknowledge.

                                                Captain,
                                                Brigade Major,
                                                121st Infantry Brigade.

Issued at 2.0 p.m.

Copy No.				
1 to	8th R. Irish Regt. ø		14 to	40th Div. Trn.
2	23rd Lancs. Fus.		15	No. 4 Coy. A.S.C.
3	23rd Cheshire Regt.		16	170th Bde. R.F.A.
4	121st T.M.Bty. ø		17	210 Coy. R.E.
5	92nd Inf.Bde. ø		18	211 Coy. R.E.
6	93rd Inf.Bde.		19	War Diary.
7	94th Inf.Bde. ø		20	Bde. Signals.
8	119th Inf.Bde.		21	Staff Captain.
9	120th Inf.Bde.		22	War Diary.
10	31st Divn(G).		23	File.
11	31st Divn(Q).		24	11th Cam. Highrs. ø
12	40th Divn(G).		25	15th K.O.Y.L.I. ø
13	40th Divn(Q).		26	10th K.O.S.B.
14	10th E. Yorks.R. ø		27	120th T.M.Bty. ø

                    ø By Special D.R.

40th Division No. 452 (Q).
120th Infy. Bde. No. 120/416.

S 98

CONFIDENTIAL.

Headquarters,
120th Infantry Brigade.
---

1. Will you kindly ensure that Divisional Routine Order 2190 dated to-day is brought to the notice of all Officers concerned.

    Various instances have occurred of Officers driving Divisional Motor Cars, of Cars being driven at high speeds, of drivers being ordered to proceed over impossible tracks and of excessive over-loading.

    Quite recently a driver was made to take 5 passengers (excluding himself).

2. The result is that damage to the Cars is done and there is a resulting shortage of cars which makes it very difficult to meet the many demands.

    It is also a matter of difficulty to get such repairs done without delay as the circumstances in which the damage was caused have to be stated and occasionally enquired into.

(Sgd) A.L.COWTAN, Major,

10th August 1918.
                D.A.A.G., 40th Division.

* 2 *.

10th K.O.S.B.
15th K.O.Y.L.I.
11th Cam. Hrs.
120th T. M. Battery.

For necessary action.

Captain,
Staff Captain,
120th Infantry Brigade.

11.8.1918.

SECRET   COPY No. 8

120TH INFANTRY BRIGADE ORDER NO. 208.

                                                12:8:18.

1. 120th Infantry Brigade Order No. 207 is cancelled and the following substituted.

2. The 120th Infantry Brigade will relieve part of the 92nd Infantry Brigade on the night of the 13/14th in accordance with attached Relief Table.

3. The boundary between 120th Brigade and Brigade on the left will be :-
   E.30.central - E.29 central - Valley Farm (inclusive to Brigade on left) SAWMILLS E.19.d.1.0 along track to D.24.a.8.0. - gird line through D.23. and D.21 central.

4. All arrangements for relief will be made by Commanders concerned, completion of reliefs being wired to 120th Brigade Headquarters by following code words :-

15th K.O.Y.L.I.	MORE
10th K.O.S.B.	HASTE
11th Cameron Hrs.	LESS
120th T.M.Battery	SPEED

5. One company of 11th E. Yorks will remain with the battalion of the 120th Brigade in the line, and will hold the extreme right of the line. This company will be under the tactical control of the Battalion Commander in the line, and will be relieved by other companies of the 92nd Brigade, under arrangements to be issued later.

6. All special maps, defence schemes, aeroplane photographs, etc. will be taken over from units relieved, receipts given, and duplicates of receipts forwarded to Brigade Headquarters by 6 p.m., 16th inst.

7. A map showing the position of platoons, and positions of posts on the flanks will be forwarded to Brigade H.Q. by noon 15th inst.

8. Brigade Headquarters will close at its present location at 6 p.m., at which hour it will re-open at FETTLE FARM, D.24.a.7.½.; and G.O.C. 120th Brigade will assume command of the sector.

9. All transport lines will be taken over in accordance with Administrative Instructions already issued with 120th Inf. Brigade Order No. 207.

10. A C K N O W L E D G E.

                                        Captain,
                                        Brigade Major,
                                        120th Infantry Brigade.

Issued through
  Signals
  at 9.45 p.m.
  To All Recipients
of 120th Inf.Bde. Order
  No. 207 dated
  10:8:18.

RELIEF TABLE TO ACCOMPANY 120TH INF. BDE. ORDER NO. 208.

Date	Unit	From	To	In relief of	Remarks.
15th	10th K.O.S.B.	Le Rôle TxOU	Reserve about D.17.b.	8th K.I.R.	Under arrangements between C.Os. concerned.
-Do-	11th Camerons	Support Centre Sector	Support Right Sector about E.25.b. & d. and E.27.d.	15th K.O.Y.L.I.	Relief to be complete by 9 p.m.
13/14th	15th K.O.Y.L.I.	Support	Line	1 Coy. 11th E. Yorks. 3 Coys 11th E. Lancs.	Under arrangements between C.Os.
-Do-	120th T.M.Bty.			121st T.M.Battery.	To be completed as early as possible.
-Do-	1 Coy. 11th E. Yorks.		Extreme right of line	1 Coy. 11th East Lancs.	Under arrangements between C.Os. To come under tactical control of O.C., K.O.Y.L.I. on completion of relief.

Any routes in Divisional area may be used.

The usual distances will be maintained on the line of march.

120th Inf. Bde. No. 120/416.

CONFIDENTIAL.

S 103

10th Bn. K.O.S.B.
15th Bn. K.O.Y.L.I.
11th Bn. Cam. Highrs.
120th T. M. Battery.

  The Brigadier wishes Commanding Officers to pay great attention to the contents of 40th Division letter No. C/124/A dated 12th August, 1918.

  A certificate is to be rendered to Brigade Headquarters by 1st D.R. on Thursday 15th August, 1918 to the effect that every Officer present with the Unit has been informed of the purport of this letter.

T. Knox-Shaw
Captain,
Staff Captain,
120th Infantry Brigade.

13-8-18.

120th Infantry Brigade No. 120/406.   S E C R E T

15th K.O.Y.L.I.
11th Cameron Hrs. (For information).
****

    The 183rd Infantry Bde., 61st Division, is relieving the 184th Inf. Bde. on the immediate right of this Divisional Sector on the night of 14/15th August.

                                         Captain,
                                     Brigade Major,
13th Aug. 1918.   120th Infantry Brigade.

120th Inf. Bde. No. 120/415.

SECRET   COPY NO......

120TH INFANTRY BRIGADE DEFENCE ORDERS

1. The following amendments are to be made to Appendix II "ANTI-AIRCRAFT DEFENCE".

    (a) After "or if in pairs" add "or single".

    (b) Add new para. as follows :-

    "An order board is to be provided at every post. Units will also arrange that the 'Letter and Colours of the Day' (particularly the latter) are communicated to each of their posts and understood by them.

    An additional reason for the restriction of A.A. Lewis Gun fire at night, particularly in back areas, is that the A.A. defences depend largely on listening for the location of hostile aeroplanes and that this is made more difficult if Lewis Guns fire unnecessarily."

2. With reference to (b) above, copies of a paper of orders for A.A. Lewis Gunners have been forwarded for distribution to each gun (vide 120th Inf. Bde. No. 120/401 dated 14:8:18 - to Battalions only). This paper should be pasted to a board of piece of tin and tied to the mounting or some part of the emplacement of the gun.

3. The Letters and Colours change daily at 12 noon and are to be communicated daily to A.A. Lewis Guns as if they were Passwords.

4. ACKNOWLEDGE (Units only).

16.8.18
Issued to
all recipients
of 120th Inf.
Bde. Defence
Orders dated
13:8:18.

                                                Captain,
                                            Brigade Major,
                                        120th Infantry Brigade.

Appendix II.

ANTI - AIRCRAFT DEFENCE.

All Units are responsible for their own protection against attacks from the air, and should ensure that they are complete in A.A. small arms, sights and mountings, according to establishment.

The following are the chief considerations which will govern the defence of the area :-

(a) Fire will be opened on low-flying aeroplanes by rifles and Lewis guns, but in every case the sentry in front line posts will continue to watch the front.

(b) Lewis guns told off for anti-aircraft purposes in the line should not be placed at greater intervals than 500 yards. Positions may be changed, but changes should be reported to Brigade Headquarters so that the anti-aircraft defence may be co-ordinated.

(c) Most implicit orders are necessary to ensure that no Lewis gun or rifle is to fire unless the "CROSS" on the hostile plane can be clearly seen with the naked eye. It is useless to fire at a range greater than 1,300 yards. This is to be made clear to every Lewis gunner, and steps will be taken to deal with those who fire wildly at aeroplanes obviously out of range.

(d) Anti-aircraft Lewis Guns will, as far as possible, be placed in groups of 4, or in pairs. If in groups of 4, they will be under an officer, or if in pairs under N.C.O's to be supervised by an officer.

Fire at night will not be opened unless :-

(i) The hostile aircraft can be seen against the sky.

(ii) The struts of the planes can be distinguished in the beams of the searchlight.

subsequently be forwarded to Battalion and thence to Brigade Headquarters as soon as possible.

(3) The Battalion Signaller on receiving the message will automatically repeat it as follows in this order :-

To   (i) The signal office of the covering artillery units.
     (ii) Covering Machine Gun units.
     (iii) Brigade Signal Office.
     (iv) Companies other than the company which originated the call.
     (v) Flank battalions.

(4) The Brigade Signal Office on receiving the message will automatically repeat in this order :-

To   (i) The signal office of the covering Artillery Group.
     (ii) The signal office of the covering Machine Gun Coy.
     (iii) Divisional signal office.
     (iv) Battalions other than the battalion which communicated the call.
     (v) Flank Brigade Signal Offices (for information only).

(5) The order of precedence given in (3) and (4) above is so given as a guide only, but it should be understood that the S.O.S. call takes precedence of all other messages, and that all other traffic should be suspended for it. The S.O.S. call should, therefore, where circumstances permit, be sent simultaneously to all concerned.

(6) In the event of a breakdown of lines, any other suitable means of communication may be used.

(7) Every signal office will warn its own H.Q. of the S.O.S. message as instructed by those H.Q.

(c) (1) The S.O.S. Light Signal consists at present of a rifle grenade bursting into :-

            RED over GREEN over YELLOW.

(2) Chains of repeating stations are established as follows :-

Sending Stn.	Repeating Station.
Any Coy. in R.1.	K.4.a.6.2.
	K.4.a.6.4. (Artillery).

(3) In order to confine the barrage to essential limits only, S.O.S. light signals will not be repeated by flank companies in the line or by repeating stations other than those in the chains given above.

(4) The signal will be repeated by the sending station until answered by artillery fire.

(d) (1) The strombos horn signal is a succession of short blasts lasting not more than 10 seconds each.

(2) The signal is taken up by all horns in the neighbourhood.

(3) It should therefore not be used when either of the other means is possible. It is intended only to cover the breakdown of signal communications combined with conditions which make it doubtful that the S.O.S. light signal will be seen.

-3-

defence of the "Z" line, and may be stationed close behind the "Z" line instead of on it, if thought desirable.

(d) The 3 Companies of the Support Battalion not in the "Z" line will remain as permanent garrisons of the works they are occupying.

(e) The two remaining companies of the Reserve Battalion will form a Brigade Reserve, for employment as the situation requires.

(f) That portion of the T.M.Battery not manning positions covering either the Forward Zone or "Z" line will remain in Brigade Reserve.

(g) The Details of the 5 Battalions of the Brigade will be formed into a composite company under the orders of the senior officer with them, and will occupy 3 posts in D.12 and D.18.a.

ACTION IN THE EVENT OF SURPRISE ATTACK BEFORE "PERCY" IS ISSUED.

In this case, the dispositions will follow as closely as is possible those made for "PERCY".

(a) Troops in the Forward Zone will hold out at all costs, but will not be reinforced.

The "Z" line will be reinforced as soon as possible as for "PERCY", but no counter-attack will be made in front of the "Z" line until the force of the enemy's attack has been broken.

7. WORKING PARTIES.

Working Parties will always move to their work fully equipped for fighting. In case of heavy bombardment or hostile action indicating an attack, working parties will at once man the nearest defences, reporting to the nearest unit (Battalion or Brigade Headquarters) that they have done so, and notifying their own unit at once.

If the situation does not require them to remain in these defences, instructions will be issued by the Brigade for them to rejoin their units.

8. RESPONSIBILITY FOR WORK.

The Battalion in the line is responsible for all work forward of the "Z" line. All battalions are responsible for the improvement and maintenance of all portions of that part of the line which they occupy. Responsibility for the work on the defences of the "Z" line rests with the Division.

9. ACKNOWLEDGE.

Captain,
Brigade Major,
120th Infantry Brigade.

Distribution :-
Copy No. 1 ... G.O.C.
2 ... Bde.Major.
3 ... 10th K.O.S.B.
4 ... 15th K.O.Y.L.I.
5 ... 11th Camerons.
6 ... 31st Div. "G".
7 ... 92nd Inf.Bde.
8 ... 183rd Inf.Bde.
9 ... 165 Bde. R.F.A.
10 ... 120th T.M.Bty.

-2-

5. The 120th Bde. ~~front~~ front is covered by :-

(a) The 165th Bde. R.F.A., whose Headquarters are at SCALLOP FM. This comprises 3 - 18 pr. batteries, and 1 - 4.5 Howitzer battery.

(b) "A" Coy. 31st M.G. Battalion with Hd.Qrs. at E.26.a.8.3.

(c) Certain 6" Newton mortars, details of which will be issued later.

6. ACTION IN CASE OF ATTACK.

There are 3 kinds of warning signals :-
(i) S.O.S.
(ii) GAS.
(iii) "PERCY".

(i) S.O.S.

See Appendix I for general instructions.

The S.O.S. lines of the covering Artillery are as follows :-

"A" Battery (18-pdr.).

K.12.a.0.0. - K.12.a.60.55. - thence along line of the BECQUE - K.12.a.75.80.

"B" Battery. (18-pdr.)

K.12.a.75.80. - K.6.c.83.00. - K.6.c.98.83.

"D" Battery. (4.5" How.)

K.6.c.98.83. - K.6.b.0.0. - E.30.c.8.0.

"C" Battery. (18-pdr.)

E.30.c.8.0. - E.30. central.

(ii) GAS.

For general instructions as to giving alarm, etc., see Appendix 2.
Special precautions against gas shelling are to be taken in this sector, as it is particularly likely to occur in the BOIS D'AVAL area. Steps will be taken to thin out the troops in the gassed area as far as is possible, and to arrange for their periodical relief.
Our guns will not open fire if no hostile attack is suspected, except at the request of the infantry.

(iii) "PERCY".
If a hostile attack on our front seems to be impending, the code word "PERCY" will be sent.
The following action will then be taken at once :-
(a) Artillery will move into battle positions.
(b) No reinforcements will be sent, nor counter-attacks made in front of the "Z" line.
(c) The battalion in reserve will send two companies to reinforce the "Z" line. These companies will be under the tactical control of the C.O. of the battalion in the ~~line~~ forward zone, who will be responsible for the

SECRET   COPY NO. 5

120TH INFANTRY BRIGADE.

DEFENCE ORDERS.

14:8:18.

1. The 120th Brigade is holding the right sector of the 31st Division, with the 92nd Brigade of the 31st Division on the left, and the 183rd Brigade of the 61st Division on the right.

2. The boundaries of the area are as follows :-

   NORTHERN BRIGADE BOUNDARY.

   E.30 central - E.29 central - VALLEY FARM inclusive to Northern Brigade - SAWMILLS, E.19.d.1.0 - along track to D.24.a.8.0 - grid line through D.23 and D.21 central.

   SOUTHERN BRIGADE BOUNDARY.

   K.11.b.7.4. - K.4.a.6.0. - K.2.a.2.0. - along Canal through K.1.c. to D.30.c.7.3. - D.29.c.8.5. - D.29.a.8.2. - D.28.a.6.2. - D.28.c.6.5. - WEEVIL Crossing.

3. METHOD OF HOLDING THE SECTOR.

   (a) The Sector will be held with one battalion in the Forward Zone and "Z" Line; one battalion in Support about the Reserve Line, and one battalion in Reserve about TIR ANGLAIS.

   (b) The battalion in the Forward Zone will have two of its own companies and one company attached to it from the 92nd Brigade in the Forward Zone. The attached company will always be on the right. Its other two companies will garrison the "Z" Line. In addition, one company of the Support Battalion will garrison the Northern portion of the "Z" line, and will be under the tactical control of the C.O. of the Battalion holding the Forward Zone and "Z" Line.

   (c) The Support Battalion will have one company in the Northern Sector of the "Z" Line, under the tactical control of the forward Battalion, as detailed in para. 3 (b), one company about E.27 central, and two companies in the Reserve Line.

   (d) The Reserve Battalion is concentrated at LE TIR ANGLAIS.

4. LIAISON POSTS.

   There are two liaison posts with the Brigade on the right :-

Front Line ...	120th Bde. post (attached Coy.)	... K.11.b.7.6.
...	183rd Bde. post	... K.11.b.7.2.
"Z" Line ...	120th Bde. Post	... K.4.c.8.8.
...	183rd Bde. Post	... K.4.c.8.8.

SECRET.   XV Corps No. I.G.50a/22.

31st Division.
============

1. In order to avoid delay in the naming of trenches a list of names which have been approved by the Army will be kept at Corps Headquarters.

2. In future, when it is required to name a trench, a map showing the limits of the trench will be sent to this office when a name will be allotted from this list.

XV Corps.   (Sgd) N.S.NESBIT, Captn.
13-8-18.   for G.B., G.S.

- 2 -

120th Infantry Brigade.
======================

    For information.
1. Please forward to this office a tracing showing :-

   (a) Any lengths of trench which have been named locally, stating the name which has been given to each. This name will, by virtue of the above letter, be cancelled and a new name allotted.

   (b) Any un-named lengths of trench which it is desired to have named.

2. It is pointed out that the practice of giving names to farms, roads, etc., locally is out of order. A list of any places which have been named locally or which it is desired to name should be forwarded to this office in order that the names may be submitted to higher authority, approved, and included in future prints of maps.

I.G.S.339   (Sgd) R.C. GREENAS, Captain,
14-8-18.   for Lieut.-Colonel, General Staff,
                                           31st Division.

- 3 -

120th Inf. Bde. No. 120/429.

10th Bn. K.O S.B.
15th Bn. K.O.Y.L.I.
11th Bn. Cam. Highrs.

    For necessary action as regards minute 2 by 16th instant.

                                              Captain,
                                          Brigade Major,
                                       120th Infantry Brigade.

14-8-18.

120th Infantry Brigade No. 120/427.   S E C R E T

10th K.O.S.B.
15th K.O.Y.L.I.
11th Cameron Hrs.
****

                    Herewith 5 copies of map showing area.

                                                    Captain,
                                              Brigade Major,
                                          120th Infantry Brigade.

14:8:18.

120th Infantry Brigade No. 120/429.   S E C R E T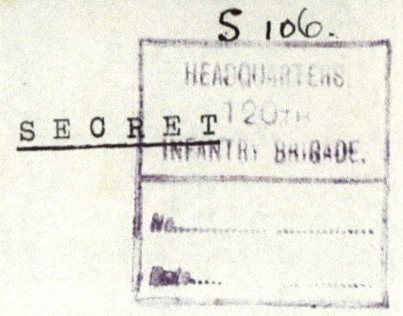

15th K.O.Y.L.I.
10th K.O.S.B.
11th Cameron Hrs.
****

    The G.O.C. wishes the policy of the front line posts to be one of active patrolling. The greatest attention should be paid to the enemy's habits and methods of holding the line, as there appear extremely good opportunities of occupying places by day which the enemy only occupies by night, and of capturing or killing Germans by lying in wait for them.
    The chief aim should be to make every man confident in patrolling.

                                          Captain,
                                       Brigade Major,
14th Aug. 1918.   120th Infantry Brigade.

120th Infy. Bde. No. 120/400.

Confidential.

S105.

10th K.O.S.B.
15th K.O.Y.L.I.
11th Cam. Hrs.

With reference to the attached correspondence re Training Officers for the Staff. Please will you forward the names of Officers recommended for Staff employment with a short summary of their services etc.

Reports to reach this office on 18th instant.

13.8.1918.

Captain,
Staff Captain,
120th Infantry Brigade.

40th Div. No. 138/2 G. CONFIDENTIAL.

119th Infantry Brigade.
120th   ,,
121st   ,,
17th Worcestershire Regt. (Pnrs).
C. R. E.
40th Div. Train.
A & Q
G.O.C.
****

The present series of courses referred to in the attached confidential memorandum " TRAINING OF OFFICERS FOR THE STAFF" commences on August 15th. Vacancies for this course have already been allotted.

Formations can help in maintaining a good standard for the Probationary Course by having officers whose names they propose to forward, attached to their Headquarters for a period of about a fortnight to test their capabilities.

A short summary of the service, age, and qualification of an officer should be forwarded with the nomination.

Nominations will be called for when required.

J. H. Stafford.
Major GS.

for. Lieut. Colonel,
11th August, 1918.   General Staff, 40th Division.

****

40th Div. No. 136/2 G.   C O N F I D E N T I A L.

TRAINING OF OFFICERS FOR THE STAFF.

1. The selection of officers for the Staff will be carried out under the following arrangements.

2. Officers will not be considered for first employment on the Staff unless they have passed either -

      1. The Probationary Course.
      2. Staff Course.

3. Probationary Course.

(i) For officers of all arms to test their suitability for the Staff.
(ii) Officers selected should be between the ages of 21 and 35 and should not be above the rank of Captain, but in special cases acting majors may be nominated.
(iii) Officers will remain on the strength of their own units during the continuance of the course.
(iv) The course will last 6 weeks and will consist of :-

    (a) Three weeks' attachment to an Infantry Brigade H.Q.
    (b) Three weeks' attachment to Divisional Headquarters.

(v) The number of officers undergoing this course will be limited to :-
    1 Officer to be nominated by Division.
    4 officers to be nominated by Army.

(vi) At the conclusion of an officer's attachment to a Brigade, the Brigade Commander will forward a report on A.F. W.3723 to Divisional Headquarters. At the completion of the course a report on A.F. W.3723 will be sent in to Corps from Divisional Headquarters.
(vii) Officers reported on as suitable for further training will be eligible for the Staff Course.

4. Staff Course.

(i) For further training of officers who have been through the Probationary Course or the Preliminary (Learners') Course which is now superseded by the Probationary Course, and are reported on favourably.

(ii) Officers will remain on the strength of their own units during the continuance of the course.

(iii) The course will last 60 days, and will consist of :-

    (a) 6 weeks' attachment to G.S. (including Intelligence) A & Q Offices. The attached officer should be placed in close touch with junior staff officers on both sides in order to gain a knowledge of their work both in the office and out of doors. He should be given work to do on his own account as opportunity offers, but he will not be employed upon purely mechanical routine work to lighten the labour of the junior staff officers concerned.

Variety.....

-ii-

Variety of employment is essential in order that the course may provide instruction as to the Staff machinery, its methods and duties.

(b) Two weeks' attachment partly to another arm -

Artillery or R.E. to Infantry
Infantry to Artillery

and partly to the administrative services.

(c) During at least 14 days in all the attached officer will officiate in the absence of an officer on leave or duty in a junior staff appointment of the type for which he is considered best suited.

(iv) A portion of the course will be carried out at Corps Headquarters. At the completion of this attachment a report will be sent by Corps Headquarters to Division.

(v) Officers to undergo the Staff Course will be selected by the Corps Commander.

(vi) At the conclusion of the course a report will be sent to Corps on A.F. W.3723, stating particularly -
  (a) The course carried out
  (b) An opinion as to the officer's suitability for the staff, manner, experience, age, ability etc., and for what appointment he is recommended.

(vii) Officers who have passed through the Staff Course will be eligible for appointment as G.S.O.3 or Staff Captain.

5. The Probationary and Staff Courses will start on the same day and nominations will be called for prior to this date.

6. Nominations for these courses will not be confined to the Infantry but will embrace all arms of the service.

7. Nominations for the Staff Courses held at Cambridge will be called for as heretofore.

8. In order to provide a reserve of qualified Staff Officers for appointment as Brigade Majors, officers holding the appointment of G.S.O.3 and Staff Captain will be attached as understudies to Brigade Majors for a period of one month. These attachments will be arranged by Army. The officers will be replaced in their permanent appointments by officers who have qualified for staff employment at a Staff Course (as in 4 above). The latter will continue to draw regimental pay.

9. Appointments up to Brigade Major will be made by the Army from the lists kept at Army Headquarters.
Appointments above Brigade Major will be made by G.H.Q.
Applications by subordinate commanders for officers by name to fill these appointments will not be considered.

****

S 105

120th Infantry Brigade.

With reference to your No 120/400 re training officers for the Staff the return for this unit is
N I L

Lt Col
Comdg 11th Cameron Highrs

15/8/18

SECRET   COPY NO. 8.

120TH INFANTRY BRIGADE ORDER NO. 209.

15:8:18.

1. On the night 17/18th August, the 10th K.O.S.B. will relieve the 11th Cameron Hrs. in Support: the 11th Cameron Hrs. will relieve the 15th K.O.Y.L.I. in the line, and the 15th K.O.Y.L.I. will move back into Reserve.

2. All arrangements for reliefs will be made between C.Os. concerned, but the relief of the 11th Cameron Hrs. by the K.O.S.B. will be complete by 9 p.m.

3. All special maps, etc. will be handed over to incoming battalions, and 11th Cameron Hrs. will take over all hot food containers and trench store petrol tins from battalion in line.

4. Battalions coming into their new positions will take over all working parties, in accordance with 120th Inf. Bde. No. 120/417 dated 14:8:18.
   All working parties for the night 17/18th, previously found by 11th Cameron Hrs., will be provided by the 10th K.O.S.B.

5. Completion of relief will be wired to Brigade H.Q. using following code words :-

       15th K.O.Y.L.I.   ...   ...   DUCK.
       10th K.O.S.B.   ...   ...   BOARD.
       11th Cameron Hrs. ...   ...   TRACK.

6. ACKNOWLEDGE.

                                                          Captain,
Issued through   Brigade Major,
   Signals   120th Infantry Brigade.
  at 2 p.m.
   *****

Distribution:-
Copy No. 1 ... G.O.C.   21 ... 121st Inf.Bde.
       2 ... Bde.Major.   22 ... Bde.Supply Offr.
       3 ... Staff Captain.   23 ... Bde.Signals.
       4 ... War Diary.
       5 ... File.
       6 ... 10th K.O.S.B.
       7 ... 15th K.O.Y.L.I.
       8 ... 11th Cameron Hrs.
       9 ... 120th T.M.Bty.
     10 ... 40th Divn. "G".
     11 ... 31st Divn. "G".
     12 ... 31st Divn. "Q".
     13 ... 92nd Inf.Bde.
     14 ... 183rd Inf.Bde.
     15 ... "A" Coy. 31st M.G.Bn.
     16 ... 165 Bde. R.F.A.
     17 ... A.D.M.S., 31st Div.
     18 ... C.R.E., 31st Div.
     19 ... 40th Div. Train.
     20 ... 119th Inf.Bde.

S 112

SECRET.

Administrative Instructions for LA MOTTE Area.

Ref. Sheets:
27.A., 36.A., (1,40,000).
36.A. N.E. (1,20,000).   15:8:1918.

120th Infantry Brigade Administrative Order No. 207 applies to the LA MOTTE Area with the following alterations.

(1) Delete para. 1 and substitute :-
"Brigade Headquarters   ...   FETTLE FARM, D.24.a.8.1.
 Front Line Batt.H.Qrs.   ...   E.26.d.9.8.
 Support Battalion H.Qrs.   ...   E.25.d.5.6.
 Reserve Battn.H.Qrs.   ...   D.11.d.7.8.
 120th T.M. Battery.   ...   D.18.c.7.3.
 211th Fd.Coy., R.E.   ...   D.5.c.9.1.

(2) Delete paras. 3(b), (c), (d) and substitute :-
    (b) Rations can be delivered close to all Company Headquarters by limber.
    (c) Limbers passing the SAWMILLS, (E.19.d.1.2) by day must go singly at an interval of at least 100 yards.
    (d) The main road passing the SAWMILLS is closed from 7.30 pm. to 9 pm., until further orders.

(3) Delete para. 5(b) and substitute :-
    5(b). The Brigade dump is established at E.27.c.1.2.
          Battalion dumps are located at E.28.a.3.2 and E.29.a.9.1.

(4) Add to para. 6(c) after "Headquarters" by 9 am.

(5) In para. 12, line 2 for D.8.a.3.0 read D.8.d.3.0.

(6) WATER.
    (a) Water points cart filling points exist at :-
            GUNEWELE   ...   D.2.a.1.1.
            WALLON CAPPEL   U.28.b.5.7.
    (b) Water points exist forward at :-
            E.28.a.5.9.
            E.19.b.9.7.

                                        Captain,
                                        Staff Captain,
                                     120th Infantry Brigade.

15.8.1918.

120th Inf. Bde.   S E C R E T   S 110
****

It is reliably reported that the enemy has adopted a method whereby they try to rush our posts by coming up to them apparently meaning to surrender. Having thus approached they then try to capture the posts.
Please warn all Battalions concerned.

        sd. R.C.Greenas, Capt.,
        for Lieut-Colonel,
        General Staff,
        31st Division.

I.G.S. 341.
15/8/18.

-ii-

120th Infantry Brigade No. 120/429.

10th K.O.S.B.
15th K.O.Y.L.I.
11th Cameron Hrs. ✓
****

For information and communication to all ranks concerned.

        Captain,
        Brigade Major,
        120th Infantry Brigade.

15:8:18.

Confidential.   120th Infy. Bde. No. 120/400

10th K.O.S.B.
15th K.O.Y.L.I.
11th Cam. Hrs.

    Names of Officers recommended for Command or Second-in-Command of Infantry Battalions is due at Division on 17th instant.

    Please confirm that the Second-in-Command of the Battalion under your command has been confirmed in his appointment.

    Also if you have any officers whom you consider suitable to command or be Second-in-Command of a battalion, the necessary recommendation should be submitted on A.F. W.3723, particular care being taken that the Record of Services of the Officer is accurately stated.

    The question of officers considered suitable for the appointment of Second-in-Command should be given particular xxxxxxxxx consideration.

                                  Captain,
                                Staff Captain,
14.8.1918.   120th Infantry Brigade.

120th Inf. Bde. No. 120/466.
11th Cameron Hrs.
~~15th K.O.Y.L.I.~~
15th K.O.Y.L.I.
****

S E C R E T.
****

The relief of "A" Coy., 31st M.G. Battalion by "D" Coy. will take place night 18/19th instead of 17/18th inst.

17:8:18.

Captain,
Brigade Major,
120th Infantry Brigade.

S 117

120th Infantry Brigade No. 120/406.　　　S E C R E T
11th Cameron Hrs.
10th K.O.S.B.
15th K.O.Y.L.I. (For information).
****

The 10th E. Yorks will be relieving the company attached to this Brigade in the line this evening.

O.C., K.O.Y.L.I., has made all arrangements.

10th E. Yorks are also relieving 11th E. Yorks in R.2.

　　　　　　　　　　　　　　　Captain,
　　　　　　　　　　　　　Brigade Major,
17:8:18.　　　　　　　　　120th Infantry Brigade.

HEADQUARTERS,
120TH
INFANTRY BRIGADE.

S E C R E T

120th Inf. Bde.
****

Commencing at 12 noon on 19th August 1918, the S.O.S. Signal on the XV Corps Front will be a rifle grenade - RED - RED - RED. The grenades will be issued under arrangements to be made by "Q".

All S.O.S. signals of the type now in use and remaining on hand after noon on 19th inst., will be collected and returned under arrangements to be made by "Q".

sd. R.O.Greenas, Capt.,
for Lieut.-Colonel,
General Staff,
51st Division.

S.G.17/359
15/8/18.

-ii-

120th Inf. Bde. No. 120/477.
10th K.O.S.B.
15th K.O.Y.L.I.
11th Cameron Hrs./
****

For information.
Instructions as to issue of new grenades and withdrawal of old will be issued by Staff Captain.

15:8:18.

Captain,
Brigade Major,
120th Infantry Brigade.

URGENT.

S 119

Secret   92nd Brigade.
==========   S.12/183/4.

120th Inf. Bde.

    *   *   *

Ref. this office S.12/183.

It is possible that if the enemy system from F.13.a.5.0. to E.24.central is penetrated by our patrols and held, the enemy may vacate his line from about E.24.b.6.0. through LA COURONNE down to about E.30.a.8.0.
Front Battalions will therefore send out two daylight camouflage patrols each (2 or 3 O.R.) to gain knowledge of the enemy's whereabouts and ensure that he does not vacate this system without our knowing. These patrols will leave our line at 3 p.m. and time of return and information will be wired to this office immediately.

                                sd.   Major,
                                  Brigade Major,
                                92nd Infantry Bde.

18:8:18.

-ii-

120th Inf. Bde. No. 120/426.   SECRET.

11th Bn. Cameron Hrs.
****

Reference above.

Left Company must keep close touch with Company on their left, in the event of the enemy withdrawing.

                                  Captain,
                                Brigade Major,
18:8:18.   120th Infantry Brigade.

120th Infantry Brigade No. 120/426.   S E C R E T

10th K.O.S.B.
15th K.O.Y.L.I.
11th Cameron Hrs.
120th T. M. Bty.
92nd Infantry Bde.
183rd Infantry Bde.

1. The final line which is at present to be aimed at by the Division runs as follows :-

   VIERHOOCK - PONT RONDIN - KEW CROSS - F.25.c.9.5. - BRACKEN FARM - BLEU -HULLEBERT FARM.

   This will be known as the "Q" Line.

2. No main posts will be established E. of the BECQUE until patrols have made good the line of the PONT-RONDIN - KEW CROSS roads,* when posts will be established on this new line, and patrols again pushed out to gain information.

   *through SLUG FARM.

3. No further advance will be made East of the "Q" Line without further orders, but patrols will be pushed out, when the line has been made good with posts, to try and gain information.

4. 11th Camerons may move up one Company, exclusive of that relieving the 10th E. Yorks., from the "Z" Line into the forward zone, if desired, but notification must be sent to Brigade Headquarters.

5. The most frequent reports possible must be sent back by patrols.

20:8:18.

Captain,
Brigade Major,
120th Infantry Brigade.

SECRET　　　　　　　　　　　　　　　　　　　　　COPY NO. 8

S 122

120TH INFANTRY BRIGADE ORDER NO. 210

20-8-18.

1. The 120th Infantry Brigade will take over the Right Battalion Sector of the 92nd Infantry Brigade on the left to-night.

2. The new Northern Brigade Boundary of the Brigade will run as follows :-

    E.22.central - Road Junction E.30.b.0.7. - F.26.c.0.0. - L.3.a.0.0. - L.5.d.0.5.

3. The 10th K.O.S.B. will take over this new Sector from the 10th E. Yorks Regt., and will carry on the latter's Patrol Scheme.
    All arrangements will be made between C.Os. concerned. Special maps, etc, will be taken over as usual.

4. The 11th Cameron Hrs. will relieve the attached Company of the 10th E. Yorks Regt. on the right to-night. On relief this attached Company will move back to TIR ANGLAIB.
    The most careful arrangements must be made to ensure that the strictest liaison is maintained with the Unit on the right.

5. The 15th K.O.Y.L.I. will move from TIR ANGLAIS to the Support Area, moving one Company to the "Z" Line, one in the area between "Z" and Reserve Line, keeping two in the Reserve Line.
    The Camp at TIR ANGLAIS will be left standing and will be handed over to the 10th E. Yorks Regt.

6. Completion of relief will be wired as under :-

    10th Bn. K.O.S.B.　...　...　STICK
    15th Bn. K.O.Y.L.I.　...　...　NO
    11th Bn. Cam. Hrs.　...　...　BILLS.

Issued through
Signals
at 3-30 p.m.

Captain,
Brigade Major,
120th Infantry Brigade.

DISTRIBUTION :-

Copy No 1 ... G.O.C.　　　　　　13 ... 92nd Inf. Bde.
       2 ... Brigade Major.　　14 ... 183rd Inf. Bde.
       3 ... Staff Captain.　　15 ... 223rd Field Coy. R.E.
       4 ... War Diary.　　　　16 ... C.R.E., 31st Divn.
       5 ... File.　　　　　　　17 ... A.D.M.S., 31st Divn.
       6 ... 10th K.O.S.B.　　18 ... 165th Bde. R.F.A.
       7 ... 15th K.O.Y.L.I.　19 ... "A" Coy. 31st Bn.M.G.C.
       8 ... 11th Cam. Hrs.　 20 ... Bde. Signals.
       9 ... 120th T. M. Bty. 21 ... Bde. Supply Officer
      10 ... 31st Divn. "G"　 22 ... "X" 31st M.T.M.Bty.
      11 ... 31st Divn. "Q"
      12 ... 40th Divn. "G"

SECRET   COPY NO. 8

120TH INFANTRY BRIGADE ORDER NO. 212.
                                                    21:8:18.

1. On night 21st/22nd, the 10th K.O.S.B. will extend their left flank northwards to F.19.d.2.6., taking over the line from the 11th E. Yorks Regt., of the 92nd Infantry Brigade, and holding R.2. and R.3. subsectors with 3 companies in the line.

2. After completion of relief, the northern boundary of the Brigade will run as follows :-

    E.16.central - Road Junction E.18.c.1.2. - F.27 central.

3. All arrangements for relief will be arranged direct between C.Os. concerned.

4. All maps, aeroplane photos, dumps, etc. will be taken over, receipts given, and duplicates forwarded to this office.

5. 10th K.O.S.B. will submit disposition sketch within 24 hours of relief.

6. Completion of relief will be wired by code word :-

    GILDY.

7. 15th K.O.Y.L.I. will be prepared to furnish carrying parties for the two battalions in the line to-night. All arrangements will be made direct.

8. On night 22nd/23rd, 119th Infantry Brigade will relieve the 10th K.O.S.B. in R.3. subsector, and the 15th K.O.Y.L.I. will relieve the 11th Camerons in R.1. subsector. The inter-battalion boundary between 10th K.O.S.B. and 15th K.O.Y.L.I. will then be brought further South.

9. ACKNOWLEDGE.

Issued through
  Signals   Captain,
  at 3.45 p.m.   Brigade Major,
                                      120th Infantry Brigade.

DISTRIBUTION :-

Copy No.			No.		
1	...	G.O.C.	12	...	31st Div. "Q".
2	...	Bde. Major.	13	...	92nd Inf. Bde.
3	...	Staff Capt.	14	...	183rd Inf. Bde.
4	...	War Diary.	15	...	"D" Coy. 31st M.G.Bn.
5	...	File.	16	...	165 Bde. R.F.A.
6	...	10th K.O.S.B.	17	...	A.D.M.S., 31st Div.
7	...	15th K.O.Y.L.I.	18	...	C.R.E.
8	...	11th Cameron Hrs.	19	...	223 Fd. Coy. R.E.
9	...	120th T.M.Bty.	20	...	Bde. Supply Officer.
10	...	40th Div. "G".	21	...	"X" 31 T.M.Bty.
11	...	31st Div. "G".	22	...	Bde. Signals.

S 128

ADMINISTRATIVE INSTRUCTIONS No. 213.

R I G H T   B R I G A D E.

Ref. Sheets 27 and 36a.

1. Transport Lines of battalions are ~~xxxxxxxx~~ located at PAPOTE - D.16.d.1.2.
    Brigade Headquarters Transport Lines are at present at D.8.d.8.1 but will move shortly to D.16.d.1.2.

2. Water. Is obtained from following water cart refilling points :-
    (1) GUNEWALE.
    (2) HAZEBROUCK.

3. Ammunition. (a) The Divisional Dump is situated in the lines of the S.A.A. Section, 40th D.A.C., at U.21.b.6.5.
    (b) Brigade dumps are established at :-
        Brigade Hd.Qrs   ...   D.24.a.8.1.
        "B" Ride   ...   E.27.c.2.3.
    (c) Demands for ammunition will be submitted to reach Brigade Headquarters by 8 am. daily.

4. (a) R.E.Dumps.
        Divisional Dump   ...   V.19.c.8.7.
        Brickstacks Dump   ...   E.20.b.7.0.
        Forestry Dump   ...   E.26.c.2.3.
        Operation Dump   ...   E.27.d.9.9.
        (end of No.2 Mule track).
    (b) All indents for material will be forwarded to reach Brigade Headquarters by 9 am. daily. Brigade Headquarters will submit requirements to affiliated R.E. Company.

5. Railhead.
        E B B L I N G H E M.

6. Refilling Point.
        Location of re-filling point and No.3 Coy., A.S.C. Train will be notified later.

7. Reserve rations and water.
        Rations are dumped for the LA MOTTE Defences at -
            D.30.d.2.6.
            E.20 central.

8. Tramway System.
        Runs from E.20.b.7.0 to K.3.a.3.8 with branches running East as under :-
        (1) E.27.a.0.4 to E.27.b.1.8.
        (2) E.27.c.2.3 forking at E.27.c.7.3 to E.27.d.9.9 and K.3.b.9.8.
        Push trucks are kept under a guard at E.20.b.7.0 and receipts must be given for all trucks issued.

9. Baths. A bath is being erected near FETTLE FARM, D.24.a.7.6., for the use of the Reserve Battalions in the line. It will have capacity for 100 men per hour.

10. Clean Clothing Store. Divisional Clean Clothing Store will be established at WALLON CAPPEL.
        Units indent direct on the Divisional Baths Officer and draw from Divisional Stores with 1st line transport

11. Gassed Clothing. Such men as have been affected with Yellow

Cross/

* 2 *

Cross Gas will be sent to the Divisional Main Dressing Station with a certificate signed by an officer stating that their clothing has been affected, when fresh clothing will be issued.

12. **Salvage.** All salvage collected will be sent by units direct to Divisional Salvage dump at WALLON CAPPEL. A solder kiln for the recovery of solder is situated at Divisional Salvage Dump.

13. **Ordnance.** D.A.D.O.S. opens at WALLON CAPPEL at 12 noon, 24th August.

14. **Medical Arrangements.**
    (a) 135th Fd. Ambce. will be responsible for the evacuation from forward area.
    (b) Relay Posts - E.19.b.8.3.
                      K.3.a.3.7.
                      K.4.a.5.4.
        A. D. S.   - D.18.a.5.3.
        Reserve A.D.S. - D.9.d.1.3.
        M. D. S.   - C.5.a.6.9.

15. **Provost Arrangements.**
    Locations of Battle stops, P. of W. cages and Stragglers Posts :-
    First Position - Battle Stops.
    D.20.d.0.3 - D.20.b.9.4 - D.15.b.4.1 - D.10.b.6.7 - D.11.b.3.7.
    Stragglers Collecting Station and Advanced P. of W. Cage :-
    D.9.b.4.2.

16. **Divisional Canteens.**
    Wallon CAPPEL   .....   U.23.c.20.35.
    LE GRAND HAZARD   .....   D.13.b.3.9.

17. **Cemeteries.**
    No burials will take place except in the cemeteries authorised in Corps and Divisional Routine Orders.

18. **Divisional Reception Camp.**
    Remains in present location.

T. Knox-Shaw

Captain,
Staff Captain,
120th Infantry Brigade.

23.8.1913.

O.C.
1/4 KOSB
15 KOYLI
11 Camerons.

**HEADQUARTERS,
120TH
INFANTRY BRIGADE.**

No. 120/47

The following dumps have been made by the 92nd Inf Bde.

(a) Top of 'B' Ride E.20.b.6.0
    Rolls of barbed wire ready for transport on Pack Animals.

(b) On road from LA BECQUE to E.23.a.9.5
    Rolls of barbed wire

(c) At Bridge over BECQUE at E.23.a.8.5
    150 shovels.

21.8.18   T. Knox Shaw Capt
           Staff Capt 120 Inf Bde

SECRET   COPY NO... 8.

120TH INFANTRY BRIGADE ORDER NO. 214.
                                                          22:8:18.

1.   On completion of relief to-night, the 120th Infantry
        Bde. line will run from COCHIN CORNER along the road PONT
        RONDIN - KEW CROSS - thence to F.25.c.7.4.

2.   119th Infantry Brigade are trying to-night to get on
        to the general line ROOSTER FARM - BECKET CORNER - OUTLET
        CORNER.
        183rd Infantry Bde. on our right are on the line
        CHAPELLE DUVELLE - RUE MONTIGNY, and from there have an
        advance flank to COCHIN CORNER.

3.   At 4 p.m., 23rd inst., the 120th Inf.Bde., in conjunction
        with 119th Infantry Bde. on the left and 183rd Inf. Bde. on
        the right, will advance to the line Cross Roads L.3.c.8.4.
        to BECKET CORNER. This line will be continued Southwards
        by 183rd Bde. 15th K.O.Y.L.I. will be on the right and
        10th K.O.S.B. on the left.

4.   The right boundary of the advance will be the line
        of the road from L.15.b.2.7. to Cross Roads L.3.c.8.4.,
        on which line touch will be continuously maintained with
        183rd Bde. on the right.
        The left boundary of the advance will be the line of
        the road from KEW CROSS to BECKET CORNER, on which line
        touch will be continuously maintained with 119th Infantry
        Bde.
        Inter-battalion boundary will be the line of the stream
        from PONT RONDIN to its junction with the LAUDICK in L.1.b.7.3.,
        thence along the ditch from L.1.b.8.1. to L.2.b.7.6.

5.   The advance will be made with fighting patrols, supported
        by platoons, and will be made in two main bounds - one, to the
        line of the LAUDICK, and the second to the final objective.

6.   Fighting patrols must push forward boldly, and must
        endeavour to work round any local points which is holding
        up the advance. To assist in this, two Stokes Mortars with
        teams will be allotted to each battalion. All arrangements
        for parties for the necessary carrying of ammunition, etc.
        will be made direct between O.C., 120th T.M.Bty. and Battn.
        Commanders concerned.

7.   In the event of the general advance being held up by
        machine gun fire from enclosures along the line of BISHOPS
        CORNER - BECKET CORNER, arrangements have been made for
        artillery to fire a 10-minutes burst on this line of
        enclosures from BISHOP'S CORNER to F.26.d.7.4. when called
        for by Company Commanders.
        The signal for this artillery support to be put down
        will be the firing of 3 Very Lights in succession, fired
        from Company Headquarters.

8.   Joint Battalion Headquarters will be formed by 15th
        K.O.Y.L.I. and 10th K.O.S.B. at present 15th K.O.Y.L.I.
        Headquarters - ~~GARS BRUGGHE~~. K.5.a.8.7.

9.   The Greatest attention must be paid to the forwarding of
        frequent reports, and to keeping the closest touch with
        units on flank.

10.   ACKNOWLEDGE.

Issued 10.30 p.m.

                                                    CAPTAIN,
                                                BRIGADE MAJOR,
                                            120TH INFANTRY BRIGADE.

DISTRIBUTION:-

Copy No.		
1	...	G.O.C.
2	...	Brigade Major.
3	...	Staff Captain.
4	...	War Diary.
5	...	File.
6	...	10th K.O.S.B.
7	...	15th K.O.Y.L.I.
8	...	11th Cameron Hrs.
9	...	120th T.M. Bty.
10	...	40th Division "G".
11	...	119th Inf. Bde.
12	...	183rd Inf. Bde.
13	...	223rd Field Coy. R.E.
14	...	165 Bde. R.F.A.
15	...	Bde. Signals.

S 126

SECRET.   120th Infy. Bde. No. 120/474.

10th K.O.S.B.
15th K.O.Y.L.I.
11th Cam. Hrs.
Bde. Transport Officer.
T.O., 15th K.O.Y.L.I.
T.O., 11th Cam. Hrs.

HEADQUARTERS,
120TH
INFANTRY BRIGADE.

No............................
Date ....

The following arrangements will be made with reference to Brigade Order No. 214.

WATER.   A dump of 80 petrol tins of water will be formed near Rear Headquarters of 15th Batt. K.O.Y.L.I. in "B" Drive.

The Brigade Transport Officer will arrange for 10 pack animals to be at this dump by 7.30 pm. on 23nd instant.

O.C., 11th Cam. Highrs. will detail one officer and a loading party to take charge of this dump; assist in roping up the tins and checking the issue. 40 tins are allotted to each of the Battalions - 10th K.O.S.B. and 15th K.O.Y.L.I.

This water is intended to be in addition to the water sent up with rations.

Battalions must notify Rear Headquarters, 15th K.O.Y.L.I number of tins required and where guides will meet convoy.

S. A. A.   Boxes of S.A.A. and Grenades can be drawn from the Brigade Dump in "B" Ride.

The O.C., 10th K.O.S.B. and 15th K.O.Y.L.I. will each detail one limber to be at dump at 8 pm. ready to take forward any S.A.A. etc. required.

Captain,
Staff Captain,
120th Infantry Brigade.

23.8.1918.

11. Full details as to tactical and administrative policies to be adopted on the front will be issued later.

12. ACKNOWLEDGE.

Issued through
Signals
at 1.30 p.m.
========

                                              Captain,
                                     Brigade Major,
                        120th Infantry Brigade.

DISTRIBUTION :-

```
Copy. No.  1  ...  G.O.C.
           2  ...  Bde. Major.
           3  ...  Staff Captain.
           4  ...  War Diary.
           5  ...  File.
           6  ...  10th K.O.S.B.
           7  ...  13th K.O.Y.L.I.
           8  ...  11th Cameron Hrs.
           9  ...  120th T.M.Bty.
          10  ...  40th Div. "Q".
          11  ...  40th Div. "G".
          12  ...  119th Inf.Bde.
          13  ...  121st Inf.Bde.
          14  ...  183rd Inf.Bde.
          15  ...  223rd Fd.Coy.R.E.
          16  ...  229th Fd.Coy.R.E.
          17  ...  C.R.E., 40th Div.
          18  ...  A.D.M.S., 40th Div.
          19  ...      -Ditto-
          20  ...  40th Divnl. Train.
          21  ...  Bde. Supply Officer.
          22  ...  Bde. Signals.
```

============================

40th Division No. C/136/Q.

   The attached copy of Winter hutting scheme for the present 40th Division Area, as prepared by 31st Division, has been sent to us by XV Corps for remarks and suggestions as the situation and the area has been somewhat changed.

   Will you please consider the scheme from point of view of location of units (and their transport lines) with which you are concerned, and the number of huts required.

   With regard to the latter attention is drawn to this Office No. C/136/Q dated 23/8/1918.

   Your report is required at Divisional Headquarters by midday 25th August, 1918, in order that one may be sent to the XV Corps on the following day.

23rd August, 1918.

(WB).

               Lieut-Colonel,
              A. A. & Q. M. G.,
               40th Division.

S 138

O.C.
11th Cam. Highrs.

For information

Any Suggestions should
be forwarded to these S.O's
by last D.R. tonight

W. Archer
/t Staff Captain
120 Infantry Brigade

24.8.1918

HEADQUARTERS.
120th
INFANTRY BGDE
No. 120/403/1
Date............

31st Division No. 2015/14A.
XV Corps No. Q.C.550/10.

Headquarters,
XV Corps "Q".

In reply to your Q.C.550/10 of 11th and 13th inst. Herewith Map and Tabular statements as requested.

This scheme is based on the assumption that the scale of accommodation as laid down in S.S.501, namely 4 Senior, 6 Junior Officers or 20 O.R's per Nissen Hut is adhered to.

The proposed camps are designed to hold 700, the additional accommodation for 200 being allowed for at Transport Lines. It may be found necessary to make slight alterations in the positions of Transport Lines, but this will be avoided as far as possible.

The number of Huts required has been given in order to assist you in estimating the number required, and to prevent the possibility of the necessity or Orderly Rooms, Messes and Medical Inspection Rooms, etc., being overlooked.

19/8/18.

(Sd) John Campbell, Maj-General,
Commanding 31st Division.

Unit.	Location.	Accommodation required for.		Accommodation existing for.		Balance required for.		Huts to be used for Offrs. O.R.		Total No. of huts reqd.	Sundries.
		Offrs.	O.R.	Offrs.	O.R.	Offrs.	O.R.				
H.Q.,R.E.	U.20.c.0.7.	3	14			3	14	1	1	2	
1 Field Coy.	D.1.b.7.5.	7	211			7	211	2	10	14	
1 do	D.5.c.9.1.	4	111	4	111	-	-	-	2	2	
Tpt.Lines.	V.22.c.8.6.	1	80			1	80	1	4	5	
1 Field Coy.	D.9.b.5.4.	6	121	3	20	3	101	English or Elephant shelters.			
Tpt.Lines.	D.1.d.8.8.	1	90			1	90		5	5	
H.Q.,R.A.	U.28.c.8.1.	5	35	4	20	1	15	1	1	2	
1 Arty.Bde.H.Q.	C.23.b.1.9.	3	25			3	25	1	2	4	
1 Batty.	C.22.b.4.7.	2	120			2	120	1	6	8	
1 Batty.	C.22.d.7.9.	2	120			2	120	1	6	8	
1 Batty.	C.23.a.3.1.	2	120			2	120	1	6	8	
1 Batty.	C.28.c.1.9.	2	120			2	120	1	6	8	
1 Arty.Bde.H.Q.	Field. at	3	30			3	30	1	2	4	
1 Batty.	C.5.d.5.1.	2	120			2	120	1	6	8	
1 Batty.	and	2	120			2	120	1	6	8	
1 Batty.	)C.5.d.99.70	2	120			2	120	1	6	8	
1 Batty.	)	2	120			2	120	1	6	8	
H.Q.,D.A.C.	C.3.d.1.6.	4	28			4	28) 14)	1	3	5	
No. 1 Section.	C.9.d.5.7.	5	155			5	155) 33)	2	10	13	
No. 2 Section.	C.9.c.3.9.	6	156			6	156) 33)	2	10	13	
No. 3 Section.	U.21.b.6.5.	6	90			6	90) 74)	2	9	12	The Huts in Col. "Sundries" are
Mob.Vet.Sectn.	C.28.d.2.3.	1	20	1	20	-	-				for Messes, Ord-
1 Fld.Amb.	C.9.a.6.8.	9	231	2	150.	7	81	2	4	7	erly Rooms, Med-
1 do.	U.5.a.5.8.	6	130			6	130	2	7	10	Insp.Rooms, Q.M.
1 do.	T.11.a.2.0.	9	210	9	14	-	196	1	10	12.	Stores, etc.
Employment Co.	U.27.c.3.2.	1	60			1	60	1	3	4.	
Total for sheet 1.		96 313	2911 7002	23 18		73 295	2576 6622	26 63	129 331	176. 469	
Grand Total.		409	9913	41		368	9198	89	460	645.	

P.T.O.

WINTER ACCOMMODATION - 1918 - 1919.

Unit.	Location.	Accommodation required for Offrs.	Accommodation required for O.R.	Accommodation existing for Offrs.	Accommodation existing for O.R.	Balance required for Offrs.	Balance required for O.R.	Huts to be used for Offrs.	Huts to be used for O.R.	Huts to be used for Sundries.	Total No. of Huts.
D.H.Q.	U.30.c.0.7.	20	174	9	114	11	60	3	3		6
Signal Co.	U.30.c.0.7.	8	119			8	119	2	6		8
Reserve Bde.H.Q.	WALLON CAPPEL	In billets.									
1 Inf. Battn.	U.30.b.6.5.	30	700			30	700	5	35	5	45
1 Inf. Battn.	U.30.a.8.8.	30	700			30	700	5	35	5	45
1 Inf. Battn.	U.24.c.2.0.	30	700			30	700	5	35	5	45
Res.Bn.Left.Bde.	U.22.d.9.4.	30	700			30	700	5	35	5	45
Res.Bn.Right.Bde.	HAZEBROUCK	In billets.									
Pioneer Bn.	D.2.c.9.1.	30	700			30	700	5	35	5	45
M.G.Battn.	-do-	8	200			8	200	2	10	4	16
-do-	V.25.d.6.1.	28	380	9	200	19	180	4	9	2	15
-do-	-do-	4	165			4	165	2	8	1	10
1 Inf.Bde.H.Q.											
T'port Lines.	C.18.b.8.5.	-	40			-	40	-	2	-	2
-do-	U.24.c.2.3.	-	40			-	40	-	2	-	2
-do-	D.13.b.1.8.	-	40			-	40	-	2	-	2
1 Battn. do.	C.18.b.8.3.	8	200			8	200	2	10	4	16
1 Battn. do.	D.13.c.6.4.	8	200			8	200	2	10	4	16
1 Battn. do.	C.18.b.9.1.	8	200			8	200	2	10	4	16
1 Battn. do.	U.30.a.4.8.	8	200			8	200	2	10	4	16
1 Battn. do.	U.30.b.1.2.	8	200			8	200	2	10	4	16
1 Battn. do.	U.30.b.7.6.	8	200			8	200	2	10	4	16
1 Battn. do.	C.5.c.8.8.	8	200			8	200	2	10	4	16
1 Battn. do.	C.6.c.4.5.	8	200			8	200	2	10	4	16
1 Battn. do.	C.5.d.5.8.	8	200			8	200	2	10	4	16
Train H.Q.	U.30.c.0.7.	8	16		16	4	-	1	1	-	1
No. 1 Coy.	C/8.b.5.6.	5	206		50	5	156	2	8	2	12
No. 2 Coy.	U.28.b.3.3.	6	122			6	122	2	6	2	10
No. 3 Coy.	U.28.a.9.9.	4	100			4	100	1	5	2	8
No. 4 Coy.	U.28.b.4.6.	4	100			4	100	1	5	2	8
Totals (to sheet 2).		313	7002	18	380	295	6622	63	331	75	469.

TRANSPORT LINES.

Unit.	Location.	No. of horses for which required.	No. of horses for which existing.	Balance for which required.
D.H.Q.	U.28.b.8.9.	66	66	-
Signal Coy.	U.29.a.3.9.	80	-	80
1 Inf.Bde.H.Q.	C.18.b.8.5.	30	-	30
1 Battn.	C.18.b.8.3.	56	-	56
1 do	D.13.c.6.4.	56	-	56
1 do	C.18.b.9.1.	56	-	56
1 Inf.Bde.H.Q.	U.24.c.2.3.	19	-	19
1 Battn.	U.30.a.4.8.	55	-	55
1 do	U.30.b.1.2.	55	-	55
1 do	U.30.b.7.6.	55	-	55
1 Inf.Bde.H.Q.	D.13.b.1.8.	22	-	22
1 Battn.	C.5.c.8.8.	56	-	55
1 do	C.6.b.4.5.	56	-	56
1 do	C.5.d.5.8.	56	-	56
Pioneer Battn.	D.2.c.9.1.	79	-	79
M.G?Battn.	V.25.d.6.1.	240	-	240
Arty.H.Q.	U.23.c.8.1.	13	-	13
1 Arty.Bde.H.Q.	C.23.b.1.9.	21	-	21
1 Batty.	C.22.b.4.7.	169	-	169
1 do.	C.23.d.7.9.	169	-	169
1 do	C.23.d.8.1.	169	-	169
1 do	C.23.c.1.9.	169	-	169
1 Arty Bds.H.Q.)		21	-	21
1 Batty.	)Fields at	169	-	169
1 do	)C.5.d.35.10.	169	-	169
1 do	) and	169	-	169
1 do	)C.5.d.99.70.	169	-	169
H.Q.,D.A.C.	C.3.d.1.6.	36	-	36
No. 1 Section.	C.9.d.5.7.	213	-	213
No. 2 do	C.9.c.3.9.	213	-	213
No. 3 do	U.21.b.6.1.	199	-	199
No. 1 Coy.Train.	C.8.b.5.6.	160	-	160
No. 2 Coy. do	U.28.b.3.3.	84	-	84
No. 3 Coy. do	U.28.a.9.9.	66	-	66
No.4 Coy. do	U.28.b.4.6.	64	-	64
1 Field Co.R.E.	D.1.b.7.6.	74	-	74
1 do	V.25.c.8.8.	74	-	74
1 do	D.1.d.8.8.	74	-	74
Mob.Vet.Sect.	C.2.d.3.3.	30	-	30
1 Fld.Amblce.	C.5.a.6.9.	45	-	45
1 do.	U.30.a.4.8.	45	-	45
	T.18.a.9.0.	45	-	45

S E C R E T   COPY NO...8
                                    S141

120TH INFANTRY BRIGADE ORDER NO. 215.

                                    23:8:18.

1. On completion of the forward movement to-night, the 120th Infantry Brigade front will be readjusted as follows :-

   (a) The Southern boundary will be altered to the grid line from K.4 central to L.5. central at 11.30 p.m., 23rd August, by which hour all troops of the 120th Infantry Brigade will be clear of the area South of that line. This area will then be taken over by 183rd Infantry Brigade.

   (b) The 11th Cameron Hrs. will withdraw their companies from the "Z" Line and the E.27 area, and will dispose all 4 companies in the Reserve Line and the LA MOTTE Switch. Any accommodation that can be found in or West of the Reserve Line within the Brigade area may be utilised by this Battalion.
   The 10th K.O.S.B. will relieve all troops of the 15th K.O.Y.L.I. in the final line reached, and will hold the outpost line with two companies, keeping two companies in Support about E.30. and K.6.a. and b.
   The 15th K.O.Y.L.I. on relief will place three companies in the "Z" line, keeping as few troops as possible in the GAUDESOURE portion of this line, and one company in the area about E.27.

   (c) Any M.G's. or T.M's. in the area to be vacated will be withdrawn by 11.30 p.m.

2. On completion of this adjustment, Battalion Headquarters will be as follows :-

   15th K.O.Y.L.I.   ...   GRENADE FARM
                           E.20.b.7.0.
   10th K.O.S.B.   ...   Advanced Headquarters -
                           by GARS BRUGGHE.
                           Rear Headquarters -
                           E.26.d.

3. All reliefs will be arranged direct between C.Os. concerned.

4. Completion of reliefs and moves will be wired as follows :-

   10th K.O.S.B. (Completion of relief)   ...   SUN.
   15th K.O.Y.L.I.("   "   move)   ...   MOON.
   11th Cameron Hrs. "   "   "   )   ...   STAR.

5. ACKNOWLEDGE.

                                    Captain,
                                    Brigade Major,
Issued through
   Signals   120th Infantry Brigade.
at 3.30 p.m.

S E C R E T   XV Corps No. 663/15 G.

40th Division.
****

S 139

1.   XV Corps No. 663/10 G. dated 5:8:18 (copy attached) is cancelled.

2.   Field Artillery Harassing fire will be maintained at a total of 300 to 400 rounds daily on each Divisional front.

3.   For Heavy Artillery the amounts of ammunition to be fired will be governed by circumstances, 10 rounds per 6" How. per 24 hours being considered normal.

                                  sd.   D.J.CORRIGALL, Major,
XV Corps,   for Brigadier-General, Genl.Staff.
23:8:18.

-2-

40th Division No. 25/12 G.
120th Infantry Brigade No. 120/402.

10th K.O.S.B.
15th K.O.Y.L.I.
11th Cameron Hrs.
****

    For your information.

                                              Captain,
                                       Brigade Major,
24:8:18.   120th Infantry Brigade.

S E C R E T   XV Corps No. 663/10 G.

   31st Division,
      etc. etc.
      ******

        The following will be the "normal" rates, for harassing fire only, for Field Artillery, until further orders.

   18-pdr.Gun.)
   4.5" How.   )   40 rounds per gun and How. per 24 hours.

                                          sd. H. KNOX,
XV Corps   Brigadier-General,
5:8:18.   General Staff.

S 145

120th Infantry Brigade No. 120/426.   SECRET

15th K.O.Y.L.I.
11th Cameron Hrs.
119th Inf. Bde.   )
184th Inf. Bde.   )   For information.
40th Division "G".)

****

1. The objective line given in 120th Infantry Brigade Operation Order No. 216 is to be attained as early as possible.

2. With this end in view, the Heavy Artillery, during the 28th instant, will bombard at different times BOWERY COTTAGES, RUE PROVOST and other points of enemy resistance.

3. At 7 p.m., 28th instant, strong active patrols will be pushed out from both Companies of the 11th Cameron Hrs. to try and seize these points, the Northern Company patrols moving on RUE PROVOST, and the Southern on BOWERY COTTAGES.

4. In the event of these points being seized, the two Companies of 11th Camerons will at once move forward to take up the line from BISHOP'S CORNER along the objective line to L.9.a.2.8.- thence to line of RUE PROVOST - COCHIN CORNER Road, including BOWERY COTTAGES. The dividing point between Companies on this line will be L.8.b.5.5.
   The forward movement will be carried out directly under the orders of the Company Commanders, who must ensure that the patrols mentioned in para. 3 send reliable reports to Company Headquarters.

5. In the event of patrols being unable to seize these points, they will report accordingly to the Company Commanders, and a regular attack under a creeping barrage from the line of the DENVER - BISHOP'S CORNER Road will be made Southwards by the Camerons on the 29th instant. Full details will be issued later.

6. ACKNOWLEDGE (K.O.Y.L.I. & Camerons).

Captain,
Brigade Major,
120th Infantry Brigade.

27:8:18.
12 p.m.

SECRET.　　　　　120th Inf. Bde. No. 120/474.

120TH INFANTRY BRIGADE ADMINISTRATIVE INSTRUCTIONS.

1. Battalions will move to-morrow to Camps located as under :-

   (a) 120th Inf. Bde. H.Qrs.　...　WALLON CAPPEL.
   (b) 10th Bn. K.O.S.B.　...　34A/C.S.d.8.8.
   (c) 18th Bn. K.O.Y.L.I.　...　27 /C.24.c.2.4.
   (d) 11th Bn. Cam. Hrs.　...　27 /U.20.a.8.8.
   (e) 120th T. M. Bty.　....　School at WALLON CAPPEL.

2. (i) For Camp (b) 200 shelters will be delivered at 1 p.m. O.C., 10th K.O.S.B. will arrange for a party to be there to take them over at that hour.

   (ii) In Camp (c) there are about 70 tents. 20 of these tents must be handed over to the 10th K.O.S.B. in exchange for 50 trench shelters. Details of exchange to be arranged between Commanding Officers concerned.

   (iii) For Camp (d) D.A.D.C.S. will deliver 20 tents and 140 shelters at 1 p.m. O.C., 11th Cam. Highrs will arrange for a party to be there to take over and erect.

3. Transport Lines will move to-morrow as under :-

   120th Infantry Brigade to WALLON CAPPEL.
   10th K.O.S.B. will take over from 23rd Lancs. Frs. C.5.c.8.8.
   18th K.O.Y.L.I." "　" 　"　 8th R.Irish. R. C.5.d.5.5.
   (these lines may not be vacated until 31st instant in which case, temporary lines for the night must be found in the same field)
   11th Cam. Hrs. will take over from 23rd Cheshires R.C.6.b.2.4.

4. Baggage Wagons will report to Units Transport Lines at 9 a.m. on 30th instant.

5. Two motor lorries will report for each battalion at LA PAPOTE at 9 a.m. on 30th instant. These lorries are to do two journeys.

6. The Transport lines at LA PAPOTE will be handed over to the 119th Infantry Brigade and a duplicate of the receipts for stores and Camp equipment handed over will be forwarded to this office.

7. The 119th Infantry Brigade will send representatives to take over trench stores by 12 noon 30th instant. Duplicates of receipts to be forwarded to this office.

8. Horse Ambulances will report as under :-
   One for 10th K.O.S.B. at FIR ANGLAIS at 1 p.m.
   One for 18th K.O.Y.L.I. at LA MOTTE at 1-30 p.m.
   One for 11th Cam. Hrs. at BRICKSTACKS (E.20.b.6.0.) at 1 p.m.

   Battalions must arrange to send representatives to act as guides.

29-8-18.

T. Knox Shaw
Captain.
Staff Captain,
120th Infantry Brigade.

~~Bn Parade~~

Bn will move today to camp in Wallon Cappel area U 30 a 8.8.

Cos will parade at 3 p.m + move in following order B Co, C Co, D, A.

T/o will arrange 2 L.G Limbers to report to A + C Cos at junct no 3 track
for 1 Limber for Bn H.Q. at B.H.Q. & Bnde. A, D, C
~~Cookers~~ Officers chargers mettre cont
About to report at 2 p.m. —

2 Cookers will meet the column at TIR ANGLAIS to cook tea for Cos en route.

B + C Cos tea ration will be taken by the Co Cookers to the leading cooker

C + D Cos tea ration by C + D cookers to the second Limber.

LAMOTTE
Route ↓ TIR ANGLAIS — D 10 c 5.5 — D 3 a 3.3.
to ~~HAZEBROUCK~~ V 26 c 2.6.

SECRET S147

XV Corps No. 83/27 G.
27th August 1918.

40th Division.

* * * *

Orders have been issued to gradually re-equip all night flying squadrons with navigation lights in place of those already in existence. Conversion to be completed by 5th Septr. 1918.

The "Orders regarding Firing at Aircraft from the ground at Night" (A.A.25 dated 15th April 1918, as amended by XVth Corps No. 83/23 G. dated 28/7/1918) will therefore be amended as under on night 5th/6th September, inclusive :-

Cancel para. 3 (a) (1) and substitute the following :-

3. (a) RIFLE & MACHINE GUN FIRE.

In "Intermediate and Back Area".

(1) Rifle and Machine Gun Fire will be opened on any aeroplane located in this area by night which does not show its navigation lights, or which is unmistakably identified as hostile in the beam of a searchlight.

N.B. The navigation lights are as follows :-

Handley Pages.
1 white light under the nacelle, shining downwards.
1 white light underneath and halfway down the fuselage, shining downwards.
1 white light on the top and in the centre of the upper plane, shining upwards.
1 small white light on the tail fin, shining backwards.

F.E's.
1 white light under each wing tip, shining downwards.
1 white light under the tail, shining downwards.
1 white light on the top and in the centre of the upper plane, shining upwards.
1 small white light on the tail fin, shining backwards.

Camels.
1 white light under the fuselage, shining downwards, just behind the pilot's seat.

sd. H.J.CORRIGALL, Major, for
Brigadier-General,
General Staff.

XV Corps
27/8/18.

40th Div. No. 9/10 G.   -11-   HEADQUARTERS,
                                                      120TH
120th Inf. Bde. No. 120/401.   INFANTRY BRIGADE.
10th K.O.S.B.
15th K.O.Y.L.I.
11th Cameron Hrs.
    ******

For information.

29:8:18.

Captain,
Brigade Major,
120th Infantry Brigade.

S149

120th Inf. Bde. No. 120/474

11th Bn. Cam. Highrs.

> HEADQUARTERS.
> 120TH
> INFANTRY BRIGADE.
>
> No.
> Date.

1. Application has again been made for an Orderly Room Sergeant and a Transport Sergeant to be posted to your Battalion.

2. Please arrange for C.Q.M.Ss. CALDWELL and HUELIN to be examined by your M. O. and for him to report upon their physical fitness to carry out their present duties.

T. Knox-Shaw.
Captain,
Staff Captain,
120th Infantry Brigade.

4-9-18.

SECRET

Second Army G.40.
3rd Septr. 1918.

XV Corps.
_____

    Aerodromes at BAILLEUL TOWN and BAILLEUL Asylum will be taken into use again shortly.

    Instructions will be issued to all concerned for the remnants of hangars, huts. etc., to be left to be disposed of by the R.A.F.

                      (sd.) W. ROBERTSON, Col.
                           for M.G., G.S.,
                              Second Army.

-ii-

40th Div. No. 21/10 G.
120th Inf. Bde. No. 120/401/1.

10th K.O.S.B.
15th K.O.Y.L.I.
11th Cameron Hrs.
120th T. M. Bty.
****

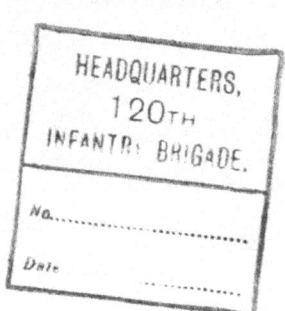

For information.

                                    Captain,
                                Brigade Major,
5:9:18.   120th Infantry Brigade.

40th Div. No. 137/4 (G).   SECRET

120th Inf. Bde.

* * *

---

1. Signals from infantry to aeroplanes have not always been satisfactory.
   The following procedure will be carried out :-

   (1) Flares are to be carried by Platoon and Section Commanders of advanced guard troops.

   (2) Contact aeroplanes will call for flares at the following hours :-

Septr. 5th.	Between	6.30 a.m.	and 7 a.m.
	"	6.30 p.m.	and 7 p.m.
Septr. 6th.	"	7 a.m.	and 7.30 a.m.
	"	7 p.m.	and 7:30 p.m.
Septr. 7th.	"	6 a.m. and 6.30 a.m.	
	"	6.30 p.m. and 7 p.m.	

   (3) All advanced troops will light flares when called for on morning of September 5th; on the subsequent occasions parties of advanced troops which have changed their position since flares were last shown will again light flares or indicate their position by discs if flares are not available.

   (4) In addition to the above if the situation requires clearing up at intermediate hours contact aeroplanes will be sent out on application by Divisions to Corps.
   Troops to be warned that if flares are called for they must be shown.

2. All Headquarters are to make use of Popham Signal panels.

                                    sd. C.H.BLACK, Lieut-Colonel,
4th Septr. 1918.   General Staff, 40th Division.

                          -ii-

120th Infantry Bde. No. 120/401.
10th K.O.S.B.
15th K.O.Y.L.I.
11th Camerons.
120th T. M. Bty.
    ******
                                For information and action
    when necessary.

                                            Captain,
                                        Brigade Major,
                                    120th Infantry Brigade.
5:9:18.

SECRET.

O.B./2246.

Armies.

In continuation of O.B./2246 dated 12th June, it has been decided that the mrthod of carrying battalion Lewis Guns in racks in accordance with the load tables already circulated by the Q.M.G. will be adopted.

Tables are attached showing the distribution of rounds carried in battalion transport and the scale of rounds carried in the field per Lewis gun and rifle, (A) for an infantry Battalion and (B) for a Pioneer battalion.

A table (C) is also attached showing the scale and total S.A.A. rounds carried in the different transport echelons of a division for infantry, pioneers and machine-guns.

General Headquarters. (Sgd) K. WIGRAM, Brig. General,
3rd September, 1918. for Lieutenant-General, O. G. S.

120th Inf. Bde. No. 120/423.

10th Bn. K.O.S.B.
15th Bn. K.O.Y.L.I.
11th Bn. Cam. Highrs.

The attached is forwarded for information and necessary action in continuation of 120th Inf. Bde. No. 120/423 dated 6-7-18.

This office No. 120/423 of 31st July, 1918 is cancelled and the G.S. wagon detailed therein will be returned to the S.A.A. Section by 12 noon 10th September, 1918.

All magazines surplus to establishment will be handed in to D.A.D.O.S., 40th Division.

Surplus SAA and grenades can be returned to Div Bomb store on the G S wagon however

Captain,
Staff Captain,
120th Infantry Brigade.

9-9-18.

(A).

INFANTRY BATTALION.

Distribution of Rounds carried in Battalion Transport.

(1) In each of four Company L.G.S. wagons, each carrying eight Lewis Guns in bags :-

    160 magazines @ 47 rds. = 7,520.

    8 boxes @ 1,248 rds.(in bundles) .. .. .. = 9,984.
                                  17,504 - 2,188 rds per L. G.

    160 magazines = 20 magazines per Lewis Gun.

(2) In one L.G.S. wagon carrying 4 A.A. Lewis Guns in bags :-

    216 magazines @ 47 rds = 10,152

    6 boxes @ 1,248 rds.   = 7,488
                              17,640 = 500 rds per A.A. gun (4)
                                        388 rds per gun   (32)
                                          4 rds. per rifle (800)

    216 magazines = (10 magazines per A.A. Lewis Gun = 40
                          (5½ magazines per Coy. Lewis Gun = 176

(3) In the remaining transport of the battalion :-

    2½ L.G.S. wagons = 55,000)
    6 pack animals   = 12,000) 67,000 = 84 rds. per rifle
                                                    (800 rifles)

    ⅛ L.G.S. wagon   = 384 grenades.

Scale of rounds carried in the field per Lewis Gun and rifle.

	On man	Regt'l Transport.	D.A.C.	M.T.Coy.	Total
Rifle . . .	120	88	70	42	320
Company Lewis gun		2,576	1,290	1,490	5,356
A.A. Lewis Gun .		500	–	–	500

CONFIDENTIAL.

40th Division No. 861 (A).

S 154

HEADQUARTERS.
40TH
DIVISION.

No.........
Date.........

Headquarters,

XV Corps.

With reference to the attached correspondence concerning Capt.(T/Major) A.E.S. CURTIS, 3rd (Reserve) Bn. The Suffolk Regt serving with 11th Bn. Cameron Highlanders.

In view of this report I recommend that this officer be re-employed with the Labour Corps.

His record of service is attached marked   and a medical officer's report marked . His age is 49 and a copy of this letter has been sent to him today.

(sd). W. E. Peyton.

Major-General,
Commanding 40th Division.

7/9/18.

(JM)

- 2 -

Headquarters,

120th Infantry Brigade.

For information and communication to Major CURTIS.

Major,
D.A.A.G., 40th Division.

7/9/18.

O.C.
11 Cameron Highrs

120/C/3.

For information and Communication to
Major Curtis

T Knox Shaw Capt
Staff Capt 120 Inf Bde

8/9/18

SECRET.

120th Inf. Bde. No. 120/477.

10th K.O.S.B.
15th K.O.Y.L.I.
11th Cameron Hrs.
120th T. M. Bty.
Bde. Signals.
Staff Captain.
******

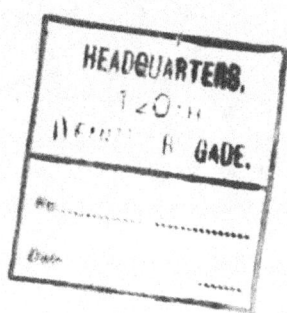

1. Herewith additions to the current List of Station Code Calls, 40th Division (Sixth Series), which came into use at midnight on 7/8th August 1918.

Please acknowledge receipt hereunder.

2. Additions to the Lists which were forwarded under 40th Division No.53/62 (G) dated 24/8/18 and 27/8/18 (forwarded under this office No. 120/477 dated 25/8/18 and 27/8/18 respectively) should be destroyed and a certificate to that effect rendered to these H.Qrs.

Captain,
Brigade Major,
120th Infantry Brigade.

9:9:18.

1.0. Inf. Bde No. 120/

10th K.O.S.B.
15th K.O.Y.L.I.
11th Cam. Highrs.
120th T. M. Btty.

CONFIDENTIAL

HEADQUARTERS,
120TH
INFANTRY BRIGADE.

No. 120/070
Date

S 164

With reference to the attached 40th Div. No. C/117/A dealing with the New Years Honours Despatch, 1919.

1- Units will prepare recommendations forthwith so that they can be forwarded as soon as the allotment is published. Single copies on A.F.W. 3121 only will be required from units not in possession of a typewriter.

2. The names of Officers and O.R. who have previously been recommended for immediate rewards and have not been passed by higher authority may be re-submitted.

3. Careful attention is to be paid to the instructions laid down in S.S. 477.

Captain,
Staff Captain,
120th Infantry Brigade.

18/9/18.

40th Division No. C/117/A.

CONFIDENTIAL.

NEW YEARS HONOURS DESPATCH - 1919.

Period. 1. Recommendations for the above Despatch will shortly be called for. The period to be covered will be from 25th February, 1918 to the night 16/17th September, 1918. Services rendered subsequent to that period are not to be brought to notice.

Allotment. 2. Will be notified as early as possible after 17th September, 1918. A separate allotment of Honours and Mentions will be made as also a separate allotment for Officers and Other ranks.

Form to be used and method of compiling. 3. (a) Recommendations will be made on A.F. W.3121 except in the case of the British Empire Order for which see para. 11.
(b) A.F's W.3121 will be rendered to Divisional Headquarters in quadruplicate by formations and units to whom the issue of a Typewriter is authorised. Other units will render a single copy only to Divnl. Headquarters.
(c) Whatever the wording of Column 5 is, it must be made clear that the period under review is embraced.
(d) Officers and men should not be shown on the same schedule and personnel of one Unit only should be shown on the same schedule.
(e) Separate schedules are to be rendered for "attached" personnel.

Mentions. 4. No description of the services rendered is necessary in cases of recommendations for "MENTION". Not more than 10 names should be submitted on one A.F. W.3121.

Care in compiling schedules. 5. The greatest care must be taken to ensure that everyone recommended is correctly described.
In the case of Officers the names should be checked with the current Army List whenever possible.

Responsibility for recommending 6. Headquarters of Formations and Units will be responsible for the submission of recommendations concerning all those who were under their Command, or administered by them at midnight September 16/17th.

Old Units of 40th Division. 7. Further instructions will be issued regarding recommendations for those Officers and men who belonged to the Units of the Division before it was re-constituted.
It is probable that they will have to be recommended from the Divisional allotment.

Recommendations for D.C.M. 8. In no circumstance must recommendations for the D.C.M. be submitted in a higher proportion than 1 to 4 M.S.M's.

/Over.

General Instructions.	9.	Careful attention is to be paid to the instructions contained in S.S.477 (Instructions regarding Recommendations for Honours and Rewards) Sections I and III.
All general information is contained therein and full particulars are given of decorations and honours for which Officers and men may be recommended.
Restrictions.	10.	The Army Council have issued instructions that except in special circumstances or for particularly gallant services, no Officer should be recommended for the January Gazette who has received two rewards in any of the following Gazettes, or supplements bearing the same date:-
    4th June, 1917.
    1st January, 1918.
    3rd June, 1918.

Two rewards are to be regarded as either two promotions, Brevet or Substantive, or one promotion and one decoration, or two decorations. Foreign decorations and immediate awards are not to be included. |
| British Empire Order. | 11. | (a) No special allotment in connection with the British Empire Order will be made but recommendations will will be submitted for such services as you consider merit this award.
(b) See S.S.477 for particulars of the different grades.
(c) Recommendations will be submitted on the special printed form which will be obtained on indent by Units in the same way as ordinary stationery. The last three headings of the form need not be filled in.
Numbers of copies required same as for A.F.W. 3121.
(d) Attached herewith as Appendix "A" is an extract from a letter to the War Office showing the relationship of the B.E.O. to other awards.

NOTE. A.F.W.3121 is not required for recommendations for the B.E.O. |
| Chaplains. | 12. | The specific denomination of all Chaplains must be inserted on a recommendation form. For example "Non C.of E." is not sufficient.
A separate form will be rendered for each Chaplain recommended. |
| Returned Immediate Awards. | 13. | In the event of any notification having been received by Units that recommendations for immediate reward were not approved, but that they would be considered for various awards in a General Despatch, such recommendations will not count against any allotment.

N.B. This only refers to recommendations which have not been passed by G.H.Q. for immediate reward, NOT to recommendations which the Corps Commander has declined to forward. The latter can be re-submitted and count against the New Year's Gazette allotment. |

/Over.

- 3 -

Special Promotion.

14. Recommendations for special promotion of non-commissioned Officers to higher rank, or Warrant Officers to Hon. Lieutenants should not be submitted in connection with despatches. They will be dealt with as they are brought to notice.

Brevet Promotions, Alternative to be stated.

15. When an Officer is recommended for Brevet promotion an alternative recommendation will always be stated.
If the alternative award is the B.E.O. the special form above referred to, duly completed, must accompany A.F.W. 3121 recommending the Brevet promotion.

17th September, 1918.

(WB).

A. L. Costan.
Major,
D. A. A. G.,
40th Division.

Distribution :-

All Units 40th Division.
All Branches 40th Divnl. Hd. Qrs.
Headquarters, 66th Divnl. Artillery.
O.C., 39th Bn. Machine Gun Corps.

Appendix "A" to 40th Division No. C/117/A.
dated 17-9-18.

EXTRACT FROM LETTER TO WAR OFFICE.

24th August, 1918.

- x - x - x - x - x - x - x - x - x -

2.   D.S.Os and M.Cs bear the same relation to the B.E.O. as do the D.C.M. and the M.M. to the M.S.M. (vide your letter 68/Gen.No./3274 (H.S.3) of 12/8/18.
    That is to say - if in the case of officers the essence of the recommendation lies in gallantry in action, or good work under fire, then the reward is the D.S.O. or M.C.

3.   To take a concrete example -
    The D.A.A.G. of a Division is recommended for reward for good work during a six months period. Divisional Headquarters have often been under shell fire, he has visited Brigade and Battalion Headquarters at considerable personal risk. But the essence of the recommendation is, that at his office desk he has kept everything straight, and spared no effort to further the efficiency of the Division. The B.E.O. will be a suitable reward.

    The D.A.Q.M.G. of a Division is similarly recommended. But it is specially brought to notice that for the offensive near ARRAS he has perfected plans for the supply of food and ammunition, and that during the offensive he personally supervised the execution of these plans, and in spite of shell fire and bombing from aeroplanes, carried them out in their entirety.
    The D.S.O. or M.C. will be a suitable reward.

    A Transport Officer is recommended for whole-hearted devotion to his especial duty. He has lavished time and labour on his animals and vehicles, with the result that the unit has frequently been complimented on their state by superior authorityand won the first prize at the Army Show.   The B.E.O. is a suitable reward.

    Another Transport Officer has never failed to deliver ammunition and rations to his unit, night after night he has been exposed to shell and machine gun fire, but has always succeeded in his task.   The M.C. would be the reward.

    True Extract.

10/9/18.
                                                Sd/ J. SCOTT, Major,
                                                  D.A.A.G., XV Corps.

CONFIDENTIAL.   40th Division No. C/117/A.

NEW YEAR'S HONOURS DESPATCH — 1919.

Addendum No. 1 to Instructions dated 17th September, 1918.

(a) Any recommendation for an officer or man who may have left a formation or unit will come out of the allotment given to the officer making the recommendation, and will be submitted by him.

(b) A copy of the recommendation will be sent "For information" to the formation or unit to which the officer or man has been transferred.

A. L. Corotan.
Major,
D.A.A.G., 40th Division.

18/9/18.

(JM) Distribution :- All Units 40th Division.
All branches 40th Divnl. Hd.Qrs.
H.Q., 66th Divnl. Artillery.
O.C., 39th Bn. Machine Gun Vorps.

120th Inf. Bde. No. 120/420.

10th Bn. K.O.S.B.
15th Bn. K.O.Y.L.I.
11th Bn. Cam. Highrs.
120th T. M. Battery.

For information.

19-9-18.

Captain,
Staff Captain,
120th Infantry Brigade.

CONFIDENTIAL.   40th Division No. C/117/A.

NEW YEAR'S HONOURS DESPATCH - 1919.

Addendum No. 2 to Instructions dated 17th September, 1918.

1. 40th Divisional Artillery complete (including No 1 Company, 40th Divisional Train etc.) will be included in the allotment of the Army to which they are now attached.

2. 66th Divisional Artillery and attached Units belonging to 66th Division will be included in the allotment of 66th Division.

A. L. Lowton

18th September, 1918.   Major,
                                                D. A. A. G.,
(WB).   40th Division.

                Distribution :- All Units 40th Division.
                                All Branches 40th Divl. Hd.Qrs.
                                H.Q., 66th Divnl. Artillery.
                                O.C., 39th Bn. Machine Gun Corps.

120th Inf. Bde. No. 120/420/1.

10th Bn. K.O.S.B.
15th Bn. K.O.Y.L.I.
11th Bn. Cam. Highrs.
120th L.T. Battery.

For information.

19-9-18.

T. Kroshaw
Captain,
Staff Captain,
120th Infantry Brigade.

HEADQUARTERS,
120TH
INFANTRY BRIGADE.

CONFIDENTIAL.   40th Division No. C/117/A.

NEW YEAR'S HONOURS DESPATCH - 1919.

Addendum No.4 to Instructions dated 17th September, 1918.

Recommendations for the BRITISH EMPIRE ORDER will be rendered on Army Form W.3121 and not on the special printed form previously referred to.

A. L. Cowtan.
Major,
D.A.A.G., 40th Division...

20th September, 1918.

(JM)   Distribution :-   All Units 40th Division.
                                     All branches 40th Divnl. Hd.Qrs.
                                     Hd.Qrs., 66th Divnl. Artillery.
                                     O.C., 39th Bn. Machine Gun Corps.

120 Inf. Bde. No. 120/420

10th K.O.S.B.
15th K.O.Y.L.I.
11th Cam. Highrs.
120th T.M.Battery.

For information.

Captain,
Staff Captain,
120th Infantry Brigade.

20/9/18.

C O N F I D E N T I A L.　　　　　　40th Division No. C/117/A.

NEW YEAR'S HONOURS DESPATCH - 1919.

Addendum No. 4 to Instructions dated 17th September, 1918.

1. When more than 1 name is entered on an A.F., W.3121 the names should be placed in "Order of Merit" and numbered.

2. A nominal roll, single copy, will accompany each batch of recommendations sent to Divisional Headquarters.

3. Reference para. 11 of Instructions dated 17th September, 1918. Five copies of recommendations for BRITISH EMPIRE ORDER are required from Formations and Units in possession of Typewriters.

4. It is to be understood that whilst every endeavour will be made by higher authority to forward all recommendations submitted in accordance with the allotment made it is not to be taken for granted that approval will be sanctioned in every case.

5. Recommendations should be prepared now as far as possible. The allotment will not be notified until 24th instant and recommendations will be required by the end of the week.

A. L. Gorotan.
Major,
D.A.A.G., 40th Division.

22nd September, 1918.
WB.

Distribution :- All Units, 40th Divn.
All Branches 40th Divl. Hd.Qrs.
Hd.Qrs., 66th Divnl Artillery. (for information)
O.C., 39th Bn. M.G.Corps.

O.C.
11th Camns.

For information & guidance.

25/9/18

CAPT.,
STAFF CAPT., 120TH INF. BDE.

120th Inf. Bde. No. 120/438/1.   SECRET

10th K.O.S.B.
11th Cameron Hrs.
15th K.O.Y.L.I.
120th T. M. Bty.
 ****

1. Commencing from noon 16th Septr., 1918, the S.O.S. Signal (now a Rifle Grenade Signal RED over RED over RED) will be changed to a rifle grenade signal bursting into three coloured stars GREEN over GREEN over RED.

2. Instructions for the return of the present signal and the issue of new signal will be issued by 40th Division "Q" and units will be notified by Staff Captain in due course as to these.

3. ACKNOWLEDGE.

                                    Captain,
                                 Brigade Major,
                              120th Infantry Brigade.

14:9:18.

120th Inf. Bde. No. 120/420.   **HEADQUARTERS, 120TH INFANTRY BRIGADE.**   CONFIDENTIAL

O.C., 11th Bn. Cam. Highrs.

No. 50259 Pte. J. LYONS, D.C.M., 11th Bn. Cam. Hrs.

While appreciating the gallant conduct of the above-mentioned man, the Divisional Commander regrets that in view of para 47(i) S.S.477 he cannot recommend him for an immediate award.

The congratulations of the Divisional Commander should be conveyed to Private LYONS.

Captain,
Staff Captain,
120th Infantry Brigade.

30-9-18.

S 173

SECRET   COPY NO. 8

120TH INFANTRY BRIGADE ORDER NO. 224.

                                                    30:9:18.

1. The 120th Infantry Brigade will relieve the 121st
    Infantry on the Right Brigade Front on the night
    1st/2nd October, in accordance with attached relief
    table.

2. All arrangements for relief will be made direct
    between C.Os. concerned.

3. (a) All special maps, aeroplane photographs,
        defence instructions, and trench and area stores,
        including hot food containers, will be taken over
        and receipts given.

    (b) Instructions as to Defence of STEENWERCK Line
        will be handed over to Battalions relieved.

    (c) Special care will be taken to ensure that all
        details of work on defensive systems are taken
        over.

4. Sketches showing dispositions down to platoons will
    be submitted to Brigade Headquarters by 12.00, 3rd prox.

5. No movement will be made East of STEENWERCK before
    xxxxx 19.00.

6. Completion of reliefs will be wired by following
    code word :-
                    N A P C O.

7. Brigade Headquarters will close at WINK COTTAGE
    and re-open at TOUQUET PARMENTIER, B.21.a.9.5. at
    10.00 on 2nd Octr., at which hour G.O.C. 120th Infantry
    Bde. will assume command of the sector.

8. A C K N O W L E D G E.

                                                    Captain,
Issued through   Brigade Major,
  Signals   120th Infantry Brigade.
  at 7 p.m.

DISTRIBUTION :-

Copy No.			No.		
1	...	G.O.C.	13	...	121st Inf. Bde.
2	...	Bde. Major.	14	...	182nd Inf. Bde.
3	...	Staff Capt.	15	...	331st Bde. R.F.A.
4	...	War Diary.	16	...	64th H.A.G.
5	...	File.	17	...	"B" Coy. 39th M.G.Bn.
6	...	10th K.O.S.B.	18	...	137th Fd. Ambce.
7	...	15th K.O.Y.L.I.	19	...	-Do- Adv. Dg. Stn.
8	...	11th Camerons.	20	...	224 Field Coy. R.E.
9	...	120th T.M.Bty.	21	...	"L" Special Coy. R.E.
10	...	40th Divn. "G".	22	...	Bde. Supply Officer.
11	...	40th Divn. "Q".	23	...	Bde. Signals.
12	...	119th Inf. Bde.	24	...	40th Div. Train.

SECRET   G.H.Q. Ie/1732 of 11/9/18-
Second Army G.I. /6/19 of 16/9/18-
SECOND ARMY.   40th Div. No. 19GG.

1- Evidence of the use of unauthorised codes and ciphers has been obtained from time to time from our listening sets and other sources. These codes have been constructed, for the most part, in such a manner as to afford little or no security; some of them could be solved by enemy experts in a very short time.

2. The use of unauthorised codes or ciphers is strictly forbidden. No code or cipher must be used until it has been submitted to G.H.Q. and authority for its use has been obtained.

3. If it is desired to use a special code or cipher for a special purpose, and none of the codes and ciphers is considered suitable for this purpose, the circumstances must be reported to G.H.Q. The precise requirements should be stated in full, together with an estimate of the probable extent to which the special code or cipher required would be used.

4. Full particulars of any special codes or ciphers which are now in use should be furnished to G.H.Q.

                          (sgd) G.P. Dawney, Major General, for
G.H.Q.   Lieut General
11/9/18.   Chief of the General Staff.

- 2 -

120th Inf. Bde. No. 120/477.

10th K.O.S.B.
15th K.O.Y.L.I.
11th Cam. Highrs.
120th T.M. Btty.

For information.

                               Captain,
                            Brigade Major,
18/9/18.   120th Infantry Brigade.

RELIEF TABLE TO ACCOMPANY 120TH INFANTRY BRIGADE ORDER NO. 224.

Serial No.	Unit.	From	To	In Relief of	Headquarters.	Remarks.
1.	15th K.O.Y.L.I.	PADDY FARM, A.11.c.2.8.	LINE Left.	23rd Cheshires.	B.22.a.3.6.	23rd Cheshire H.Q. at present at TOUQUET PARMENTIER. 15th K.O.Y.L.I. will go into new H.Q. at B.22.a.3.6.
2.	10th K.O.S.B.	GRAND BEAUMART.	LINE Right.	8th Royal Irish Regt.	PUNGENT FARM, B.26.a.2.6.	To arrange march with 15th K.O.Y.L.I. so that K.O.Y.L.I. have priority of movement.
3.	11th Camerons.	TRIMBLE FARM.	RESERVE.	23rd Lancs. Fusiliers.	LETT FARM, B.25.c.3.6.	Not to move off till 10th K.O.S.B. are clear.
4.	120th T.M.Bty.	A.21.a.4.6.	LINE	121st T.M.Bty.	A.24.a.6.4.	

SECRET.　　　　　　　　　　　　　　　　　　　S 180.
　　　　　　　　　　　　　　　　　　　　　　　COPY NO. 8

　　　　120TH INFANTRY BRIGADE INSTRUCTIONS NO. 1.

　　　　　　　　　　　　　　　　　　　　　　　5-10-18.

1.　　On completion of relief of the 119th Infantry Brigade the 120th Infantry Brigade, with attached troops, will operate as the Advanced Guard to the Division.

2.　　The Advanced Guard will be composed as follows :-

　　　　Advd. Guard Commander　...　G.O.C. 120th Inf. Bde.

　　　　　　120th Infantry Brigade.
　　　　　　331st Bde. R.F.A.
　　　　　　"A" Coy. 39th Bn. M.G.C.
　　　　　　½ Coy. XV Corps Cyclist.

3.　　The Advanced Guard Brigade will be responsible for the defence of the NIEPPE System South of the LYS in addition to the Outpost Line.
　　　　For this purpose the Reserve Battalion will keep a nucleus garrison of 1 Company in the NIEPPE System from the LYS to the Division Southern boundary.
　　　　Machine Gun positions for the defence of this portion of the LYS line are being reconnoitred and will be notified later.
　　　　The responsibility for the defence of the rest of the NIEPPE system will be with the 119th Infantry Brigade, who are being withdrawn into that neighbourhood.

4.　　The following communications are being opened up and maintained under the direction of the C.R.E. :-

　　(a)　A main route running forward through ORVILLE JUNCTION - ERQUINGHEM - Southern edge of ARMENTIERES - CHAPELLE D'ARMENTIERES.

　　(b)　Supplementary route through LE BIZET - C.14.a., c and d, to C.20.b. and d to bridge at C.20.d.9.0. A connection with the main route will be made East of the LYS as soon as possible.

　　(c)　Pontoon bridges exist :-

　　　　　　H.2.c.1.9.
　　　　　　H.3.c.4.7.
　　　　　　H.4.c.1.4.
　　　　　　C.20.d.9.0.

　　(d)　Foot bridges exist at :-

　　　　　　H.3.d.5.5.
　　　　　　C.15.d.6.8.
　　　　another in under construction at
　　　　　　C.21.d.3.5.

5.　　In two or three days time R.E. assistance will be available for the improvement of forward and second line defences.

　　　　　　　　　　　　　　　　　　　　　　M. Ensly
　　　　　　　　　　　　　　　　　　　　　　Captain,
To all recipients　　　　　　　　　　Brigade Major,
of 120th Inf. Bde.　　　　　　　　120th Infantry Brigade.
Order 225 dated
5-10-18.

S 149

SECRET.   COPY NO. 8

120TH INFANTRY BRIGADE ORDER NO. 225.

5-10-18.

1. The 120th Infantry Brigade will relieve the 119th Infantry Brigade in the outpost positions on the night 5/6th and 6/7th October in accordance with attached table of reliefs.

2. All arrangements for relief will be made direct between C.Os. concerned.

3. Boundries on completion of relief will run as follows :-

   <u>Northern</u>. Grid line through C.16.central and C.17.central.
   <u>Southern</u>. I.10.central I.11.central.

4. The 11th Bn. Cameron Highrs. are relieving the 10th Bn. K.O.S.B. in the outpost position of the 120th Infantry Brigade front on the night 5/6th October. If the 11th Bn. Cameron Highrs. are not squeezed out of the line by the 119th Infantry Brigade extending as far south as Southern Boundary, the 15th Bn. K.O.Y.L.I. will take over on the night 6/7th the portion of the outpost line still occupied by the 11th Bn. Cameron Highrs.

5. All special maps, aeroplane photographs, etc. and all trench stores will be taken over from Units being relieved.

6. Dispositions of battalion in the line, giving locations of all posts, will be sent to Brigade Headquarters by 1800 7th inst.

7. Completion of relief will be wired by the following code word :-

   "BUCKSHEE"

8. Brigade Headquarters will close at TOUQUET PATMENTIER and re-open at a site to be notified later at 1000 7th inst. at which hour G.O.C. 120th Infantry Brigade will assume Command of the sector. H 5 d 4 1 Advanced 17 b 5 7.
   Up to 1000 7th inst, all troops in the outpost area will be under the tactical control of G.O.C., 119th Infantry Brigade.

9. On completion of relief dispositions of 120th Infantry Brigade will be as follows :-

Brigade Headquarters	...	To be notified later.
15th Bn. K.O.Y.L.I.	...	In Outpost Line.
11th Bn. Cam. Highrs.	...	In Support about HOUPLINES.
10th Bn. K.O.S.B.	...	In Reserve in ERQUINGHEM. and H.5.d.

10. ACKNOWLEDGE.

Issued through Signals
at 16/15

                                                Captain,
                                             Brigade Major,
                                        120th Infantry Brigade.

DISTRIBUTION.:-

Copy No.		
1	...	G.O.C.
2	...	Brigade Major.
3	...	Staff Captain.
4	...	War Diary.
5	...	File.
6	...	14th A.S.E.B.
7	...	13th K.O.Y.L.I.
8	...	11th Bn. Cam. Hrs.
9	...	120th T.M. Battery.
10	...	40th Division "G"
11	...	40th Division "Q"
12	...	119th Inf. Bde.
13	...	121st Inf. Bde.
14	...	176th Inf. Bde.
15	...	330th Bde. R.F.A.
16	...	331st Bde. R.F.A.
17	...	39th Bn. M.G.C.
18	...	"A" Coy. 39th Bn. M.G.C.
19	...	"C" Coy. - do -
20	...	64th H.A. Group.
21	...	137th Field Ambce.
22	...	A.D.S. 137th Fd. Ambce.
23	...	224th Field Coy. R.E.
24	...	Bde. Supply Officer.
25	...	Brigade Signals.
26	...	40th Div. Train.

RELIEF TABLE TO ACCOMPANY 120TH INFANTRY BRIGADE ORDER NO. 225 dated 5-10-18.

Serial No.	Date	UNIT.	FROM	TO	IN RELIEF OF	Hd. Qrs.	REMARKS.
	October						
1	5/6th	15th K.O.Y.L.I.	NIEPPE.	Support Area about below HOUPLINES.	12th E.Lancs.R.	C.22.c.2.5.	
2	5/7th	11th Cam. Hrs.	ERQUINGHEM area.	Line – 10th Inf. Bde. Front.	10th K.O.S.B.	H.12.b.3.7.	
3	5/6th	10th K.O.S.B.	Line – 120th Bde. front.	ERQUINGHEM area		SKINDLES Fm.	
4	6/7th	15th K.O.Y.L.I.	Support Area about HOUPLINES.	LINE.	12th N.Staffs.R.	C.22.c.7.0.	
5	6/7th	12th N.Staffs.	LINE	Support Area camps about HOUPLINES.		C.22.c.2.5.	
6	7/8th	11th Cam. Hrs.	CHAPELLE D' ARMENTIERES area.	Support Area about HOUPLINES.	12th N.Staffs.R.	C.22.c.2.5.	

SECRET.   COPY NO 10

S 189.

120TH INFANTRY BRIGADE ORDER NO. 227.

11-10-18.

1. **OBJECTIVE:** On the 12th instant a Minor Operation will be carried out by the 120th Infantry Brigade to gain an identification and the objective shown on the attached map.

2. **TROOPS.** The attack will be carried out by one Company of the 10th Bn. K.O.S.B.

3. **ASSEMBLY POINT – METHOD OF ATTACK.** The Company of the 10th K.O.S.B. will be assembled in INCANDESCENT Support just North of the railway by Zero – 60 minutes.
   At Zero this party will advance Northwards along INCANDESCENT SUPPORT under a creeping barrage, while another barrage will comb out the ground to the East of this trench. Details of Artillery barrages are given in para 5.
   The Company 10th K.O.S.B. will make good the line of INCANDESCENT SUPPORT as far North as the road in I.5.d.5.5., and will also send a party to mop up INCANDESCENT Front Line as far North as the road.

4. (O.C., 11th Can. Highrs.) will be responsible for gaining touch between the left of this Company on completion of the attack, and the Cameron Post in L'EPINETTE.

5. **ARTILLERY.** At Zero hour the Field Artillery will open two barrages :-
   (a) One on the line of INCANDESCENT SUPPORT from I.11.a.9.5. to I.5.d.6.8., which will move Eastwards lifting 100 yards every two minutes up to Zero plus 20, when it will jump back to the line from I.11.d.6.9. to I.6.c.3.6., where it will remain as a protecting barrage till Zero plus 44.
   As much smoke as can be obtained will be fired in this barrage in its early stages.
   (b) One on the line from I.11.a.7.9. to I.11.b.3.7. and will move Northwards up the INCANDESCENT TRENCH and SUPPORT, lifting 100 yards every 3 minutes, until it reaches the line from I.5.d.3.9. to I.5.d.6.8 where it will remain as a protecting barrage till Zero plus 44.

   From Zero till Zero plus 44 the Heavy Artillery will keep the trenches and strong points in the area I.6.c., I.12.a., I.12.c. under fire, and also the strong point at C.29.central.

6. **COMMUNICATIONS.**
   1. The signal that the objective has been taken will be the firing of 3 Very Lights in quick succession.
   2. The Company of the 10th K.O.S.B. will have four pigeons.
   3. A runner relay post will be established by Brigade Signals at I.3.d.3.0. at the Level Crossing, where all runner messages for Brigade Headquarters should be sent.
   A wire will be laid by Brigade Signals from this relay post to Advanced Brigade Headquarters by Zero – 60 minutes

- 2 -

7. **GENERAL.** (a) Special arrangements for the supply of bombs, rifle grenades and Very Lights to the Company operating must be made.
   6 boxes of 'P' bombs are being sent up to H.Qrs. 10th K.O.S.B. to-night.
   (b) The co-operation of the Stokes Mortars up by GRAND PORTE EGAL FARM will be arranged direct with O.C., 120th T. M. Battery, if required.
   (c) Arrangements for tools for consolidation must be made.

8. **SYNCHRONISATION OF WATCHES.** An Officer from Brigade Headquarters will be at Headquarters, 10th K.O.S.B. at 19.00 to synchronise watches.

9. **BRIGADE HD. QRS.** Advanced Brigade Headquarters will open at H.7.b.5.6. at 05.00 12th instant.

10. O.C., 15th K.O.Y.L.I. will send up one Company to-night to replace the Company of the 10th K.O.S.B. All arrangements will be made direct between C.Os.

11. **PRISONERS.** Any prisoners or identifications obtained will be sent at once to Brigade Headquarters.

12. **ZERO HOUR.** ZERO hour for the operation will be 05.15.

13. ACKNOWLEDGE.

                                              Captain,
                                              Brigade Major,
                                              120th Infantry Brigade.

Issued through Signals
         at   18.20

Copy No. 1..G.O.C.   12.."C" Coy. 39th Bn. M.G.C.
         2..Brigade Major,   13..331st Bde. R.F.A.
         3..Staff Captain,   14..330th Bde. R.F.A.
         4..War Diary,   15..64th H.A.Group,
         5..File,   16..176th Inf. Bde.
         6 to 8 10th K.O.S.B.   17..94th Inf. Bde.
         9..15th K.O.Y.L.I.   18..40th Divn. "G".
         10..11th Cam. Hrs.   19..Brigade Signals.
         11..120th T. M. Battery.

120th Inf. Bde. No. 120/426/1.

S 188

SECRET

O.C., 11th Bn. Cam. Highrs.
==========

  Reference 120th Infantry Brigade Order No. 227 of to-day.

  The Heavy Artillery will be bombarding the enemy strong point in C.29.central to-morrow from Zero to Zero plus 44. Precautions must be taken that no troops are within 600 yards of this strong point during the bombardment.

             Captain,
            Brigade Major,
11-10-18.   120th Infantry Brigade.

"C" FORM.
MESSAGES AND SIGNALS.   Army Form C. 2123
(In books of 100.)
No. of Message ....

Prefix	Code 0735 Words 70	Sent, or sent out.	Office Stamp.
Received from *Two* By *H. [illegible]*		At .... m. To .... By	
Service Instructions			

Handed in at .... Office 07.25 m. Received 08.15 m.

TO .... PoGI

*Sender's Number.	Day of Month.	In reply to Number.	AAA
BM 76	4		

PoGi will not move into
the 4 div point 5 area tonight
but will move in
following *[illegible]* 2 coys to
about T 2 B and C
2 coy to about
C 10 C and D with Bn
HQrs near latter two coys
AAA Bn will have OP
[illegible] out by N Ref C
and E of the hq AAA ,
[illegible] *[illegible]* *[illegible]*
[illegible] out at once *[illegible]*

FROM ....
PLACE & TIME ....

"Q" FORM.
MESSAGES AND SIGNALS.

Prefix	Code	Words	Sent, or sent out.	Office Stamp.
Received from	By		At .... m.	POGL
Service Instructions			To	
			By	

Handed in at 12.9 POG   Office 1150 m.   Received 1152 m.

TO   POGL

*Sender's Number.	Day of Month.	In reply to Number.	A A A
BM52	6		
Ref J WVO order 225 para 8			
AAA site selected H.5.D.4.1			
with advanced at I.1.B.5.7			
AAA Aslsbd all recipient			
order 225			

FROM
PLACE & TIME

"C" Form.
MESSAGES AND SIGNALS.

Army Form C. 2123.
(In books of 100.)

No. of Message ....

Prefix: SB Code: 1010 Words: 49

Received. From: JUVO By: Liddiard

Sent, or sent out. At ...... m. To ...... By ......

Office Stamp. TOG1 5·10·18

Charges to Collect

Service Instructions: Priority

Handed in at 120 Bde HQ Office 1010 m. Received 1041 m.

TO TOG1

*Sender's Number	Day of Month	In reply to Number	AAA
BM 42	5		
TOG1	will	relieve	POVO
tonight	under	arrangements	
between	Co's	AAA	POVO
will	move	into	accomodation
occupied	by	TOG1	AAA Suggested
Dispositions	for	TOG1	one
company	outpost	line	one
company	in	I 7 B	one
company	along	road in	H 12 B
one	coy	about	H 5 D
AAA		Addsd	Btns

FROM JUVO.

PLACE & TIME

120th Inf. Bde. No. 120/426.

10th Bn. K.O.S.B.
11th Bn. Cam. Highrs.
331st Bde. R.F.A.

S 187

SECRET

    Reference 120th Infantry Brigade Order No. 227 of to-day.
    After Zero plus 44, all artillery fire will cease unless called for by S.O.S. signal. In this case the S.O.S. lines will be on a line 400 yards East of the INCANDESCENT SUPPORT as far North as I.5.b.8.0. thence INANE TRENCH and along old German front line. Special fire will be concentrated about I.5.b.5.8. to prevent the enemy working down from C.29.central.

Captain,
Brigade Major,
120th Infantry Brigade.

11-10-18.

<u>120th Inf. Bde. No. 120/406.</u>　　　　　　　　　　S E C R E T.

11th Bn. Cam. Highrs.
10th Bn. K.O.S.B.
=========

    The 26th Battn. R. W. Fusrs. will relieve the 17th Royal SUSSEX Regt. on the right of this Brigade on the night 11/12th October, 1918.

　　　　　　　　　　　　　　　　　　　　　　　Captain,
　　　　　　　　　　　　　　　　　　　　Brigade Major,
<u>10-10-18.</u>　　　　　　　　　　　　　　　120th Infantry Brigade.

SECRET.

40th Divn. No. 55/13 (G).

S 183.

Headquarters,
    120th Infantry Brigade.
    ========

1. The attached copy of G.H.Q. letter No. O.B./1919 dated 28-9-18 is forwarded for information.
2. Sufficient copies are enclosed for distribution down to Battns.
3. The memorandum and tables mentioned in para 2 of the above letter are being issued to Divisions and Brigade Headquarters by D.A.P.S.S.
4. The date on which the organisation will be brought into force will be notified later.

(Sgd) R. McL. CHAPMAN, Captain, G. S.
8-10-18.   40th Division.

120th Inf. Bde. No. 120/429.

10th Bn. K.O.S.B.
15th Bn. K.O.Y.L.I.
11th Bn. Cam. Highrs.

For information.

8-10-18.
                                            Captain,
                                        Brigade Major,
                                    120th Infantry Brigade.

SECRET.
O.B./1919.

Second Army.
───────────

      With reference to G.H.Q. letter No. O.B./1919 of the 14th June, it has now been decided by the Army Council that the strength of a British Infantry Battalion shall in future be fixed at 900 other ranks.

2.   The attached memorandum and tables explain in detail the organisation of the battalion and the distribution of the personnel. This organisation will be brought into force on a date to be notified later.

3.   The tables represent the provisional establishment which will be adopted as the basis of the tactical organisation of the battalion. They are not to be regarded as authority for any change in the existing War Establishment (No. 1247) the supersession of which is under consideration.

4.   The principle difference between this organisation and that laid down in the G.H.Q. letter quoted above lies in the re-expansion of the double Lewis Gun Section into two Lewis Gun Sections for the sake of greater tactical elasticity.

5.   Allowance has been made for 44 signallers only. This is due to the fact that arrangements are being made whereby the Divisional Signal Company will be responsible for carrying out all communications by wireless, the battalion signallers being responsible for communications by telephone or visual signalling only. Until this re-organisation of the Divisional Signal Company is effected however, the full number of signallers should be maintained in the battalion.

6.   The importance of preserving a uniform organisation throughout the British Armies must be impressed on all concerned, and the Field Marshal Commanding-in-Chief looks to commanders of units and formations to see that the attached instructions are thoroughly understood and strictly followed.

7.   Printed copies of the memorandum and tables are being issued to battalion commanders direct through the medium of D.A.P.S.S.

                                                    (Sgd). G.P. DAWNAY,
                                                           M.G.,
General Headquarters,   for Lieutenant-General,
28th September, 1918.   C. G. S.

SECRET.   COPY NO. 1

120TH INFANTRY BRIGADE INSTRUCTIONS NO. 2.

7-10-18.

1. 120th Infantry Brigade Instructions No. 1 of 5-10-18 will be modified as below.

2. The 330th Brigade R.F.A. has been added to the troops of the Advanced Guard, remaining in action about LE BIZET.

3. The Advanced Guard will be disposed as follows :-
(a) One Battalion holding the Outpost Line.
(b) One Battalion in Support with two Companies about I.2.b. and c. and I.7.b., and two Companies about C.20.d. which will maintain permanent posts covering the bridges over the LYS.
(c) One Battalion in Reserve about ERQUINGHEM, with a permanent nucleus garrison of one Company in the ERQUINGHEM SWITCH. This Battalion will be responsible for the defence of the ERQUINGHEM SWITCH from the river LYS to the Divisional Southern Boundary.

4. The two Companies of the Support Battalion North of ARMENTIERES will be tactically under the control of the C. O. of the Battalion in the Outpost Line, but will only be used for guarding the bridge heads and will under no circumstances be used East of the river LYS without the authority of Brigade Headquarters.

5. The Outpost Line will be held with three Companies, with one Company in Reserve on the left flank, and will be organised in a series of strong posts, each consisting of a force which is a complete fighting unit, and whose strength should not be less than a platoon.

6. Owing to the wide frontage and the consequent large gaps between posts special patrol precautions must be taken. All patrols must be strong fighting patrols, capable of dealing with any small parties of the enemy encountered.
For the same reason Officers going round their line from post to post must take a small fighting escort with them capable of dealing with any of the enemy suddenly encountered, who may have got in between our posts.

7. 8 Machine Guns are allotted to the defence of the Outpost Line, and will be placed in depth; four are left in Support North of ARMENTIERES covering the river crossings, and the battery line, four will be in Support on the South of ARMENTIERES covering the Southern Brigade of Artillery.

8. All troops will be responsible for improving the posts they occupy as far as possible.

9. ACKNOWLEDGE.

Issued to all
recipients of
120th Inf. Bds.
Instructions
No. 1. d/5-10-18.

Captain,
Brigade Major,
120th Infantry Brigade.

120th Inf. Bde. No. 120/418.

S/205.

10th K.O.S.B.
15th K.O.Y.L.I.
11th Cam. Highrs.
120th T.M.Battery.
Sgt. Isaachi.

XVth Corps Anti-Gas Instructions dated 21/10/1918 forwarded under 120th Infantry Brigade No. 120/418 dated 23/10/1918 are cancelled and will be destroyed.

T. Knox Shaw
Captain,
A/Brigade Major,
120th Infantry Brigade.

29/10/1918.

SECRET.

XV Corps No. 89/26 G.
26th October 1918.

XV CORPS ANTI-GAS INSTRUCTIONS

(The instructions contained in XV Corps
No. 89/126 G. dated 21/7/1918 are cancelled.)

1. GENERAL.

Standing orders for Defence against Gas are contained in
S.S. 534, Appendix (iv) dated March 1918.

During the present advance orders contained therein which
are applicable to the general situation are in no way to
be relaxed, for it is possible the enemy will make considerable
use of gas during his retreat.

Owing to the frequent changes of positions, Units will not
receive the same amount of supervision from Anti-Gas personnel
attached to formations, and they must therefore, use their own
personnel which has been trained at Army and Corps Gas Schools.

Frequent and careful inspections of Respirators must be carried
out and it is important that all Units maintain their authorised
reserve of Anti-Gas appliances (respirators, containers, rattles etc.)

Attention must be paid to the ALERT ZONE, the boundaries of
which are liable to change often, and to the orders relating
to the carriage of the respirator, and precautions to be taken
in this area. (S.S. 534 Appendix IV)

2. CLOUD GAS.

An attack of this nature is on the whole improbable, and only
likely if we approach an organised enemy defensive system.

In such an eventuality, Units must bear in mind that alarm
devices, with the exception of gas shell rattles, have not been
brought forward, and they must therefore rely on the vigilance
of their sentries, telephonic communications, and improvised
gas alarms.

3. GAS SHELL BOMBARDMENT.

Attention is directed to S.S. 534 Appendix I, para iv.

(1) Owing to the extended use of H.E. gas shell all ranks
should be warned that gas shell cannot be recognised by its
degree of detonation or sound during flight.

(2) Particular danger may arise through houses in which
troops are billeted being hit by gas shell. In such circumstances
the building must be evacuated immediately.

(3) Batteries in action are particularly liable to surprise.
All batteries or sections will, therefore, whenever in action
by day or night have a sentry posted to windward, who will give
warning in case of gas shelling.

(4) Unless the tactical situation precludes, areas which have been gas shelled should at once be evacuated. Owing to the lack of means at the present moment of dealing with gas shell holes and the total lack of gas proof accommodation, this way of meeting the situation will give best results.

4. TRAPS.

(1) The enemy has on several occasions, before retreating, infected cellars, dugouts, etc., with Mustard Gas, and therefore, such places lately vacated by him should be entered with caution. His usual method is either to scatter the liquid gas about or else to open a shell, thereby allowing the contents to leak into the ground.

(2) Water from shell holes must on no consideration be used either for washing, cooking, or drinking purposes.

Wood must not be handled or burnt if there are any signs of gas shelling or gas in the vicinity.

5. OUR OWN GAS SHELL BOMBARDMENTS.

In an advance following our own gas shell bombardments Divisions will issue suitable instructions to the troops to prevent gas casualties while passing over the late target.

While the length of time during which such an area is dangerous, unless respirators are worn, depends to a great extent on the weather conditions, the following figures are issued for guidance:-

Gas.	Ground dangerous for	Remarks.
With C.G.	½-2 hours.	No under surface persistency.
,, N.C.	4-12 ,,	Digging may not be possible for 96 hours.
,, H.S.	48-90 ,,	Under surface may remain dangerous for weeks.

NOTE:-

The persistence of the liquid of the ground is diminished by heavy rain, by sunshine or strong wind. During frosty and dull weather the persistency is increased.

120th Inf. Bde. No. 120/476   S/204

18th H.L.I.
18th K.O.Y.L.I.
11th Cam. Highrs ✓
120th T.M.Battery.

The following extracts from 40th Division Order No. 293 dated 21/10/1918 is forwarded for information :-

1. The enemy is continuing his preparations for the destruction of roads and railways East of the SCHELDT.

2. Should the enemy defence weaken, the Divisions in the line are to :-
   (a) Establish advanced Guards East of the inundations.
   (b) Be prepared to carry out a further advance to capture the spur which runs Northwards from I.17. through D.18. and D.3.

3. With this in view -
   (a) The advanced Guard Brigade will continually test the enemy defences. Patrols if successful in crossing the inundations will be supported and any success gained exploited.
   (b) The arrangements already made for a main crossing at PACK and the subsidiary crossing N. of GARCOING will be maintained in a state of complete readiness.

4. Forward boundaries as far as can be laid down at present will be as follows :-

   34th Division on Right.

   N.1.3.central due East.

   9th Division on Left.

   C.10.c.0.0. to D.20. central.

5. The 119th Infantry Brigade will move forward to-morrow to the LILLE ROAD area.

6. All resting artillery of the Division will move into action to-night.

In view of the above order, the 120th Infantry Brigade will hold itself in readiness to move at short notice. Training will however, be carried out as usual, until further orders are issued.

                                        Captain,
                                        A/Brigade Major,
                                        120th Infantry Brigade.

21/10/1918.

40th Division No. 169 (Q)

SECRET.

With reference to para 2 of 40th Division Instructions No. 10 dated 16th October 1918 :-

1. The Mobile Reserve of Ammunition within Infantry Brigades will not be reduced.

   (a) In order to make this possible, and to carry out the above quoted instructions, that is, of releasing sufficient pack animals to carry the 3" Stokes Mortars and Ammunition the O.C. S.A.A. Section, 40th D.A.C. will detail two L.G.S. wagons (complete turnsout less ammunition) to report to each Infantry Brigade Headquarters for duty forthwith, and until further notice.

   (b) In addition to carrying the S.A.A. (loads taken from pack animals) these limbered G.S. wagons may be utilized by Brigades to carry the remaining 3" Stokes Mortars and equipment.

23/10/1918.

(sgd) S.Dawson, Major,
D.A.Q.M.G.
40th Division.

10th K.O.S.B.
15th K.O.Y.L.I.
11th Cam. Highrs.
120th T.M.Battery.
==============

For information.

The 2 G.S. limbered wagons will be retained with Brigade Headquarters Transport and under command of Brigade Headquarters.

Application for their use other than when the Brigade is moving will be made to Brigade Headquarters by O.C. 120th T.M.Battery. as required

24/10/1918.

Lieut,
A/Staff Captain,
120th Infantry Brigade.

S 202

G.H.Q.,O.A./228.

SECRET.
****

Second Army.
****

      Now that the fighting is assuming a character more approximating to open warfare, it is no longer desirable to continue the use of large scale maps which were essential in trench warfare.

      The general use of comparatively small scale maps (1/100,000) will lead to a truer appreciation of essentials; in the present phase the situation is affected by the position of our troops in regard to tactical features, and not by the question as to whether they occupy the support or reserve trench of a certain system.

      So long as it is necessary to support our advance by a close artillery barrage it will not be possible to dispense with large scale maps altogether. At the same time, the difficulties of supply and issue of large numbers of these maps during a war of movement will necessitate a more general use of the 1/100,000, and it is essential that all Commanders should accustom themselves to its use.

      (sd) H. A. LAWRENCE, Lieut-General,
Chief of the General Staff.

Adv. G.H.Q.
19th Oct.1918.

120th Inf. Bde. No. 120/427.

10th Bn. K.O.S.B.
15th Bn. K.O.Y.L.I.
11th Bn. Cam. Highrs.
120th T.M.Battery.
****

      For information.

T. Knox Shaw

Captain,
A/Brigade Major,
120th Infantry Brigade.

24/10/18.

120th Inf. Bde. No. 120/474.   SECRET   S 193

ADMINISTRATIVE INSTRUCTIONS FOR RELIEF OF
120th Infantry Brigade by 121st Infantry Brigade.
===

1. Transport lines will not change.

2. The following area stores will be handed over on demand :-

	Hot food containers.	Water carriers	Pack-saddlery.
10th K.O.S.B.	17	12	6
15th K.O.Y.L.I.	-	number returned by 23rd Cheshire Regt.	
11th Cameron Highrs.	16	-	-

3. Any S.A.A, Grenades etc. is excess of mobile reserve on charge at Transport lines will be returned to the Divisional Bomb Store at B.21.b.3.9.

4. Units will prepare lists of trench stores to be handed over and forward a copy to this office by mid-day D.R. on 13th inst.

5. Units on relief will move to camps as under :-

	Location	Taken over from.
10th K.O.S.B.	B.9.d.8.6.	23rd Lanc. Fus.
15th K.O.Y.L.I.	B.19.a.2.3.	23rd Cheshire Regt.
11th Cameron Highrs.	H.3.a.5.1.	8th R. Irish Regt.
120th T.M.Battery.	B.9.c.2.6.	121 T.M.Battery.

6. Battalions will arrange for a representative to take over the Recreation huts or tent and contents in their new camp early on 13th inst.

T Knox Shaw
Captain,
Staff Captain,
120th Infantry Brigade.

Distribution

1. 10th Battn. K.O.S.B.   (2 copies)
2. 15th Battn. K.O.Y.L.I. (2 copies)
3. 11th Cam. Highrs.   (2 copies)
4. 120th T.M.Battery.
5. Brigade Q.M.Sergeant.
6. 121st Infantry Brigade.

SECRET. COPY NO. 8

120TH INFANTRY BRIGADE ORDER NO. 228.

12-10-18.

1. The 120th Infantry Brigade will be relieved in the Advanced Guard Position by the 121st Infantry Brigade on the night 13/14th October, in accordance with the attached relief table.

2. All arrangements for relief will be made direct between C.Os. concerned.

3. All special maps, aeroplane photos, defence instructions, details of work and trench stores will be handed over to incoming Units.

4. Completion of relief will be wired to Brigade Headquarters using following code word :-

   "POZZIE"

5. All details of defence of Divisional Main Line of Resistance will be taken over from relieving Units.

6. Brigade Headquarters will close at its present site and re-open at TOUQUET PARMENTIER at 10.00 14th instant, at which hour Command of the Advanced Guard will pass to G.O.C. 121st Infantry Brigade.
   Up to 10.00 14th instant all troops in the Advanced Guard Area will be under the tactical control of G.O.C. 120th Infantry Brigade.

7. Particular attention will be paid to handing over the Liaison Posts and Bridge Head Guards on both flanks.

8. ACKNOWLEDGE.

Issued through Signals
   at 11.30

Captain,
Brigade Major,
120th Infantry Brigade.

DISTRIBUTION :-

Copy No.				
1	G.O.C.	14	176th Inf. Bde.
2	Brigade Major	15	94th Inf. Bde.
3	Staff Captain,	16	331st Bde. R.F.A.
4	War Diary.	17	330th Bde. R.F.A.
5	File.	18	64th H.A. Grp.
6	10th K.O.S.B.	19	"C" Coy. 39th Bn. M.G.C.
7	15th K.O.Y.L.I.	20	137th Field Ambce.
8	11th Cam. Hrs.	21	A.D.S. - do -
9	120th T.M.Bty.	22	224th Field Coy. R.E.
10	40th Divn. "G"	23	"L" Special Coy. R.E.
11	40th Divn. "Q"	24	Brigade Supply Officer.
12	119th Inf. Bde.	25	Brigade Signals.
13	121st Inf. Bde.	26	40th Divnl. Train

RELIEF TABLE TO ACCOMPANY 120TH INFANTRY BRIGADE ORDER NO. 228 dated 12-10-18.

Serial No.	UNIT	FROM.	TO	RELIEVED BY	REMARKS.
1.	15th K.O.Y.L.I.	Reserve in ERQUINGHEM	B.29.a.2.3.	23rd Cheshires.	Relief to be carried out by day in small parties.
2.	10th K.O.S.B.	Support. 2 Coys. N. of ARMENTIERES. 2 Coys. S.E. of do.	B.9.d.7.6.	23rd Lancs.Frs.	
3.	11th Gen. Hrs.	Outpost line.	GOSPEL VILLA	8th R.Irish R.	
4.	120th T.M.Bty.	-	B.9.c.2.6.	121st T.M.Bty.	

SECRET.   COPY NO. 8

120TH INFANTRY BRIGADE ORDER NO. 226.

8-10-18.

1. On the night 9/10th October, the following reliefs will take place :-

   (a) The 10th Bn. K.O.S.B. will relieve the 11th Bn. Cameron Highrs. in support.

   (b) The 11th Bn. Cameron Highrs. will relieve the 15th Bn. K.O.Y.L.I. in the Outpost Line.

   (c) The 15th Bn. K.O.Y.L.I., on relief, will move back into the ERQUINGHEM Area.

2. All details of relief will be arranged direct between C.Os. concerned.

3. Special attention will be paid by O.C., 11th Bn. Cameron Highrs. to taking over liaison posts with troops on the flanks.

4. All special maps, aeroplane photographs and trench stores will be taken over by relieving Units.

5. On completion of relief the two Companies of the 10th Bn. K.O.S.B. North of ARMENTIERES will be under the tactical control of O.C. 11th Bn. Cameron Highrs. as laid down in Instructions No. 2 dated 7-10-18.

6. Completion of reliefs will be wired to Brigade Headquarters using following code word :-

   "RABBITS"

7. Detailed dispositions will be forwarded by O.C. 11th Bn. Cameron Highrs. by last D.R. 10th instant.

8. The policy of work will be continued as ordered in Instructions No. 2.

9. ACKNOWLEDGE.

Issued through Signals
   at 20.00
                                                       Captain,
                                                   Brigade Major,
                                              120th Infantry Brigade.

Copy No. 1 G.O.C.   8. 11th Cam. Hrs.   15. 94th Inf. Bde.
         2 Bde. Major.   9. 120th T.M.Bty.   16. 330th Bde. R.F.A.
         3. Staff Captn. 10. 40th Div. "G"   17. 331st Bde. R.F.A.
         4. War Diary.   11. 40th Div. "Q"   18. "C" Coy. 39th
         5. File.   12. 119th Inf. Bde.   Bn. M.G.C.
         6. 10th K.O.S.B. 13. 121st Inf. Bde. 19. 137th Fd. Ambce.
         7. 15th K.O.Y.L.I. 14. 176th Inf. Bde. 20. A.D.S. - do -
                     21 ... 224th Field Coy. R.E.
                     22 ... Bde. Supply Officer.
                     23 ... Bde. Signals.
                     24 ... 40th Divnl. Train.
                     25 ... 64 HAG

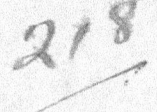

CONFIDENTIAL. 40th Division No. C/2/A.
　　　　　　　　　120th Inf. Bde. No. 120/400/1.

Headquarters,
　　120th Infantry Brigade.

　　With reference to your 76/65/Q dated 28/1/19.

　　Please arrange direct with Headquarters 120th Infantry Brigade for T/Lieut. C.H.WITHAM, 13th Bn. East Lanc. Regt to releive an officer detailed by Headquarters 120th Infantry Brigade for duty at the Halte Repas at BAISIEUX, in accordance with this office wire No.A.520 dated 22/1/1919.

　　On relief the Officer of 120th Infantry Brigade will rejoin his Unit.

　　　　　　　　　)sgd) S.DAWSON, Major,
29/1/19.　　　　　　　D.A.Q.M.G., 40th Division.

　　　　　　　- 2 -

O.C. 11th Bn. Cameron Highlanders.

　　For information.

　　　　　　　　　　　　　　　　Captain,
　　　　　　　　　　　　　　Staff Captain,
30/1/19.　　　　　　　　120th Infantry Brigade.

| HEADQUARTERS. |
| 120TH |
| INFANTRY BRIGADE. |
| No. |
| Date. |

120th Inf. Bde. No. 120/407.

O. C. 11th. Cameron Highrs.
===============

    Herewith reports on officers who attended Infantry Course at XV Corps School from 10-2-1919 to 3-3-1919.

8/3/1919.

Lieut.,
Brigade Major,
120th Infantry Brigade.

XV CORPS SCHOOL.
Report on Officers attending Infantry Course 10/2/19 to 3/3/19.

RANK. 2/Lt.   NAME. Shields, Rbt. S.t Clair   REGT. 3rd (att) 11th Cameron Highlanders   DIVN. 40th

DRILL.	Fairly good with a good word of command.
TACTICS.	His military knowledge is only average
REMARKS.	I am sure this officer will with more experience & age develop greater stability & with that knowledge which will come with more experience, he will, I feel sure make a useful Officer.

A promising young officer who should, after the steadying influence of the life in his regiment, make quite a good useful officer.

J. McCulloch Capt for Major,
C/I Infantry School.

J. Amphlett Evans Major,
Commanding XV Corps School.

XV CORPS SCHOOL.
Report on Officers attending Infantry Course 10/2/18 to 3/3/18.

RANK. 2 Lieut **NAME.** Bantock J.R.G. **REGT.** 3rd att 11th Cameron H'rs **DIV.** 40th

DRILL. Fairly Good with a good Word of Command. He handles men well

TACTICS. His military knowledge is average and his powers of imparting knowledge are above the average

REMARKS. An officer of determination with a cheerful disposition. His Topography & Musketry were Good.

He has confidence in himself and should make a good useful officer.

J. McCulloch, Capt for Major,
O/I Infantry School.

J. Amphlett Isaacs, Major,
Commanding XV Corps School.

CONFIDENTIAL.　　　　　　　　　XV Corps No A.C. 47/154
　　　　　　　　　　　　　　　　　40th Division No 84 A.

S220

120th Infantry Brigade.

　　　　　It has been brought to notice that Sentries in the Divisional Area are not presenting arms to General Officers as they pass through the Area in their Motor Cars.

　　　　　Please issue necessary instructions to ensure that all Sentries realise that a Motor Car flying an authorized flag contains a General Officer, and that the proper compliments are invariably to be paid.

　　　　　　　　　　　　　　(sgd) S.DAWSON, Major,
31/1/19.　　　　　　　　　　　　D.A.Q.M.G., 40th Division.

120th Inf. Bde. No. 120/416.

10th K.O.S.B.
18th K.O.Y.L.I.
11th Cam. Highrs.

　　　　　　　Forwarded for information.

　　　　　　　　　　　　　　　　　　Captain,
　　　　　　　　　　　　　　　　Staff Captain,
　　　　　　　　　　　　　　120th Infantry Brigade.

1/2/19.

120th Inf. Bde. No. 120/401.

    10th Bn. K.O.S.B
    15th Bn. K.O.Y.L.I.
    11th Bn. Cam. Highrs.

Herewith "Daily Table of Letters and Colours (February 1st to March 1st)"

Acknowledge on adjoined receipt.

                                  Lieut.,
                              A/Brigade Major,
6-2-19.   120th Infantry Brigade.

SECRET. A.A./25.

NOT TO BE TAKEN IN FRONT OF BRIGADE HEADQUARTERS.

DAILY TABLE OF LETTERS AND COLOURS

From Noon, 1st February, 1919, to Noon, 1st March, 1919.
(Reference G.H.Q. Letter A.A./25, dated 24th July, 1918.)

FEBRUARY From noon	To noon	Letter	Colours	FEBRUARY From noon	To noon	Letter	Colours
1	2	D	Green and Red	15	16	U	Green and White
2	3	J	Red and White	16	17	Z	White and Red
3	4	O	Green and Red	17	18	C	White and Green
4	5	M	White and Green	18	19	B	Red and White
5	6	X	Red and White	19	20	O	Red and Green
6	7	A	Green and Red	20	21	M	White and Green
7	8	K	White and Green	21	22	X	Green and White
8	9	X	White and Red	22	23	A	White and Red
9	10	I	Green and Red	23	24	H	White and Green
10	11	F	Red and White	24	25	F	Green and White
11	12	Z	White and Green	25	26	U	White and Red
12	13	A	Green and Red	26	27	L	Green and White
13	14	J	White and Red	27	28	I	White and Green
14	15	D	White and Green	28	1	C	Red and White

P.T.O.

Scale of Issue.

	Copies.
G.H.Q.:	
General Staff	10
Armies—Each—	
Army Headquarters	30*
G.O.C., R.A.	1
Corps Headquarters	20†
G.O.C., R.A.	1
Corps H.A., H.Q.	1
Corps Mounted Troops	1
H.A. Brigade or Group, H.Q.	1
Divisional Headquarters	10‡
Divisional M.G. Battalion	5
Infantry Brigade H.Q.	5§
Artillery Brigade, H.Q.	1
A.A. Defence Commanders	30‖
Brigade, R.A.F.	1
Wing, R.A.F.	1
Group, R.A.F.	1
Squadron, R.A.F.	2

	Copies.
Cavalry—Each—	
Cavalry Corps H.Q.	5
Cavalry Divisional H.Q.	10‡
Cavalry Brigade H.Q.	4§
Artillery Brigade H.Q.	1
Machine Gun Squadron	1
Motor Machine Gun Battery	1
Miscellaneous—	
Headquarters, R.A.F.	20
Headquarters Ind. Force, R.A.F.	10
Commandant, G.H.Q. Troops	14
G.O.C., L. of C. Area	2
A.A. Defence Commander, L. of C.	30‖
Each—	
A.A. Battery Commander	1
A.A. Section	1
A.A. Searchlight Section	1
Base Commandants:—Calais, Boulogne, Dieppe, Havre and Rouen	2
Commandants:—Abancourt, Abbeville, Etaples and Dunkirk	2

* Includes copies for Army Troops not otherwise provided for.
† Includes copies for Corps Troops not otherwise provided for.
‡ Includes copies for Divisional Troops, other than Artillery or M.G. units.
§ Includes copies for Regiments and Battalions.
‖ Includes copies for Garrison Guard Companies.

SECRET. 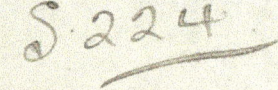 A.A./25.

<u>NOT TO BE TAKEN IN FRONT OF BRIGADE HEADQUARTERS.</u>

AMENDMENT TO DAILY TABLE OF LETTERS AND COLOURS
From Noon, 22nd February, 1919, to Noon, 1st March, 1919.
(Reference G.H.Q. Letter A.A./25, dated 24th July, 1918.)

FEBRUARY		Letter	Colours
From noon	To noon		
22 — 23		L	Red and Green
23 — 24		C	White and Red
24 — 25		F	Green and White
25 — 26		K	Green and Red
26 — 27		Z	White and Red
27 — 28		H	Red and Green
28 — 1		D	Green and Red

P.T.O.

Scale of Issue.

G.H.Q.:   Copies.
- General Staff ... 10

Armies—Each—
- Army Headquarters ... 30*
- G.O.C., R.A. ... 1
- Corps Headquarters ... 20†
- G.O.C., R.A. ... 1
- Corps H.A., H.Q. ... 1
- Corps Mounted Troops ... 1
- H.A. Brigade or Group, H.Q. ... 1
- Divisional Headquarters ... 10‡
- Divisional M.G. Battalion ... 5
- Infantry Brigade H.Q. ... 5§
- Artillery Brigade, H.Q. ... 1
- A.A. Defence Commanders ... 30‖
- Brigade, R.A.F. ... 1
- Wing, R.A.F. ... 1
- Group, R.A.F. ... 1
- Squadron, R.A.F. ... 2

Cavalry—Each—   Copies.
- Cavalry Corps H.Q. ... 5
- Cavalry Divisional H.Q. ... 10‡
- Cavalry Brigade H.Q. ... 4§
- Artillery Brigade H.Q. ... 1
- Machine Gun Squadron ... 1
- Motor Machine Gun Battery ... 1

Miscellaneous—
- Headquarters, R.A.F. ... 20
- Commandant, G.H.Q. Troops ... 14
- G.O.C., L. of C. Area ... 2
- A.A. Defence Commander, L. of C. ... 30‖
  - Each—
  - A.A. Battery Commander ... 1
  - A.A. Section ... 1
  - A.A. Searchlight Section ... 1
- Base Commandants:— Calais, Boulogne, Dieppe, Havre and Rouen ... 2
- Commandants:— Abancourt, Abbeville, Etaples and Dunkirk ... 2

* Includes copies for Army Troops not otherwise provided for.
† Includes copies for Corps Troops not otherwise provided for.
‡ Includes copies for Divisional Troops, other than Artillery or M.G. units.
§ Includes copies for Regiments and Battalions.
‖ Includes copies for Garrison Guard Companies.

120th Inf. Bde. No. 120/429.

10th Bn. K.O.S.B.
18th Bn. K.O.Y.L.I.
11th Bn. Cam. Highrs.
****

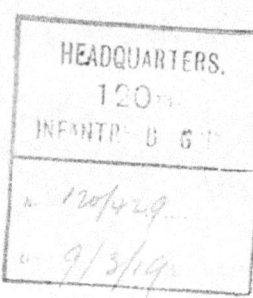

SECRET.
*****

Herewith one copy of "Daily Table of Letters and Colours", from noon, 1st March, 1919, to noon 1st April, 1919.

ACKNOWLEDGE.

J. Bonella Stuart

Lieut.
Brigade Major,
120th Infantry Brigade.

8/3/19.

SECRET. A.A./25.

NOT TO BE TAKEN IN FRONT OF BRIGADE HEADQUARTERS.

DAILY TABLE OF LETTERS AND COLOURS
From Noon, 1st March, 1919, to Noon, 1st April, 1919.
(Reference G.H.Q. Letter A.A./25, dated 24th July, 1918.)

MARCH From noon	MARCH To noon	Letter	Colours	MARCH From noon	MARCH To noon	Letter	Colours
1	2	C	Green and White	16	17	O	Red and Green
2	3	H	White and Green	17	18	K	Red and White
3	4	U	Red and White	18	19	L	Green and Red
4	5	M	Green and White	19	20	M	White and Red
5	6	Z	White and Green	20	21	I	Red and Green
6	7	A	White and Red	21	22	X	Green and White
7	8	B	Red and White	22	23	F	Red and Green
8	9	H	Green and Red	23	24	H	White and Green
9	10	D	White and Green	24	25	D	Green and Red
10	11	O	Red and White	25	26	I	Red and White
11	12	C	Green and Red	26	27	C	Red and Green
12	13	F	White and Red	27	28	M	White and Red
13	14	Z	Green and White	28	29	U	Green and Red
14	15	U	Red and Green	29	30	A	White and Green
15	16	J	Green and Red	30	31	B	Green and White
				31	1	L	White and Red

P.T.O.

SCALE OF ISSUE.

	Copies.
G.H.Q.:	
General Staff	10
Armies—Each—	
Army Headquarters	30*
G.O.C., R.A.	1
Corps Headquarters	20†
G.O.C., R.A.	1
Corps H.A., H.Q.	1
Corps Mounted Troops	1
H.A. Brigade or Group, H.Q.	1
Divisional Headquarters	10‡
Divisional M.G. Battalion	5
Infantry Brigade H.Q.	5§
Artillery Brigade, H.Q.	1
A.A. Defence Commanders	30‖
Brigade, R.A.F.	1
Wing, R.A.F.	1
Group, R.A.F.	1
Squadron, R.A.F.	2

	Copies.
Cavalry—Each—	
Cavalry Corps H.Q.	5
Cavalry Divisional H.Q.	10‡
Cavalry Brigade H.Q.	4§
Artillery Brigade H.Q.	1
Machine Gun Squadron	1
Motor Machine Gun Battery	1
Miscellaneous—	
Headquarters, R.A.F.	20
Commandant, G.H.Q. Troops	14
G.O.C., L. of C. Area	2
A.A. Defence Commander, L. of C.	30‖
Each—	
A.A. Battery Commander	1
A.A. Section	1
A.A. Searchlight Section	1
Base Commandants:—Calais, Boulogne, Dieppe, Havre and Rouen	2
Commandants:—Abancourt, Abbeville, Etaples and Dunkirk	2

* Includes copies for Army Troops not otherwise provided for.
† Includes copies for Corps Troops not otherwise provided for.
‡ Includes copies for Divisional Troops, other than Artillery or M.G. units.
§ Includes copies for Regiments and Battalions.
‖ Includes copies for Garrison Guard Companies.

PRINTED IN FRANCE BY ARMY PRINTING AND STATIONERY SERVICES.   PRESS A—3/19-9117S—pkR

UBJECT.

A.& E.W.

Contents.	Date.
Bdl 1915	
DW	

A.& E.W.

S E C R E T.　　　　　　　　　　O.B./1831/A.

Attention is called to the fact that the British Armour piercing bullet will not pierce the plates of a German Tank and that consequently fire with Armour piercing bullets has little effect against them.

On the other hand, concentrated fire with ordinary S.A.A. has a very good chance of putting a German Tank out of action owing to the fact that the machine gun, gun and loop-hole shields fit very badly and allow the lead 'splash' of ordinary bullets to enter the Tank freely.

Cases have occurred in which fire has been brought to bear on Hostile Tanks with a mixture of A.P. and ordinary bullets with good effect. This effect has generally been attributed to the Armour piercing bullets.

Experience proved conclusively, however, that the effect is really obtained by the 'splash' of the ordinary bullets.

In one case which has been reported, it is stated that the strike of the bullets was marked by long sheets of flame. This is the common appearance of 'splash'.

Hostile tanks, therefore, should be engaged by concentrated bursts of fire from machine guns, Lewis Guns and rifles, using ordinary S.A.A., particular attention being paid to the loopholes. Armour piercing ammunition should not be used.

G.H.Q.　　　　　　　　　　　　(Sgd) K. WIGRAM, B. G.
2nd July, 1918　　　　　　　　　　for Lieut.-General,
　　　　　　　　　　　　　　　　　　　　C. G. S.

(2).

120th Inf. Bde. No. 120/429.

10th Garr. Bn. K.O.S.B.
15th Garr. Bn. K.O.Y.L.I.
11th Garr. Bn. Cam. Highrs.
120th T. M. Battery.

For information and guidance.

HEADQUARTERS,
120TH
INFANTRY BRIGADE.
No. 120/429
Date..............

Captain,
A/Brigade Major,
120th Infantry Brigade.

6-7-18.

SECRET.   120th I. B. No.120/415.

120TH INFANTRY BRIGADE WARNING ORDER.

A practice manning of the WEST HAZEBROUCK LINE will be carried out by the 120th Infantry Brigade and affiliated Labour and R.E. Companies, on Wednesday, 10th instant.

Battalions will be in position in the line by 10 a.m.

Affiliated Labour and R.E. Companies will report at their allotted assembly positions by 9-30 a.m.

Detailed Orders and revised Appendix 'A' to 120th Infantry Brigade Order No. 201 will be issued shortly.

W B Kew

Captain,
A/Brigade Major,
120th Infantry Brigade.

8-7-18.

Issued to :-

10th Garr. Bn. K.O.S.B.
15th Garr. Bn. K.O.Y.L.I.
11th Garr. Bn. Cam. Highrs.
64th Labour Group.
26th Labour Group.
258th Tunnelling Coy. R.E.

S E C R E T.
....

40th Divn. No. 105/6 G.
XV Corps No. 228/1 (G).

40th Division.
....

1. Will you please ensure that all ranks of the battalions of your Division undergoing training in the EAST HAZEBROUCK LINE are instructed that no damage is to done to the trenches which they occupy.

2. A Staff Officer of the Corps reports that certain number of recesses have been dug in the sides of the trenches and that at D.9.c.62.20. two walls have been built across the trench, it is believed with the object of forming a Company Headquarters. Action of this nature detracts from the defensive value of the trench system.

(Sgd) A.E.OSBORNE, Major,
for B.G., G.S.

5-7-18.

- 2 -

120th Inf. Bde. No. 120/415.

10th Garr. Bn. A.O.S.B.
13th Garr. Bn. K.O.Y.L.I.
11th Garr. Bn. Cam. Highrs.

Please issue orders accordingly.

Captain,
A/Brigade Major,
12th Infantry Brigade.

7-7-18.

120th Inf. Bde. No. 120/415/1.   SECRET.

Headquarters, "G"

    31st Division.

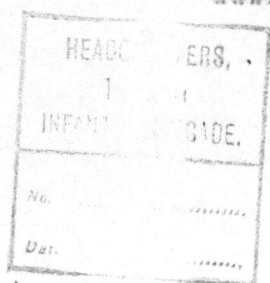

Reference the attachment to Battalions in this Brigade of Officers and N.C.Os. as instructors in trench duties, Battalions are ordered to occupy the WEST HAZEBROUCK LINE as follows :-

10th G.Bn. K.O.S.B. ... 3rd to 7th instant.
   H.Q. at C.23.a.9.2.

15th G.Bn. K.O.Y.L.I. ... 7th to 11th instant.
   H.Q. at C.18.c.5.9.

11th G.Bn. Cam. Hrs. ... 11th to 15th instant.
   H.Q. at C.11.d.4.8.

Can you please arrange for the Officers and N.C.Os. to report to Battalion Headquarters concerned, at 6 p.m. on the 3rd inst. in the case of 10th G. Bn. K.O.S.B. and at times suitable to you in the other cases.

        (Sgd) C.J.HOBKIRK, Brig. Gen.
1-7-18.   Comdg., 120th Infantry Brigade.

10th Garr. Bn. K.O.S.B.
15th Garr. Bn. K.O.Y.L.I.
11th Garr. Bn. Cam. Highrs.

Battalions will arrange to meet these Officers and N.C.Os. at above mentioned places if their Headquarters are not situated there.

1-7-18.   CAPTAIN.

40th Div. No. 27/5 G.   S E C R E T.

NOTES ON CONFERENCE,

held at Divl. Headquarters, 29th June, 1918.

1. **Manning of West Hazebrouck Line.**

   (a) It was reported by all Brigades that the concentration of Labour units carried out in accordance with Div. Order No. 175 dated 24/6/18 had been quite satisfactory.

   (b) The Divl. Commander decided that Labour Companies were not to be employed forward of the Support Line to the Main Line of Resistance unless during battle it became imperative to advance them.

   (c) The Divl. Commander emphasised the point that he did not want Labour Companies allotted an independent sub-section of the line, but that they were to be attached to Battalions vide para. 13 of Order 175.

   (d) The G.O.C. 120th Brigade asked that the trenches which the Brigade has to man be named. Application has been made through XV Corps.

   (e) It was decided that there will be three ammunition dumps in each Brigade Area and that ammunition will not be distributed in the trench system until it is occupied by troops.

   (f) Brigadiers asked that Field Companies and A.T.Coys should devote some time to training, as for some time they have been employed exclusively on work.
   Application has been made to VIIth Corps, under whom the troops are working.

   (g) That 17th Bn: Worcestershire Regiment (Pioneers) be allotted an assembly position now that it has become Div. Troops.
   This has been done, vide Amendments to 40th Div. Order No. 175 issued to-day.

   (h) The Major General decided that when Battalions go up to man the EAST HAZEBROUCK Line for instructional purposes, that Battalions should go as complete as possible and training should be continued there. If, however, it is not possible to man all Lewis Guns, classes of instruction in Lewis Gunnery may be carried on in the present camps with personnel and guns detailed from the Battalions occupying the line.

Lieut. Colonel,
General Staff, 40th Division.

29/6/18.

SECRET

O.C. 11th Gdn. Com. Hrs.

Forwarded.

[Stamp: HEADQUARTERS, 120TH INFANTRY BRIGADE. No......... Date......]

30/6/18.

H. B. Kerr
CAPTAIN,
A/BRIGADE MAJOR,
120th INFANTRY BRIGADE.

S E C R E T.   Hd.Qrs. 40th Divn. No. 858 (A).

The Training Staff of 12th Yorkshire Regt. (P) is being absorbed into the 17th (G) Bn. Worcestershire Regt. and the latter Unit is becoming this Divisional Pioneer Battalion.
The 17th (G) Bn. Wrocestershire Regt.(P) will be administered direct by Divnl. Head Quarters from and including 29th June, 1918.

(Authority - G.H.Q. O.B./1851/A dated 23rd June, 1918).

27th June, 1918.

A. L. Cowton.
Major,
D. A. A. G.,
40th Division.

HEADQUARTERS.
120TH
INFANTRY BRIGADE.

Distribution :--

All Units 40th Division.
All branches Divnl.Hd.Qrs.

For information.

S E C R E T.   40th Division No. 835(A).

1. 135th and 136th Field Ambulances are rejoining the Division from First Army.

   They march on 24th June, under orders of First Army staging night 24/25th June, at QUERCAMP and NIELLES LES BLEQUIN, respectively.

2. Rations for consumption 25th June being carried. Rations for consumption on 26th June to be drawn from R.S.O., LUMBRES.
   40th Divisional Train will ration for consumption on 27th June.

3. Headquarters, Second Army, has been asked to arrange for these Field Ambulances to report as under on arrival in Divisional Area.

   135 Field Ambulance to Headquarters, 120th Infantry Brigade, for allotment of Camping ground in 120th Brigade area.

   136 Field Ambulance to Headquarters, 119th Infantry Brigade, for allotment of Camping ground in 119th Brigade area.

4. A.D.M.S., 40th Division, will report arrival and exact locations.

A. L. Corot

Major,
D.A.A.G., 40th Division.

22nd June, 1918.

(JM)   Distribution :-   All Units 40th Division.
                                      All branches 40th Div'l. Headquarters.

1st Gai Bn Cameron Highrs

For information

28/6/18

V. Hatcher Lt
A/SC 120 Bde

HEADQUARTERS,
120TH
INFANTRY BRIGADE.
No.
Date.

SECRET.   VII Corps No. A/130/125.
                           Hd.Qrs.40th Divn.No. 680(A).

40th Division.

PREVENTION OF TRENCH FOOT.

1. In view of the low medical category of the men in many of the Units which may have to occupy the WEST HAZEBROUCK and LE PEUPLIER Lines, and that the weather may be wet and the trenches waterlogged, it is necessary for all concerned to consider measures for the prevention of Trench Foot.

2. Attention is therefore directed to G.R.O. 1275.

3. It is realised that units will not have at their disposal hot food containers and gum boots, but Commanding Officers must take every precaution possible to prevent Trench Foot if the weather conditions happen to be adverse.

Headquarters.   (sgd). A.R.Gordon, Lt-Col. for Brig-Gen.,
20. 6. 18.   for D.A. & Q.M.G. VII Corps.

                    (2).
C.R.E., 40th Division.
Head Qrs.,119th Infy.Brigade.
Head Qrs.,120th Infy.Brigade.
Head Qrs.,121st Infy.Brigade.

A.D.M.S., 40th Division.

For information and necessary action.

21st June, 1918.
                                    Lieut-Col.,
                                    A.A. & Q.M.G.,
                                    40th Division.

For information.

SECRET.   40th Div. No. 19/12 (G).

H.Q., 119th Inf. Bde.
H.Q., 120th Inf. Bde.
H.Q., 121st Inf. Bde.
C.R.E., 40th Division.
Div. Signal Coy.
A.D.M.S.,
Div. Train.
A. P. M.

1.   It is reported by the French that a German aviator coming from SOISSONS, and captured on the 14th instant, near ST. MENEHOULD, states that he had landed a German agent behind our lines.

2.   To be noted in continuation of 40th Div. No.19/9 (G) dated 16-6-18.

                                          W Carter Major,
                                    General Staff, 40th Division.

21-6-18.

O.C. 11th G.Bn. Cam. Hrs.

For information, reference this office letter No. 120/429 d/16/6/18

                                          H B Kerr
                                          CAPTAIN.
                                          BRIGADE MAJOR,
                                          120TH INFANTRY BRIGADE.

21/6/18

S E C R E T.   40th Division No. 843(A).

1. No. 2 Coy. 40th Divisional Train (less Supply Details) will move from STAPLE to join 119th Infantry Brigade in ST. MOMELIN Area on 19th June 1918. Billeting parties to report Headquarters, 119th Brigade, NIEURLET.
Location of Company to be reported to Div'l. Headquarters on 19th June, by Headquarters, 119th Brigade.

2. Supply Details No.2 Coy. 40th Divisional Train will remain at STAPLE.

A. L. Coictan.
Major,
D.A.A.G., 40th Division.

18th June, 1918.

(JM) Distribution :-

All Units 40th Division.
All branches 40th Div'l. Headquarters.
Area Commandant
ST MOMELIN.

1/11th Gar. Bn. Cameron Highrs.

For information

[signature]
Lieut
a/ STAFF CAPT., 120TH INF. BDE.

HEADQUARTERS,
120TH
INFANTRY BRIGADE.

19/6/1918.

S E C R E T.   H.Q., 40th Division No. 835/A/21.

    17th Garrison Battn. Worcester Regiment and 23rd Garrison Battn. Lancashire Fusiliers joined the Division to-day.

    They are posted to 121st Inf. Brigade and located respectively at LONGUENESSE and SALPERWICK.

                                                         signature

                                                     Major,
H.Q., 40th Division.   D.A.A.G.,
18th June, 1918.   40th Division.

Distribution:-
                  All Units, 40th Division.
                  All Branches, 40th Divnl. Hd.Qrs.

(RSJ)

11th Bn. Cameron Highrs

For information.

[signature]
a/ STAFF CAPT., 120TH INF. BDE.

19/6/1918.

40th Div. No. 19/9 (G).

SECRET. .... G.H.Q. No. I(b) 6357
VII Corps No. I.G.83
....

Second Army.
.....

    Two prisoners of war captured on 10-6-18 by Fourth Army have stated under examination that the Germans had called for volunteers to be dropped by aeroplane behind our lines in order to get in touch with a German Officer dressed as a French Officer who would give them instructions as to blowing up certain bridges in the SOMME Area on 15-6-18.

    As it is possible that similar attempts may be made in other areas, it is of importance that special measures should be taken to guard important bridges, and to look out for low-flying aeroplanes at night.

    In this connexion it is to be noted that on 23-5-18 an escaped German prisoner of war was arrested near AMIENS and under interrogation stated that a German Officer in French Sous-Lieutenant's uniform had approached him on the AMIENS-POIX road and suggested to him that he should undertake acts of sabotage.
    The description of the German Officer was as follows :-

    Height 1m70, 35 years, strongly built, heavy brown moustache, wore steel helmet, Sam Browne belt, revolver, and leggings. Rode a bicycle with a carrier.

                  (sd). S.J. MENZIES, Major,
                      for Lt. Colonel, G.S.

G.H.Q.I(b).
13-6-18.

                2.   40th Div. No. 19/9 (G).

H.Q., 119th Inf. Bde.
H.Q., 120th Inf. Bde.
H.Q., 121st Inf. Bde.
C.R.E., 40th Division.
Div. Signal Coy.
A.D.M.S.,
Div. Train.
A. P. M.
....

            For information.

                            for Major,
16-6-18.   General Staff, 40th Division.

120th Inf Bde. No 120/429.
O/C. 11th Cameron H'rs.
        For information.

16/6/18

11th Garr Bn Cameron Highrs

SECRET. 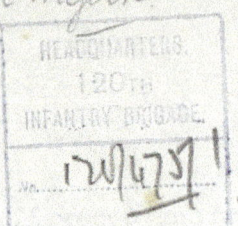 40th Division No.035/11/A.

The Garrison Battalions of this Division are at present disposed as follows:-

119th Infantry Brigade.

New Designation.	Old Designation.	Composed of	Remarks.
13th Gar. Bn. Royal Inniskilling Fusiliers.	No. 7 Garrison Battalion.	"G", "H", "I", "J" Garrison Companies from Second Army	Companies not yet joined but expected.
13th Gar. Bn. East Lancashire Regt.	No. 8 Garrison Battalion.	"K","L","M","N" Garrison Companies from Second Army.	Companies not yet joined but expected.
12th Gar. Bn. North Staffordshire Regt.	No.11 Garrison Battalion.	"U","V","W","X" Garrison Companies from Fourth Army.	Companies expected to-day.

120th Infantry Brigade.

New Designation.	Old Designation.	Composed of	Remarks.
11th Gar. Bn. Cameron Highlanders.	No.6 Garrison Battalion.	"A","B","C","D", Garrison Companies from First Army.	Companies have joined.
10th Gar. Bn. K.O.S.B.	No.9 Garrison Battalion	"E" & "F" Coys from First Army. "O" & "P" Coys from Third Army.	Companies have joined.
15th Gar. Bn. K.O.Y.L.I.	No.10 Garrison Battalion	"Q","R","S","T" Coys from Third Army.	Companies have joined.

121st Infantry Brigade.

17th Gar. Bn., Worcester Regt.)
23rd Gar. Bn., Lancs Fusiliers.)
2nd Gar. Bn., Royal Irish Regt.)
23rd Gar. Bn., Cheshire Regiment.)

Origin not known. These Battalions are going to be transferred to this Division from 59th Division but have not yet arrived.

A. L. Ingotan Major.
D.A.A.G.
for Major General,
Commanding 40th Division.

15th June, 1918.

- 2 -

Distribution :-

Adjutant General, General Headquarters,
Deputy Adjutant General, G.H.Q., 3rd Echelon,
Headquarters, Second Army "A",
Headquarters, VII Corps.

All Units, 40th Division.
All branches 40th Divisional Headquarters.

(JM)

SECRET.   40th Division No. 835/10 (Q).

1.   Information has now been received that Garrison Battalions will be made up to the full scale of 1st Line Transport for an Infantry Battalion.

2.   Further instructions will be issued to those concerned regarding the drawing of the transport and the provision of transport personnel.

                                         A. L. Cowtan.
                                              Major,
                                     D.A.A.G., 40th Division.

15th June, 1918.

(JM)

Distribution :-
                All Units 40th Division,
                All Branches 40th Divisional Headquarters.

11th Garr. Bn Cameron Highrs

for information.

H.B. Kerr
Capt.
STAFF CAPT., 120TH INF. BDE

15/6/1918.

SECRET.

40th Division No.835(A).

G.H.Q., No. A.G/833 (H).

1. Reference para. 4, 40th Division letter No.835(Q) dated 9th June, 1918.

The following permanent designations are allotted to Garrison Battalions and will come into force at 9 a.m. 12th JUNE, 1918 :-

Old Designation.	New Designation.
No.6 Garrison Battalion - 11th Garrison Bn.	Cameron Highlanders.
No.7 " " - 13th " "	R. Inniskilling Fsrs.
No.8 " " - 13th " "	East Lancashire Regt.
No.9 " " - 10th " "	K.O.S.B.
No.10 " " - 15th " "	K.O.Y.L.I.
No.11 " " - 12th " "	N. Staffs. Regt.

2. Permission is given for the transfer, if desired, of men from one unit to another, in order to separate nationalities; but all such transfers will be reported to the D.A.G., 3rd Echelon, by Headquarters, 120th Infantry Brigade, who will approve the proposed transfer before it is effected.

3. The transfers of records will be carried out by the D.A.G., 3rd Echelon, who will allot new regimental numbers.

A.B. 64 and Identity Discs will then be altered accordingly.

Major,
D.A.A.G., 40th Division.

11th June, 1918.

(JM)

Distribution :- All Units 40th Division.
All branches 40th Div'l. Headquarters.
O.C., 65 Labour Group (WATTEN).
Area Commandant, LEDERZEELE.

O.C.
Nº 6 Gar. Battn.

For information.
Ref para 2, a nominal roll of all other ranks on the strength will be prepared and forwarded to this office as early as possible. This roll to show:—
(a). The NCOs. or mans present Regt. and
(b). Native County.

Thatcher Lieut.
for Staff Captain
120' Infy Bde.

6/
18

SECRET.   40th Division No. 835/15 (A).

With reference to the four Garrison Battalions arriving from 59th Division for 121st Infantry Brigade.

1.   2nd Garrison Battalion Royal Irish Regiment and 23rd Garrison Battalion Cheshire Regiment were formed in ENGLAND and are stated to have complete transport (to Infantry Battalion scale).

2.   17th Garrison Battalion Worcester Regiment and 23rd Garrison Battalion Lancashire Fusiliers were formed recently in this country and are stated to have transport at modified scale only.   59th Division have indented for balance to complete Infantry Battalion scale.

3.   Personal equipment of all four Battalions is reported to be complete except for minor deficiencies.

4.   The exact state of these Battalions as regards mobilization equipment is not known at present but it is understood that they are in possession of vital requirements.

5.   One Battalion will probably arrive on 18th June, and three Battalions on 19th June, 1918. Further details will be issued early and the question of accommodating the fourth Battalion will also be settled at that time.

15th June, 1918.
(WB).
              Major,
              D. A. A. G.,
              40th Division.

Distribution :-

H.Q., 121st Infantry Brigade.
O.C., 40th Divisional Train.
D.A.D.O.S., 40th Division.
All branches 40th Divnl. Hd. Qrs.

11th Gar. Bn. Cameron Higlrs

For information

15/6/1918.

CAPT.,
STAFF DAPT., 120TH INF. BDE.

S 2

SECRET.

Second Army

G. 42.

11th June, 1918.

VII Corps.

A report received on the use of gas shell by the enemy during the bombardment at the commencement of the AISNE battle on May 27th brings the following points to light :-

(a) Heavy gas shelling for neutralising effect is to be regarded as normally used by the enemy at the beginning of an offensive. (E.g. SOMME, LYS, KEMMEL & VILLERS BRETONNEUX).

(b) Whilst "Mustard Gas" may be used beyond the limits of the objective, gas of low persistence is used against the area to be occupied. It is fired in such quantity as to make it necessary to wear masks during practically the whole bombardment, and the drift of the gas may carry to several miles from the actual spots shelled. Particular attention as usual is paid to battery positions, villages and woods.

(c) No new enemy gases have been used. The box respirator has given complete protection in every case.

(d) Avoidable casualties were due to -

(i) ignorance on part of men of properties of gases used, with resulting unnecessary moral effect.
(ii) men removing respirators to see,
(iii) gas shells being mistaken for H.E. shells,
(iv) men surprised when asleep.

(e) The remedies for (d) are -

(i) More gas training of officers, particularly senior and more responsible officers,
(ii) more practice in wearing respirators at night and better use of anti-dimming composition,
(iii) general recognition that gas shells can no longer be infallibly picked out by the sound of their explosion and that the enemy uses Blue Cross shell in most H.E. bombardments,
(iv) strict adherence to be paid to the posting of gas sentries.

(f) The value of gas-proof shelters has again been demonstrated.

(sd) W. ROBERTSON, Lt.Col,
for M.G.G.S.,
Second Army.

S E C R E T. VII Corps G.C.R.829/84.

34th Division.
39th Division.
40th Division.
41st Division.
G.O.C.,R.A.
C.E.
C.A.
B.G.C.,H.A.
"Q".
D.D.M.S.
O.C. Corps Troops.
----

1. Copy of Second Army G.42 of 11th June, on reverse, is forwarded for your information.

2. The necessity for continued training in anti-gas precautions is emphasised.

                                              Brigadier-General,
12th June, 1918.   General Staff, VII Corps.

11th G.Hr. Cameron Hrs.

For information

P.T.O.

CAPTAIN,
BRIGADE MAJOR,
120TH INFANTRY BRIGADE.

Confidential

G.H.Q. No. A.G.833/4(a).
40th Division No.835/23/A.

Headquarters,
    40th Division.

    Now that your Division has been reconstituted, I wish to take the opportunity of greeting the Officers, Non-Commissioned Officers and men who are about to take their part in the defence of the British Line.

    I am keenly sensible of the sacrifices which they have been called upon to make, and of the ready spirit in which they have responded to the call: many of them, I know, have already seen much fighting, many are no longer young men, and all are in some way handicapped in physical efficiency.

    I recognise to the full these undoubted limitations, and I do not intend to throw upon them a greater strain than they can bear.

    They will not be called upon to carry out long marches, or to take part in battles of movement.

    At the present stage in this year's great campaign, when we are fighting not only for our liberty as an empire of free peoples, but also for our vital interests, and our very existence, I look to them with complete confidence to help in filling the breach; our American Allies are arriving in a ceaseless and ever increasing stream to take their part in the struggle.

    I know that I can rely upon the veterans among them to inspire their fellows with the same spirit of courage, doggedness, and devotion to duty that they have themselves so often displayed in the past, and upon those that are entering the line for the first time not to fall short of the example already set by the regiments to which they belong.

                    Sd/ D. HAIG,
                          F. M.

28th June, 1918.

- 2 -

    The above letter is to be read out on parade, in order that it may be brought to the notice of all ranks. It is not to appear in the form of Orders.

                      Lieut-Colonel,
              A.A. & Q.M.G., 40th Division.

1st July, 1918.

(JM)

Please have the above read on parade before your battalion proceeds with Inspection today

a/Staff Captain

SECRET.   XV Corps No. 57/135 G.

40th Division.

1.   A case occurred recently where certain messages were sent in cypher between Battalion and Company Headquarters of a Division in line, and the text of the message was written both in clear and in cypher on the same form. If a Battalion or Company Headquarters was captured by the enemy with one of these messages, the key word of the cypher would at once be discovered by the enemy. Such instances indicate that Staffs and Signal Service of formations are not yet exercising sufficient control over the traffic on forward telephone and telegram lines.

2.   Signal Officers of formations must be made responsible for the scrutiny of messages passing over the lines which they control, and for bringing to the notice of their Staffs any cases where messages, or the means by which messages are sent may lead to information being supplied to the enemy. *See amendment attached*

3.   It is pointed out that the Amplifiers in possession of Divisions form a valuable means of intercepting telephone messages passing over our lines, and when not actually employed to receive power buzzer messages a certain number should be used to police our own lines.

4.   It is fully realised that Staffs of formations have not the time to carry out the necessary scrutiny of messages themselves, and the responsibility for undertaking this work, should therefore, devolve upon ~~Officers of the Signal Service.~~ *Signal officers*
     Staffs of formations should, however, ensure that the arrangements made by Signal Officers to check telephone and telegraph traffic are efficient, and that all cases of carelessness, contravention of orders, and improper use of telegraph service, are brought to their notice promptly.

                           sd. H. KNOX, Brigadier-General,
                                            General Staff.
XV Corps,
1-7-18.

                           R.   40th Div. No. 66/5 (G).

119th Infantry Bde.   17th (P) Garr Bn Worc. Rgt.
120th Infantry Bde.   C.R.E.,
121st Infantry Bde.   Div. Sig. Coy.

          For information and communication to all concerned.

          O.C., Signals will issue any necessary instructions to Signal Officers and report to D.H.Q., that he is satisfied with the measures taken.

                                        Lieut-Colonel,
                                 General Staff, 40th Division.
2-7-18.

SECRET.   XV Corps No. 57/135/1 (G).

40th Division.

Reference XV Corps No. 57/135 G. dated 1-7-18.

Para 2 will be amended to read as follows :-

"2". Signal Officers of formations must be made responsible for the scrutiny of messages which have been despatched over the lines they control, and for bringing to the notice of their Staffs any cases, where messages, or the means by which messages are sent may have led to information being supplied to the enemy."

Para. 4. At the end of first sentence for "Officers of Signal Service" read, "Signal Officers".

sd. E.A. OSBORNE, Major,
XV Corps,   for Brigadier-General,
7-7-18.   General Staff.

2.

		40th Div. No. 66/5/1 (
119th Infantry Bde.	17th (P) Garr Bn Worc. Rgt.	
120th Infantry Bde.	C.R.E.,	
121st Infantry Bde.	Div. Sig. Coy.	

....

For information and communication to all concerned with reference to these Headquarters minute of the 2nd July No. 66/5 (G).

Trevor L C Wood
for Lieut-Colonel,
8-7-18.   General Staff, 40th Division.

OC 11th Ghn. Cavan Hy

For information
WBKerr

8/7/18

SECRET.

G.H.Q. No. A.G.80/6 (O).
XV Corps No. AC/9085/29.
40th Division No.120(A).

Headquarters,
Second Army.

Will you please forward by the 14th inst. the names of any subaltern officers (Yeomanry or Infantry) recommended for employment as Company Transport Officers with Machine Gun Battalions.

A short statement as to the qualifications of each officer will be forwarded with the recommendation.

The number of officers recommended will not exceed 25 per Army.

G.H.Q.
3rd July, 1918.

Sd/ D. CAMERON, Major,
D.A.A.G., for Adjutant General.

- 2 -

H.Q., 119th Infantry Brigade.
H.Q., 120th ,,
121st ,,
O.C., 17th (S) Bn. Worcester.Regt.(P).

Please forward names of any officers recommended, together with short statement of qualifications, to reach this office by first D.R. on 9th July, 1918.

Major,
D.A.Q.M.G., 40th Division.

6th July, 1918.
(JM)

- 3 -

The return called for in Minute 2 will be forwarded to these Headquarters by first D.R., 8th July. Nil returns required.

Lieut.,
A/Staff Captain,
120th Infantry Brigade.

6.7.1918.

S 54

S E C R E T.

Second Army No. G.T.887,
dated 10th July, 1918.

XV Corps No. 593/15 G.
dated 11/7/1918.

In order to test the penetration of the bullet when fired from a rifle through standing corn, experiments have recently been carried out at Second Army School of Musketry with the following results :-

Conditions under which experiments were carried out -

(a) Fired by School N.C.O. Instructors.
(b) Each rifle carefully sighted to ensure that line of fire actually passed through the corn.
(c) Auxiliary aiming marks used (Lewis Gun instructional targets) and screens placed at far side of belt of corn.
(d) Ammunition - tracer and ordinary.
(e) Firers about 4 yards from corn.
(f) Weather dry (practically no rain for two months).

Experiments and results.-

1. Width of belt of corn = 60 yards.
   Penetration obtained = 15% direct, 42% turned hits.

2. Width of belt of corn = 150 yards.
   Penetration obtained = 10% direct, 27% turned hits.

3. Width of belt of corn = 200 yards.
   Penetration obtained = .5% direct, 3.5% turned hits.

Although penetration was obtained up to 200 yards, it would appear that when firing under battle conditions without auxiliary aiming marks, fire effect through a belt of corn wider than 50 or 60 yards would be very much reduced. From observation it would also appear that the majority of bullets are deflected after passing through wheat for 60 or 70 yards.

Further experiments will be carried out in different weather conditions.

(Sd) F.C. TANNER, Lt-Col.

for M.G.G.S.
Second Army.

2.

119th Infantry Bde.   40th Div. No. 134 G.
120th Infantry Bde. 17th (P) G.B. Worc Regt.
121st Infantry Bde. C.R.E.

For information.

12-7-18.

Lieut-Colonel,
General Staff, 40th Division.

S90

40th Div. No. 10/32/1 G.   S E C R E T.

119th Inf. Bde.	Div. Sig. Co.	Div. Empl. Coy.	"Q".
120th ,,	A.D.M.S.	A.P.M.	
121st ,,	Train.	D.A.D.O.S.	
17th Worc. (P).	M.T.Coy.	D.A.D.V.S.	
C.R.E.	Camp Comdt.	Div. Gas Off.	

****

Reference XV Corps No. 99/128 G. dated 2nd August, forwarded under 40th Div. No. 10/32 G dated 4/8/18.

Para. 2 (2) Lines 11 and 12 for No. 89/109/1 G. of 9/5/18 read No. 69/136 G. of 21/7/1918.

J. H. Stafford
Major Gl
for. Lieut. Colonel,
General Staff, 40th Division.

7/8/18.

****

120th Inf. Bde. No. 120/4/18
II
11th Cameron H'rs.

Forwarded with reference to this Office No. 120/4/18 d. 5/8/18

8/8/18

SECRET.   XV Corps No. 89/128 G.

40th Division.
----

1.   The attention of all units is drawn to the recent amendments to SS 534, "Defence against Gas".

2.   During a recent inspection of the gas defence arrangements in the Corps the following points were noticed :-

(1). Gas curtains in many cases dry and not properly rolled up.

(2). Orders regarding carrying of respirators in the READY ZONE and the wearing of them in the ALERT position in the ALERT ZONE are being flagrantly disregarded.
Divisions will make the necessary arrangements to ensure strict obedience to these orders within their areas; more energetic supervision is required on the part of the military police.

Application is being made to Army to bring the limits of the ALERT and READY ZONES further east. Pending further orders, however, the limits laid down in Second Army G.54, forwarded under XV Corps No. 89/109/1 G of 9-5-18, will be observed for the ALERT and READY ZONES.

(3). A certain number of men are arriving at Divisional Reception Camps with defective respirators. Arrangements will be made at all Divisional Reception Camps to pass all troops through a fitting chamber before they proceed to their units.

3.   Attention is drawn to the provision in War Establishments for a Gas N.C.O. attached to Battalion Headquarters. Such appointment should be made in cases where it has not already been done.
It is suggested that greater use might be made of gas N.C.Os. particularly in the matter of upkeep of gas proofing arrangements.

                        sd.   H. KNOX,   Brigadier-General,
XV Corps.   General Staff.
2-8-18.

                                    2.

                                            40th Div. No. 10/32 G.
119th Infantry Bde.   Div. Sig. Coy.   Div. Emp Coy.   Camp Cdt.
120th Infantry Bde.   A.D.M.S.   A.P.M.   Div.G.O.
121st Infantry Bde.   Div. Train.   D.A.D.O.S.   "Q".
17th (P) Worc. Rgt.   Div. M.T. Coy.   D.A.D.V.S.
C.R.E.   *=*=*=*=*=*=*=*=*=*=*

        For information and communication to all concerned.

                                J. H. Stafford.
                                  Major G.S.

                                for Lieut-Colonel,
                                General Staff, 40th Division.
4-8-18.

O.C. 11th Cam. Sts.

For information and necessary action

SECRET.

40th Division No. 874/2/Q.

Ref. Map Sheet 36 A.

1. On the night 4/5th August, 1918, the 121st Infantry Brigade are being relieved on the right of the STRAZEELE Sector by the 29th Division.

2. From the night of 4/5th August, 1918, the 121st Infantry Brigade will cease to be attached to the 29th Division and will be attached for training to the 31st Division to hold a front of about 1000 yards in the centre of LA MOTTE Sector.

3. **ACCOMMODATION.**
After relief the 121st Infantry Brigade and Battalion Headquarters and accommodation is as follows :-

Headquarters 121st Infantry Brigade.	D.17.a.7.3.
Front Battalion.	E.14.d.5.3.
Support Battalion.	E.20.a.70.95.
Reserve Battalion.	D.11.d.7.8.

Transport Lines.
Brigade Headquarters and 1 Bn.	D.8.c.1.2.
2 Battalions.	C.12.b.9.9.

Details of accommodation are being arranged by 31st Division.

4. **RATIONS AND ORDNANCE SERVICES.**
During the period of attachment to the 31st Division the 121st Infantry Brigade will remain under the 40th Division for rations and Ordnance Services.
Rations for consumption 6th August, 1918, and onwards will be delivered to the Transport Lines at D.8.c.1.2. and C.12.b.9.9. for the 121st Infantry Brigade by arrangements of O.C., 40th Divl. Train.

5. **BAGGAGE WAGONS.**
Baggage wagons will be sent to Units on the night prior to the move.
After Baggage has been cleared on the day of the move of Units all Baggage wagons will be returned to their A.S.C. Companies, 40th Divisional Train same day, as they will be required for Supply Services.

6. **BATHS and CLEAN CLOTHING.**
Baths and clean clothing for 121st Infantry Brigade during the period of attachment will be obtained from the 31st Division.

7. **CASUALTIES.**
All casualties of the 121st Infantry Brigade will be reported to 31st Division and repeated to 40th Division.

8. **MEDICAL ARRANGEMENTS.**
Medical arrangements will be notified direct by the A.D.M.S., 40th Division.

2nd August, 1918.

(WB).

Major,
D. A. Q. M. G.,
40th Division.

Distribution :- All Units and Branches, 40th Divn.
29th Division
31st Division.

11th Cam. Hts.

For information

2/8/18.

S E C R E T.

40th Division No. 844 (Q).

Reference 40th Division No. 844 (Q) of 18th July, 1918.

Increase forthwith by 50 % dumps mentioned in para. 3 (c) and (d) to feed "D" and "F" Machine Gun Battalions in case of necessity arising for 40th Division to man the West HAZEBROUCK Line.

Major,
D. A. Q. M. G.,
40th Division.

29th July, 1918.
(WB).

Distribution :-   All Units 40th Division.
                  All Branches 40th Divisional Hd.Qrs.

11th Bn Cam. Highrs.

For information.

This ammunition has been indented for, and instructions will be issued when it can be drawn.

120/454

J W Swanson 2/Lieut
o/Staff Captain
130th Inf. Bde.

30/7/1918

SECRET.

XV Corps.

Second Army No. G.216.
XV Corps No. 143/32 G.
40th Division No. 137/1 G.

*   *   *   *   *   *

3. WHITE PANELS.

It has been suggested that a suitable supplementary signal from Infantry to Aircraft would be a WHITE panel formed of WHITE American cloth with a Khaki back; this could be attached to the front of the box respirator as worn in the "Alert" position.

When not in use, the panel could be folded in two and buttoned up.

Experiments should be carried out to test the practicability of this suggestion, and reports submitted before authority to purchase large quantities of White American cloth is obtained.

(sgd) W. ROBERTSON, Colonel,
for M.G., G.S.
Second Army.

21-7-18.

120th Inf. Bde. No. 120/401.   - 2 -

10th Bn. K.O.Y.L.I.
15th Bn. H.L.I.
11th Bn. Cam. Highrs. ✓

Report on the advisability of introducing WHITE panels of American cloth should reach Brigade Headquarters by 1st D.R. to-morrow, 24th July, 1918.

23-7-18.

W. ...... MAJOR,
120TH INFANTRY BRIGADE.

HEADQUARTERS,
120TH
INFANTRY BRIGADE.
No. ....
Date ....

S 67

SECRET.
Second Army G. 990/
13th July, 1918.

XV Corps.

A case occurred recently in Third Army Area of gas being introduced into a dugout under construction by sandbags.

The area round the dugout had been subjected to a two hours gas bombardment six hours previously, but owing to the direction of the wind, no gas had come near the dugout itself. The dump of sandbags was however in the shelled area, and investigation established that the gas had been brought into the dugouts by the sandbags, some of which were found to still retain gas.

(sgd) J. HOBART. Major,

for Major-General,
General Staff, Second Army.

- 2 -

XV Corps No. 599/22 G.
15th July, 1918.

1st Australian Division.
9th Division.
29th Division.
31st Division.
40th Division.
G.O.C., R.A.
C.E., XV Corps.

For information.

Brigadier-General,
General Staff.

XV Corps.
15/7/1918.

Copies to :- "Q".   D.D.M.S.
A.D.A.S.   Chemical Adviser.
XV Corps Cyclist Battn.

HEADQUARTERS,
120TH
INFANTRY BRIGADE.
No. 120/418
Date........

For information

CAPTAIN,
BRIGADE MAJOR,
120TH INFANTRY BRIGADE.

17/7/18.

S.95.

SECRET.   XV Corps No. 656/15 G.

40th Division.
==*=*=*=*

    There have recently been several cases in the Second Army Area of men crowding round aeroplanes which have fallen to the ground, and removing fittings and parts as souvenirs.

    It is the duty of the unit nearest the spot where an aeroplane (hostile or friendly) has fallen to provide a guard and to prevent any unauthorized interference with the aeroplane.

                    sd. D.J. CORRIGALL,   Major
                         for Brigadier-General,
8-8-18.   General Staff.

2.
                              40th Div. No. 21/6 G.

119th Inf. Bde.	C.R.E.,	Div. Train.	Camp Cdt.
120th Inf. Bde.	A.D.M.S.	Div. M.T. Coy.	A.P.M.
121st Inf. Bde.	D.A.D.V.S.	Div. Sig. Coy.	"Q".
17th (F) Worc. Rgt.	D.A.D.O.S.	Div. Empl. Coy.	

==*=*=*=*=*=*=*=*=*=*

For information and necessary action.

                              for Lieut-Colonel,
9-8-18.   General Staff, 40th Division.

-3-

O.

120th Inf. Bde. No. 120/401.

10th Bn. K.O.S.B.
15th Bn. K.O.Y.L.I.
11th Bn. Cam. Highrs.
120th T. M. Battery

For information and necessary action.

                              Captain,
                            Brigade Major,
10-8-18.   120th Infantry Brigade.

S 99

CONFIDENTIAL.

Hd.Qrs.40th Divn.No. 169(Q).
Q.M.G.No. 10049. (Q.C.2).
Second Army No. Q.C./959.
XV Corps No. Q.C. 7/22.

Second Army.

It is possible that British Troops arriving from other theatres of War may be in possession of pistol ammunition with flat nosed bullets. This ammunition must not be carried, and steps should be taken to ensure that any that may be in possession of troops is collected and sent to the Base, where it will be destroyed.

G.H.Q.
12th May, 1918.

(sgd). C.W. Scott, B.G.,
for Quartermaster General.

(2).

XV Corps.

It has been ascertained that certain R.A. Details that left Egypt for France on 3rd or 4th July, had flat nosed bulletted pistol ammunition in their possession. Your attention is directed to the instructions contained in Q.M.G. No. 10049 (Q.C.2) of 12th May, 1918, forwarded under this office No. QC/959 dated 13th May, 1918.

7.8.18. (sgd). R.S.Matcher, Major for M.Gen.
D.A. & Q.M.G. Second Army.

(3).

For information and action if necessary.

10th August, 1918.

Major,
D.A.Q.M.G.,
40th Division.

(4)

11th Batn. Hrs

For information and action if necessary.

T. Knox-Shaw
CAPT.,

11.8.1918.

SECRET.　　　　　　　　　　　　　Second Army No. G.709.
　　　　　　　　　　　　　　　　　XV Corps No.656/10 G.

Second Army.
─────────

　　It is notified for information that the white ring of the National Markings on British Night Flying Machines (Handley Pages, F.E.2 b's and Night Flying Camels) will be eliminated leaving only red and blue rings.

　　The conversion of markings will be gradual and existing markings may remain in use until the 15th August, 1918.

　　These machines may fly by day as well as by night. Special care should be taken, therefore, to ensure that all units are notified accordingly.

　　　　　　　　　　　　　sd. M.C. NAPIER, Colonel,
　　　　　　　　　　　　　　　　for Lieut-General,
　　　　　　　　　　　　　　　　Chief of the General Staff.

G.H.Q.

8-8-18.

　　　　　　　　　　　　　2.

　　　　　　　　　　　　　　　　　　40th Div. No. 21/7 G.

119th Inf. Bde.　　C.R.E.,　　　Div. Train.　　　Camp Cdt.
120th Inf. Bde.　　A.D.M.S.　　　Div. M.T. Coy.　　A.P.M.
121st Inf. Bde.　　D.A.D.V.S.　　Div. Sig. Coy.　　"Q".
17th (P) Worc. Rgt.　D.A.D.O.S.　　Div. Empl. Coy.

　　　　　　　　　　==*=*=*=*=*=*=*

　　　　　For information and communication to all concerned.

　　　　　　　　　　　　　　　I.H. Stafford
　　　　　　　　　　　　　　　　Major. G.S.
　　　　　　　　　　　　　　　for. Lieut-Colonel,
　　　　　　　　　　　　　　　General Staff, 40th Division.

11-8-18.

To
OC A Coy
B Coy
C Coy
D Coy
2Lt [?]

CONFIDENTIAL.   H.Q., 40TH DIVISION No. M...

1. It has been brought to the notice of the Divisional Commander by higher authority that much information is still being conveyed to the enemy by his agents in the area of the British Armies in France owing to the indiscriminate conversations of Officers and men about operations and movements of troops.

2. Two definite instances are quoted for example.

(a) A Division in the back area was ordered to the line. The owner of the house where one of the Divisional Headquarters Mess was situated was told of the move by an Officer's Mess waiter. The next day having occasion to visit BOULOGNE the landlady informed several friends with the result that the move of this particular Division from rest to the line was probably known by enemy agents within 24 hours after its being ordered.

(b) Most of the large number of Officers who visit the "Cafe Panorama" next door to the Casino at CASSEL are heard to talk of operations and movements in a most free manner.

3. Everything possible is to be done to impress on every Officer and man the necessity of keeping silent and of the danger and iniquity of talking in such a manner as to convey information to the enemy.

4. It is to be understood clearly by everyone that the leakage of information if traced to an individual officer or man will lead to his trial by Court Martial and that by some unguarded utterance the lives of comrades may be endangered.

5. The following Divnl. Routine Order is being published tomorrow :-

"LEAKAGE OF INFORMATION.

IT IS FORBIDDEN, EXCEPT IN THE COURSE OF DUTY, TO DISCUSS OR REFER TO ANY MOVEMENT OF TROOPS, OR TO THE SITUATION OF ANY BODY OF TROOPS, OR TO OPERATIONS OF ANY KIND WHATSOEVER.

WHERE EVIDENCE IS FORTHCOMING THAT ANY OFFICER, WARRANT OFFICER, NON-COMMISSIONED OFFICER OR PRIVATE SOLDIER HAS DISOBEYED THIS ORDER, HE WILL BE TRIED BY COURT-MARTIAL.

This order is to be repeated in Unit Orders on three consecutive days and is to be read out on three consecutive parades."

6. Apart from the observance of the last lines of the Order the Divnl. Commander requires a certificate to be rendered to Divnl. Hd.Qrs. by the last D.R. on Thursday, 15th August, 1918, by all units to the effect that every Officer present with the unit has been informed of the purport of this letter.

6. He also wishes the subject dealt with in the ordinary lectures given during training and special steps taken to inform the most likely offenders. In this connection clerks, officers' servants, mess men, etc., are not to be overlooked.

7. Arrangements are to be made whereby Officer and Other Rank reinforcements are warned and instructed in this matter immediately after their arrival with their Unit.

A. L. Cowtan.
Major,
D.A.A.G., 40th Division.

H.Q., 40th Division.
12th August, 1918.

Distribution:- All Units, 40th Division.
All Branches, 40th Divnl. Hd.Qrs.

Appendix III.

ANTI-GAS INSTRUCTIONS.

In the event of:-

A. **HEAVY GAS SHELLING OR GAS PROJECTOR SHOOTS.**

(1) Warning will be conveyed by :-

(a) Signal communications.
(b) sound signals - rattles
  gongs
  shouting ' Gas Shelling'
  after adjusting the
  Small Box Respirator,

BUT NOT STROMBOS HORNS.

(2) The telegram indicating heavy gas shelling or a projector shoot consists of the words "POISON HEAVY" (followed by the Battalion Sector or map square).

(3) The procedure for dealing with this message is the same as for the GAS message, except that it does not go higher than Divisional Headquarters and the D.G.O., unless the Gas Shelling is in a back area. In any case, the Divisional Signal Office will obtain the instructions of the General Staff before forwarding it higher, or to flank Divisions.

(4) The procedure for warning units occupying areas is also as above.

(5) The Signal on Rattles and Gongs will be taken up by similar instruments, but will NOT be taken up by Strombos Horns.

In the event of

B. **LIGHT GAS SHELLING.**

(1) Warning will be conveyed by :-
(a) signal communications.
(b) sound signals - rattles
  gongs
  shouting, as above,

BUT NOT STROMBOS HORNS.

(2) The telegram indicating Light Gas Shelling consists of the words "POISON LIGHT (followed by the Battalion Sector or map square)".

(3) The procedure for dealing with this message is the same as for the GAS message, except that it does not go higher than Infantry or Artillery Brigade Headquarters, unless the Gas Shelling is in rear of the line of Brigade Headquarters. In any case the Brigade Signal Office will obtain the instructions of the Brigade Staff before forwarding it higher.

(4) The procedure for warning units occupying areas is also as above.

(5) The Signal on Rattles and Gongs will be taken up by similar instruments, but NOT by Strombos Horns.

The expression "POISON" alone, or "POISON SHELL", is not to be used.

(e) As soon as possible after sending the S.O.S., the officer who originated the call will inform his Battalion Commander of the situation.

7. REPEAT S.O.S. SIGNAL.
If any part of the front which is attacked is covered by a machine gun barrage, the S.O.S. signal should be repeated at 10 minutes interval if the continuation of the S.O.S. beyond that time is required. This should be done even if information has been passed to the Brigade that a prolongation of fire is desired, as it is difficult to pass this information on to individual machine guns.

8. TEST S.O.S. CALLS.
Frequent tests of the S.O.S. arrangements will be made. The procedure is exactly the same as for an actual S.O.S., except that the word "TEST" will be substituted for "S.O.S." in the message.
Artillery procedure is also the same, except that one round per Battery only will be fired.
Any Company Commander may make one "TEST" during his tour of duty in the line. He will note the following points and report them to his Battalion Commander by whom they will be transmitted through Infantry Brigade Hd.Qrs. to H.Q. Div. Artillery.
 (a) Time of delivery of message to signaller.
 (b) Time of transmission.
 (c) Time of round fired by Battery.
 (d) Result of fire.
The Battery should normally fire at once, as for an actual S.O.S., but is permitted to delay if another target is being engaged, or if hostile planes or balloons are observing. In the latter case, instead of firing one round the Battery will reply by a message " PLANE (followed by Section to which TEST referred)".
The Battalion Commander will enquire from the Battery Commander as to the cause of any delay or badly laid rounds.
No Tests will be made with light signals or Strombos horns.

9. Instructions as to sending S.O.S. and "TEST" calls will be hung in every Signal Office in the line.

10. CANCELLATION OF S.O.S.
When fire is no longer required, the message "CANCEL S.O.S." will be sent immediately. This message is distributed in the same way as the S.O.S. call.

--*-*-*-*-*-*-*-*-*

S 113

SECRET.   40th Division No. S/142/Q.

ADMINISTRATIVE ARRANGEMENTS - 40TH DIVISION in connection
with XV CORPS DEFENCE SCHEME - ADMINISTRATIVE
ARRANGEMENTS.

With reference to para.1 of above Instructions forwarded under this office No. S/142/Q dated 22/7/18.

DISPOSAL OF SURPLUS TRANSPORT.

The following will be the composition of the two Echelons therein stated and transport of Brigades and Pioneer Battalion will be divided accordingly on orders being issued from this office.

Echelon 'B'

    Baggage Wagons.
    Officers' Mess Carts.

Note: Mess Carts can be sent forward from time to time if found necessary.

Echelon 'A'.

    Remainder of 1st Line Transport.

                            Major,
                      D.A.Q.M.G., 40th Division.

5th August, 1918.

(JM)

Distribution :-
    To all Units and Branches of
    40th Division.

OC 11 Cameron Highrs

Forwarded

T Kruse Shaw Capt
Staff Captain 120 Inf Bde

14.8.18

0137/5232 (M.S.3). XV Corps No. A.G.6618/21.
40th Division No. G/18/A.

War Office,
Whitehall,
LONDON, S.W.1.

1st August, 1918.

Sir,
    I am commanded by the Army Council to inform you that it has been decided that subsequent to this date the DISTINGUISHED SERVICE ORDER, the MILITARY CROSS and the DISTINGUISHED CONDUCT MEDAL shall be regarded as distinctions to be awarded for "Services in action" only.

2.   The definition of the term "Services in action" shall be held to mean:-
    (i)   Services under fire.

    (ii)   Distinguished individual services in connection with air raids, bombardments, or other enemy action which at the time produces conditions equivalent to services in actual combat, and demands the same personal elements of command, initiative or control on the part of individuals and, in a lesser degree only possibly, entails the same risks.

3.   In no circumstances will any exception be permissible, and recommendations must clearly show that the above conditions are fulfilled.

4.   It is recognised by the Army Council that the order of the British Empire will be in future the usual form of award for "Other services" except where Brevet promotion is deserved and it is in the interests of the Service that such promotion should be made.

5.   You will in due course be informed as to the facility in the matter of recommendations for the Order of the British Empire which are to be placed at your disposal, in order that you may be in a position to meet all necessary requirements in the matter of recommendations for reward.

                        I, am sir,
                        Your Obedient Servant,
                        (Sd) R.H. BRADE.

The Field Marshal,
    Commanding-in-Chief,
        British Armies in France.

- 2 -

For information and guidance.

14th August, 1918.
                                    Major,
(WB).   D.A.A.G.,
                                    40th Division.

For information and guidance.

14.8.1918.

Secret

40th Division No. 169 (Q).

1. The following S.A.A. is dumped in 'B' Line in Locations as given :-

Location.	No. of boxes S.A.A. dumped	Location.	No. of boxes S.A.A. dumped.
1. D.27.d.5.7.	5.	18. D.18.c.00.65.	10.
2. D.27.d.7.8.	5.	19. D.18.c.1.9.	5.
3. D.27.d.70.98.	10.	20. D.18.a.25.10.	10.
4. D.28.a.15.35.	5.	21. D.18.a.72.	16.
5. D.28.a.50.50.	5.	22. D.18.a.6.8.	10.
6. D.28.a.85.80.	9.	23. D.12.c.75.20.	5.
7. D.22.d.0.0.	6.	24. D.12.d.2.7.	10.
8. D.22.d.55.65.	10.	D.12.d.3.6.	5.
9. D.22.d.95.95.	5.	25. D.12.b.5.3.	5.
10. D.23.a.05.10.	5.	26. E.7.a.2.7.	10.
11. D.23.a.25.25.	10.	27. E.1.c.	10.
12. D.23.a.50.30.	5.	28. E.1.c.	10.
13. D.23.b.0.6.	10.	29. E.1.d.	5.
14. D.23.b.25.65.	5.	30. E.1.d.	10.
15. D.23.b.40.75.	10.	31. E.1.d.	5.
D.23.b.40.90.	10.	32. E.1.d.	5.
16. D.17.d.75.10.	5.	33. E.1.d.	10.
17. D.17.d.90.40.	5.	34. E.2.a.	10.

2. The following dumps also exist :-

Location.	No. of boxes S.A.A. dumped.	Location	No. of boxes S.A.A. dumped.
House at D.46.b.8.5.	32 boxes.	Cross Roads, D.11a.5.4.	31 boxes.
AU SOUVERAIN, D.11.b.2.2.	30 "	Railway Crossing D.20.d.0.5.	20 "

NOTE. The above dumps are controlled by Officer i/c Divnl. Bomb Store.

Major,
D.A.Q.M.G., 40th Division.

23/8/18.
(JM).

Distribution:-
All Units 40th Division
Officer i/c Divnl. Bomb Store.

OC 11 Camerons

Forwarded

24.8.18

S 137.

XV Corps Q.C. 550/12

....

WINTER ACCOMMODATION.

Before the Winter Scheme for hutting is finally put into operation, it is necessary to ensure that full use is being made of present accommodation. Some units, particularly small units with two or three officers and less than 100 men, are rather apt to spread themselves, at the expense of the larger units moving to and from the line.

In the first place, it is necessary to make full use of available billets in factories, houses and barns, especially in the evacuated area, where it is not desirable to erect too many huts. Where stone or mud floors exist, wire beds can be installed, and material for repairs to windows, floors or walls can also be supplied.

Huts for N.C.O.s and men's messes and recreation rooms should not be sanctioned until sleeping accommodation is fully provided. These will be specially arranged for by Corps as soon as material is available.

As a general rule, the approximate floor space required for sleeping, messes, etc. is as follows:-

Class of Accomdn.	Personnel.	Scale of floor space per Individual Sq.ft.	Remarks.
Sleeping.	Field Officer	100	
	Junior "	72	
	Warrant "	72	
	N.C.Os & men.	21	
Accessories.	Officers' Mess	45)	Inc. area of
	Sergts. Mess.	15)	kitchen.
Offices	Orderly Room.	1 sq.ft. per	
Q.M. Stores,	& Q.M. Stores.	total strength.	
Technical Offices.		Special as necessary.	

EXAMPLES:-

1 Nissen Hut, 27' x 16'.

Sleeping.	4 Field Officers in Cubicles.
	6 Junior Officers or W.Os.
	20 N.C.Os and men.
Accessories.	Mess for 10 officers.
	Mess for 20 Sergeants.
Offices.	Orderly Room & Office for Battalion.
	Orderly Room, Office & Q.M. Store for Field Co.R.E.
Sleeping and Mess	3 Junior Officers.

Where the height of a hut permits and in houses, etc. great economy of floor space can be obtained by installing two or three tiers of wire beds. (This is not possible in the Nissen type of Hut.)

/Area Commandants.

2.

Area Commandants will immediately visit the various units in their areas and make sure that units are not exceeding their actual requirements, and will report to this office any unit (and location) which can dispense with accommodation. Arrangements will then be made to reallot it, or to move the huts to a more convenient position.

Separate instructions will be issued for Field Ambulances, etc.

20/8/18.
HL.

W.T.C. Hurtam, Major,
D.A.Q.M.G., XV Corps.

DISTRIBUTION — O.R.O.

H.Qrs., 40th Division No. C/136/Q.

For information and guidance.

23rd August, 1918.
(WB).

C.T. Moores
Lt-Colonel,
A. A. & Q. M. G.,
40th Division.

O.C. Cameron High
For information
[signature]
for Staff Captain
120 Infantry Brigade

SECRET.   XV Corps No. 89/I?C. G.,

XV Corps ANTI-GAS INSTRUCTIONS.

1. **STANDING ORDERS.**

   Standing Orders for Defence against Gas are contained in Appendix IV. S.S. 534, dated March, 1918.

2. **GAS ZONES.** (S.S. 534, Appendix IV, Paragraph 1.)

   (a) The rear boundaries of the ALERT and READY Zones are as follows :-

   ALERT ZONE:-
   LA MOTTE - PETIT SEC BOIS - PRADELLES - ROUGE CROIX - THIEUSHOUK (all inclusive).

   (Steel helmets will be worn by all ranks East of this lin

   READY ZONE:-
   OXELAERE - THIENNES Road to Road junction U.5.a. - East of ST. MARIE CAPPEL.

   (b) Divisions in the forward area will be responsible, within their respective areas, for the erection and maintenance of the necessary Notice Boards on all roads to mark the limits of the ALERT Zone.
   The C. E., XV Corps will arrange for the erection and maintenance of Notice Boards to mark on all roads the limits of the READY Zone.

   (c) Reference S.S. 534, Appendix IV, paragraph 3, Sub-paragraph A (ix) and B (ii).
   In order to ensure that all units pay attention to the direction of the wind, at all Headquarters, and at such other places as Divisional Commanders may direct within the ALERT Zone, Notice Boards will be placed stating when the wind is "DANGEROUS".
   "WIND SAFE" Boards will not be put up, and any already erected will be removed.

3. **GAS SHELL BOMBARDMENT.**

   (a) Attention is called to para. 4 (vi) of S.S. 534, Appendix IV.
   Units occupying positions in Woods, Valleys and Villages, within range of a gas shell bombardment, will be warned of the persistent effect of the gas which is liable to be dangerous even after several days have elapsed.

   (b) Enemy gas shell bombardments should invariably be reported, and it is important that any new gas or projectile should be investigated at once.

   (c) All ranks should be warned that the recognition of gas shell by the degree of detonation is not to be relied upon.

4. **GAS SHELLING AND GAS BOMBING OF BACK AREAS.**

   In view of the fact that the enemy has gas shelled villages up to eight or ten miles behind the line, and that there is a possibility of gas bombs being dropped by hostile aeroplanes, Anti-gas precautions must not be neglected in the back areas.
   A reserve of 28 lbs. of Chloride of Lime will be kept at Area Commandant's Offices and at Labour Group Headquarters.

                                                    5 INSTRUCTIONS

ii.

INSTRUCTIONS FOR WARNING IN EVENT OF HOSTILE CLOUD GAS ATTACK.
(S.S. 534 Appendix IV, paragraph 5).

(a) Divisions are responsible for warning all troops in their areas.
Divisions will also warn the necessary civil authorities in their respective areas to ensure the warning and protection of all civilians in their areas. Arrangements to be made with French Mission.

(b) **WARDRECQUES AND BLARINGHEM AREAS.**

Area Commandants will be responsible for warning all troops in their respective areas. They will also warn the necessary civil authorities responsible for warning all civilians in their areas. Arrangements to be made with French Mission.

(c) **WARNING MESSAGES.**

Reference S.S. 534, Appendix IV, paragraph 5 (iv).
Messages conveying the warning of gas cloud attack will take the form of the letters "G.A.S", followed by the map reference of the trench opposite to which the gas is being liberated and the sheet number of the map reference. If, for any reason, the map reference cannot be given, the name of trench or sector may be sent, but local or unauthorised names of trenches or sectors must not be used.

To minimize delay, messages which are to be telegraphed or sent by Despatch Rider or Orderly, will be kept ready filled in, with the names of the recipients and the letters "G.A.S". The message to be completed before despatch.

(Sd) W.P.Lipscombe, Captain.
for Brigadier-General, General Staff.

XV Corps.
21/7/18.

2. 40th Div.No. 10/86. (G).

119th Inf. Bde.	A.D.M.S.,	D.A.D.V.S.
120th Inf. Bde.	Div. Train.	Div. Gas Officer.
121st Inf. Bde.	Div. R.T.Coy.	Div. Claims Officer.
17th (P) Worc. R.	Div. Employ. Coy.	Sen. Chap. For. D.C.G's Dep.
C.R.E.,	Camp Comdt.	Sen. Chap. For. P.C's Dept.
Div. Signal Coy.	Div. Recept. Camp.	Q.
31st Bn. M.G.C.	D.A.P.M.	French Mission.
104th Bn.M.G.C.	D.A.D.O.S.	

****

For information and guidance.

J.H.Stafford.
Major G.S. for Lieut-Colonel.
General Staff, 40th Division.

26/8/18.

3.

120th Inf. Bde. No. 120/418.
10th K.O.S.B.
15th K.O.Y.L.I.
11th Cameron Hrs.
120th Trench Mortar Bty.
****

Forwarded.

27:8:18.

CAPTAIN,
BRIGADE MAJOR,
120TH INFANTRY BRIGADE.

40th Div. No. 10/51. (G).   SECRET.   5148

119th Inf.Bde.   104/M.G.Bn.   D.A.P.M.   Sen.Ch. D.C.G.D.
120th Inf.Bde.   28th A.F.A.Bde. D.A.D.O.S.   Sen.Ch. P.C.D.
121st Inf.Bde.   A.D.M.S.   D.A.D.V.S.   French Mission.
17th Worc.R.(P)   Div.Train.   Div.Recep.Camp.   Camp Comdt.
C.R.E.   Div.L.T Coy.   Div.Gas Off.   "Q".
Div.Sig.Coy.   Div.Empl.Coy.   Div.Claims Off.

****

1. The "Gas Alert" Zone is again amended, and from this date inclusive will be the area East of the following line :-

    L.5.central - F.12.a.central to S.31.central.

2. Notice boards showing the new boundary will be erected within the divisional area and all notice boards marking the old boundary will be removed.

3. The Corps Commander brings to notice that the orders regarding the carriage of box respirators and wearing of steel helmets are not being observed. It is to be noted that the "Gas Alert" Zone is the area in which steel helmets are to be worn.

4. Brigadiers and other officers commanding will take the necessary steps to ensure that these orders are rigidly enforced at all times.

                                        for Lieut-Colonel.
3/9/18.   General Staff, 40th Division.

120th Inf. Bde. No. 120/418.

10th K.O.S.B.
15th K.O.Y.L.I.
11th Cameron Hrs.
120th T.M. Bty.

For information and necessary action.

Captain,
Brigade Major,
120th Infantry Brigade.

4:9:18.

40th Div. No. 10/54. (S).   S E C R E T.

119th Inf. Bde.	104th M.G.Bn.	Div.Emplt.Co.	Div.Claims Off.
120th Inf. Bde.	66th Div. Arty.	D.A.P.M.	Sen.Ch.D.C.G.D.
121st Inf. Bde.	28th A.F.A.Bde.	D.A.D.O.S.	Sen.Ch.P.C.D.
17th Worc.R.(P)	A.D.M.S.	D.A.D.V.S.	Camp Commdt.
C.R.E.	Div.Train.	Div.Rec.Camp.	French Mission.
Div. Signal Co.	Div.M.T.Coy.	Div.Gas Off.	"Q".

****

ANTI-GAS INSTRUCTIONS.

The rear boundaries of the ALERT and READY ZONES in the Corps area are now as follows :-

ALERT ZONE.   Along road running N.E. in G.9.a. - Cross Roads G.3.b.8.5 - thence Northwards along road (exclusive) to G.10.central - LA CRECHE (inclusive) - CRUCIFIX CORNER (S. 18.b).

READY ZONE.   VERTE RUE - VIEUX BERQUIN - MERRIS - METEREN (all inclusive) - ST JANS CAPPEL (exclusive).

J.H. Stafford.
Major G.S.
for Lieut-Colonel.
General Staff, 40th Division.

8/9/18.

120th Inf. Bde. No. 190/418 II

11th Cameron H{\i}s.

For information

HEADQUARTERS,
120TH
INFANTRY BRIGADE.

9/9/18.

CAPTAIN,
BRIGADE MAJOR,
120th INFANTRY BRIGADE

SECRET.   XV Corps No. 89/141 G. 21-9-18.

AMENDMENTS TO XV CORPS ANTI-GAS INSTRUCTIONS

Paragraph 3 is cancelled and the following substituted :-

3. **GAS SHELL BOMBARDMENTS.**

(1) Attention is called to paragraph 4 (vi) of S.S. 534, (Appendix IV).

Gas casualties are frequently caused by neglect of proper precautions being taken after a gas shell bombardment. Mustard Gas will persist for long periods after a bombardment, and respirators must be worn and protective clothing and gloves put on where available, by all troops in the affected area, as long as the smell of gas, no matter how faint, can be detected.

(2) As the persistency of the mustard Gas may extend under suitable conditions over several days, units in the forward area will select alternative positions to which, in the event of a gas bombardment, they can move if the tactical situation permits.

The exchange of positions, either to the alternative or back to the original position, should not be made until a Gas N.C.O. has reported the area which is to be occupied is free from gas.

(3) Enemy gas bombardments should invariably be reported, and it is important that any new gas or projectile should be investigated at once.

(4) All ranks should be warned that the recognition of gas shell by the degree of detonation is not to be relied upon.

```
                    sd. W.P. LIPSCOMB,    Captain
XV Corps,                    for Brigadier-General,
21-9-18.                         General Staff.
```

2.

40th Div. No. 10/67 G.

119th Inf. Bde.	66th D.A.	D.A.D.V.S.,
120th Infan. Bde.	A.D.M.S.,	Div. Gas Officer.
121st Inf. Bde.	Div. Train.	Div. Claims Officer.
17th (P) Worc. R.	Div. M.T. Coy.	Sen. Chap for D.C.G's D.
C.R.E.,	Div. Empl. Coy.	Sen. Chap. for P.C's D.
Div. Sig. Coy.	Camp Cdt.	French Mission.
30th Bn. M.G.C.	Div. Recept Camp.	"Q".
S.A.A. Sec. D.A.C.	D.A.P.M.,	D.A.D.O.S.,

For information and guidance.

```
                              for Major,
22-9-18.            General Staff, 40th Division.
```

120th Infantry Brigade No. 120/418.

    10th K.O.S.B.
    15th K.O.Y.L.I.
    11th Cameron Hrs.
    120th T. M. Bty.
    ****

For information and guidance.

22:9:18.

**HEADQUARTERS,
120TH
INFANTRY BRIGADE.**

Captain,
Brigade Major,
120th Infantry Brigade.

SECRET. 40th Division No. 23 (A).

1. The situation as regards Reinforcements for the Division, particularly Infantry Reinforcements, is not, at the moment, entirely satisfactory. Hence it becomes more than ever necessary to conserve, as far as possible, Officers and men.

The Divisional Commander looks to Unit Commanders for their whole hearted co-operation in this.

He feels that much can be done in saving Officers and men unnecessary fatigue and exposure; in ensuring that they are well and regularly fed; in taking precautions about drinking water used, etc.

2. In the forward area there is not always sufficient attention paid to the avoidance of unnecessary movement, nor when movement is necessary is cover intelligently made use of.

The necessity of wearing steel helmets and box respirators in the defined zones must be insisted on.

3. All matters of this sort which tend to prevent wastage must receive the attention of all Commanders.

It is appreciated that much has been done already but it is felt that there is still more to do.

A. L. Cowtan.

H.Qrs., 40th Division. Major,
6th September, 1918. D. A. A. G.,
  40th Division.

Distribution :-
  All Units, 40th Division.
  All Branches, 40th Divnl. Headquarters.

Forwarded

SECRET.

XV Corps No. 100/70 G.

All Divisions.

1. The Counter Battery organization exists for the benefit of the Corps as a whole.

All units, Infantry and Artillery, should understand the necessity of sending to the Counter Battery Office, at all times, such information as exists, concerning enemy Artillery fire. All shelling must be reported at its commencement or as soon after as possible. Officers should not wait to see whether it becomes heavy or damaging.

Reports should be made by telephone direct to the Counter Battery Office - not to the Heavy Artillery - in the following form :-

    1. Time of first round.
    2. Area shelled.
    3. Nature of Gun or Howitzer firing.
    4. Rate of fire.
    5. Rough sound bearing of report of gun.
    6. Point from which sound bearing is taken.
    7. Code word HELP if neutralisation is required.
       Code word HARMLESS if hostile shells are doing no damage.

2. All bearings to be Grid bearings.

3. It is important to report always when shelling has ceased.

                      (sgd) H.KNOX.

XV Corps.   Brigadier-General,
13th December, 1917.   General Staff.

- 2 -

XV Corps No. 100/84 G.

1st Australian Division.
51st Division.
29th Division.
G.O.C., R.A.

With reference to the above, which is re-issued, information concerning the enemy artillery is specially desired at the present time. This can best be obtained at the moment by a careful analysis of all shelling reports, and it is therefore of first importance that these should be complete.

Endeavours must be made that no shelling, whether damage is done or not, passes without being reported to the Counter Battery Office.

                      (sgd) H.KNOX.

XV Corps.   Brigadier-General,
19/4/1918.   General Staff.

Copies to :-   1st Australian Divnl. Artillery.
                57th Divisional Artillery.
                34th Divisional Artillery.   XV Corps H.A.
                33rd Divisional Artillery.   S.O., Counter Batteries.

SECRET.

XV Corps No. 100/90 G.
6th September, 1918.

29th Division.
31st Division.
40th Division.

Attention is directed to XV Corps No. 100/70 G. dated 13th December, 1917, and No. 100/84 G. dated 19th April, 1918. (Copies attached).

No doubt largely owing to difficulty of communications under existing conditions very few reports of hostile shelling are at present being forwarded by units to the Counter Battery Office. This absence of information handicaps the efforts of the Counter Battery Staff.

Additional Heavy Artillery is now being brought forward and it is of the utmost importance that shelling reports should be forwarded as regularly as possible.

Every effort should be made to keep the Counter Battery Office fully supplied with information.

H. Knox
Brigadier-General,
General Staff.

XV Corps.
6/9/1918.

Copies to :- G.O.C., R.A.
XV Corps H.A.
S.O. Counter Batteries.
9th Division.
66th Divisional Artillery.

P.T.O.

2.

40th Div. No. 19/38. (G).

119th Infantry Bde.
120th   ,,
121st   ,,
17th Worc. Rgt. (P).
104th Bn. M. G. C.

For information.

Lieut-Colonel.
General Staff, 40th Division.

7/9/18.

S 162

S E C R E T.　　　　　　　　　　　　40th Division No. S/146/Q.

AMENDMENT No. 1
TO　40TH DIVISION ADMINISTRATIVE INSTRUCTION No.1,
DATED 8th SEPTEMBER, 1918.

1. Supply Railhead is "HAZEBROUCK" instead of "STRAZEELE".
2. The Divisional Bomb Store is located at F.23.c.2.3.

J.M. informed Jr.

Major,
D.A.Q.M.G., 40th Division.

10th September, 1918.
(JM) *OC 11th Cam Hrs.*

For information

HEADQUARTERS,
120TH
INFANTRY BRIGADE.

No. ....
Date ....

S E C R E T.   40th Div. No. 10/61 (G).

119th Inf.Bde.	C.R.E.	A.D.M.S.	Div. Emplt. Co.
120th Inf.Bde.	Div.Sig.Co.	D.A.P.M.	Camp Commdt.
121st Inf.Bde.	17th Worc.(P)	D.A.D.O.S.	Div. Gas Off.
66th Div. Arty.	Div.Train.	D.A.D.V.S.	"Q"
39th M.G.Bn.	Div.M.T.Coy.	S.A.A.Sec.	

****

1.   As the result of recent experiments it has been found that Chlorine gas destroys Yellow Cross and its use as an external disinfectant has given very satisfactory results in treating clothing and equipment contaminated with this gas, thus saving 'gas' casualties among men who have not actually been in contact with the gas itself, but who come into contact later with the men who have.
     In an Army on our right many 'gas' casualties have been saved in this way.

2.   A small chlorine gas chamber will therefore be established and maintained at the Advanced Dressing Station, A.24.d.2.1. under arrangements to be made between the A.D.M.S. and 40th Division Gas Officer: all personnel who have been in contact with Yellow Cross gas and are therefore likely to be contaminated with it, will be despatched as soon as possible to the A.D.S. and there passed through the chamber: this treatment should be carried out, if possible, before the men are allowed to congregate in any confined space. A period of 10 minutes in a concentration of about 1:1000 is sufficient.

3.   When their condition permits of it, wounded men who are contaminated, and Yellow Cross gas casualties should also be passed through the chamber.

4.   It has also been found that shell holes and inhabited localities such as dugouts, huts, gun positions, etc. that are contaminated with Yellow Cross Gas can be disinfected by being sprayed with chlorine Gas: 40th Divisional Gas Officer will therefore arrange as soon as possible for the Gas N.C.O's of all units to receive instruction in this and that they are in possession of the necessary equipment to carry out this disinfecting process as soon as possible in any locality which may have become contaminated. The necessary orders ensuring that this be done on all such occasions will be issued by all concerned.

5.   It may possible be found necessary and adviseable to establish additional chlorine gas chambers, as mentioned in para. 2, in the Divisional Area, in which case further instructions will be issued.

                                                                 Major.

                                    General Staff, 40th Division.

18/9/18.

-ii-

120th Inf. Bde. No. 120/418.

10th K.O.S.B.
18th K.O.Y.L.I.
11th Cameron Hrs.
120th T. M. Bty.

For information.

19:9:18.

Captain,
Brigade Major,
120th Infantry Brigade.

S.E.C.R.E.T. Second Army G.T.420,
9th Sept. 1918.

XV Corps.

The gas casualties in the Army during the past month have been unusually high.

In order to combat these excessive casualties the Army Commander wishes Corps Commanders to go thoroughly into this question and to ensure that the responsibilities of the General Staff of formations and of all Commanders for successful anti-gas measures is fully realised.

C.Os should be constantly reminded that they are responsible for casualties occurring in their units which prove to be the result of lack of training in defensive gas measures in accordance with the orders which have been issued on the subject from time to time.

        sd. J. PERCY,
        M.G., G.S., Second Army.

    2.   XV Corps No. 89/137 G.
            11th September, 1918.

40th Division.

Forwarded.

Attention has been drawn frequently to the importance of this subject.

Arrangements will be made to have further 1 day courses for C.Os and Second-in-Command.

The question is, however, largely one of discipline; the strictest gas discipline is always to be enforced.

XV Corps,   sd. H. KNOX, Brigadier-General,
11-9-18.   General Staff.

    3.   40th Div. No. 10/56 G.

119th Inf. Bde.	C.R.E.,	A.D.M.S.,	Div. Train.	D.G.O.
120th Inf. Bde.	Div. Sig. Coy.	D.A.P.M.,	Div. M.T. Coy.	"Q"
121st Inf. Bde.	17th (P) Worc.R.	D.A.D.V.S.,	Div. Empl. Coy.	
C.R.A., 66th Div.	39th Bn. M.G.C.	D.A.D.O.S.,	Camp Cdt.	

==*=*=*=*=*=*=*

The G.O.C., is confident that the most careful attention will be given to this matter by all concerned and the strictest supervision exercised in the anti-gas training of all units, both in the knowledge of all anti-gas precautions and in the care and upkeep of anti-gas equipment. In order to assist formations and units in this connection, the Divisional Gas Officer will make the following arrangements :-

(a) In the case of the Infantry Brigade in rest :
    (i) To inspect all box respirators and anti-gas equipment at least once during the period the Brigade is out.
    (ii) To hold a short refresher course for all Battn and Coy Gas N.C.Os during the period of rest, to ensure their being up to date and efficient in anti-gas measures.

    He will make similar arrangements regarding the resting Company of the 39th M.G.Bn. taking each Coy. in turn as it comes into Reserve.

(b) In the case of other units he will arrange direct with the units concerned, to carry out similar inspections and refresher courses for the Gas N.C.Os so that each unit will receive periodically his assistance and attention.

(c) On the completion of his inspection of each unit, he will render to Div. Hd. Qrs. a report on the state of the anti-gas training and equipment in that unit.

                      Major,
13-9-18.   General Staff, 40th Division.

-iv-

120th Infantry Bde. No. 120/418.

10th K.O.S.B.
15th K.O.Y.L.I.
11th Cameron Hrs.
120th T. M. Bty.
****

For information and action where necessary.

Captain,
Brigade Major,
120th Infantry Brigade.

15:9:18.

120th Inf. Bde. No. 120/400.

10th Bn. K.O.S.B.
15th Bn. K.O.Y.L.I.
11th Bn. Cam. Highrs.

    The attached 40th Division letter No. 485 (A) is forwarded for future guidance.

    The names of candidates will be reported to Brigade Headquarters by 1st D.R. on 18th instant.

    NIL returns required.

                                               Captain,
                                            Staff Captain,
                                120th Infantry Brigade.

16-9-18

40th Division No. 483 (A).

1. In future candidates for commissions will be interviewed by a specially selected Committee consisting of an Infantry Brigadier, a R.F.A. Brigade Commander and a G.S.O. 1st Grade (Division).

2. The president of this Committee will sign form M.T. 393 A on page 3 of that form against the words "Signature of above Officer" in para (IV).

3. (a) The Committee will sit at the XV Corps Troops Reception Camp at D.4.b.7.8. (Sheet 36A) at 10 a.m. on 20th September, 1918.

   (b) You will send to this Committee any candidates for INFANTRY commissions only recommended by you. Efforts are to be made to send as many good N.C.O's as possible.

   (c) Names and Units will be reported to Divisional Headquarters, by 1st D.R. 19th instant.

4. If convenient Units may send their candidates to the Corps Troops Reception Camp on 19th September where they can stay the night and return to their Unit after they have been examined.

5. In any case rations for the time candidates are away from their Unit must be taken.

6. Each candidate will report his arrival at the Corps Troops Reception Camp to the Commandant and will be accompanied by a certificate signed by the Commanding Officer to the effect that he is a "candidate for commission". The Map reference of his final destination will also be stated on the certificate.

   A.F. M.T. 393 A duly completed is to be taken by every candidated

7. Candidates who pass the Committee will return to their Unit and will not proceed home until instructions are issued from this Office.

   No applicant for a commission in the Infantry will be sent to England during October unless he passes this Committee.

8. Candidates who are not eligible for admission to a Cadet School without first doing an attachment in the line will be sent to the Committee and special instructions will be issued as to their ultimate disposal if they pass the Committee.

9. Attention is drawn to the fact that only Category "A" men are eligible for Temporary Commissions in the Infantry.

Major,
D. A. A. G.,
40th Division.

15th September, 1918.

(WB).

Distribution :- C.R.E., 40th Division.
Headquarters,
119th Infantry Brigade.
120th Infantry Brigade.
121st Infantry Brigade.
O.C., 17th Bn. Worcester Regt (P).
O.C., 39th Bn. M.G. Corps.
O.C., 40th Divisional Train A.S.C.
A.D.M.S., 40th Division.
O.C., Divnl. Employment Coy.
"Q" 40th Division.
Commandant, 40th Divl Reception Camp) For information

S 177.

40th Div. No. 10/76 G.

119th Inf. Bde.	66th D.A.	D.A.D.V.S.,
120th Inf. Bde.	A.D.M.S.,	D.A.D.O.S.,
121st Inf. Bde.	Div. Train.	Div. Gas Officer.
17th (P) Worc. R.	Div. M.T. Coy.	Div. Claims Officer.
C.R.E.,	Div. Empl. Coy.	Sen. Chap для D.C.G's Dept.
Div. Sig. Coy.	Camp Cdt.	Sen. Chap. for P.C.'s Dept.
39th Bn M.G.C.,	Div. Receptn Cp.	French Mission.
S.A.A. Sec. D.A.C.	D.A.P.M.	"Q".

****

Reference XV Corps Anti-Gas Instructions forwarded under 40th Div. No. 10/69 G dated 23-9-18.

From noon to-day the boundaries of GAS ZONE will be advanced as follows :-

ALERT ZONE.   River LYS at H.7.b.6.0 along the LYS to JESUS FARM - NIEPPE (excl) Cross Roads B.4.b. WHITE GATES - WULVERGHEM (excl) Cross Roads N.36.b.2.9.

READY ZONE.   Along road running N.E. in G.9.a. - Cross roads G.3.b.8.5. - thence Northwards along road (excl) to A.10.central - LA CRECHE (incl) - CRUCIFIX CORNER (S.18.b.) Northwards to DRANOUTRE (excl)

NOTE.-   The GAS ALERT Line will also be the line in front of which STEEL HELMETS will be worn by all ranks.

3-10-18.

for Lieut-Colonel,
General Staff, 40th Division.

For information & necessary action

CONFIDENTIAL.   O.B.2272.

Second Army.
****

In continuation of G.H.Q. letter NO. O.B/2272 dated 1st August, 1918, approval is also given to the following extensions of leave being given to Brigadier-Generals, General Staff, Deputy Adjutant and Quartermasters General, General Staff Officers 1st Grade Administrative Staff Officers, at the discretion of Army Commanders, for the purpose of visiting the Cambridge Staff School or in the case of General Staff Officers one of the tactical schools -

   (a) One day for a visit to the Cambridge Staff School or a tactical school.

   (b) One additional day's extension when visits are made both to the Staff School and to a tactical school (total 2 days).

2. A Staff Officer, who, under the provisions of para. 1 is desirous of visiting one or both of these Schools and has obtained the authority of the Army Commander, should communicate direct with the Director of Staff Duties, War Office.

3. For these visits railway expenses and railway warrants to and from Cambridge Staff School or a tactical school will be granted, and allowances in accordance with G.R.O. 4346 will be admissible.

4. It is pointed out that the grant of the one day or two days extension of leave, travelling expenses, railway warrants and detention allowance will not be made unless the visit is made on the authority of the Army Commander.

5. One additional day's leave will also be granted on the same terms to Brigade and Battalion Commanders and Artillery Brigade Commanders for the purpose of visiting an Officers' Cadet Battalion or School.
   Officers who have obtained the Army Commander's permission should report in writing to D.S.D. on arrival in England stating the Battalion or School and the date of their proposed visit so that the unit may be informed.

6. In all cases in which additional leave is approved under this letter or under G.H.Q. letter O.B/2272 dated 1st August, 1918, the leave warrant will be marked :-

   "Extended Leave, authority G.H.Q. O.B.2272".

             sd. G.P. DAWNAY, M.G.

           for Lieut-General, C.G.S.

General Headquarters,
29th September, 1918.

S 175.

40th Div. No.160/2 G.

119th Infantry Bde.
120th Infantry Bde.
121st Infantry Bde.
39th Bn M.G.C.
66th D.A.
17th (P) Worc. Rgt.
****

For information and communication to officers concerned.

A copy of G.H.Q. letter O.B/2272 of the 1st August and a List of Schools and Training Battalions at home (2nd Army letter G.T.66 dated 24th August are attached.

[signature]
Capt.
for Lieut-Colonel,
General Staff, 40th Division.

1-10-18.

OC 17th Cam. Hrs.

For information

[signature]

5/10/18.

SECRET.　　　　　　　　　　　　　　　Second Army, G.T. 86.
　　　　　　　　　　　　　　　　　　　24th August, 1918.

XV Corps.
******
　　　With reference to G.H.Q. No. O.B.2272 of the 1st August, para 2 (b), the following is a list of the "Training Centres" at Home which may be regarded as such for the purposes of the above-mentioned letter :-

(a) Infantry Brigades.

```
191 Infantry Brigade, THETFORD              )
192     "         "   HOLT                  ) 64th Div. NORWICH.
193     "         "   TAVERHAM              )

201     "         "   FOXHALL HEATH, IPSWICH )
202     "         "   COLCHESTER.            ) 67th Div. IPSWICH.
214     "         "   COLCHESTER.            )

203     "         "   HERRING FLEET          )
204     "         "   BURY ST. EDMUNDS       ) 68th Div. BUNGAY.
205     "         "   HENHAM PARK (WANGFORD) )

206     "         "   GUISBOROUGH (YORKS)    )
207     "         "   THORESBY (NOTTS)       ) 69th Div. RETFORD.
208     "         "   WELBECK  (NOTTS)       )
```

(b) Training Reserve Brigades.

```
1st Training Reserve Brigade, RUGELEY CAMP, CANNOCK CHASE.
2nd     "        "      "     BROCTON  "      "      "
4th     "        "      "     NORTHAMPTON.
8th     "        "      "     ROLLESTON.
14th    "        "      "     KINMEL PARK, RHYL.
15th    "        "      "     DONEGAL SQUARE, BELFAST (South).
20th    "        "      "     CLIPSTONE.
23rd    "        "      "     ALDERSHOT.
25th    "        "      "     CORK.
27th    "        "      "     LIMERICK.
28th    "        "      "     CLIPSTONE.
```

(c) Special Reserve Brigade.

```
CHATHAM Special Reserve Brigade.
1st DOVER   "      "      "
2nd DOVER   "      "      "
EDINBURGH   "      "      "
FELIXTOWE   "      "      "
HARWICH     "      "      "
IRISH       "      "      "    (LARKHILL, WILTS).
SHEPPEY     "      "      "
SITTING-    "      "      "
BOURNE
```

(d) Territorial Reserve Brigades.

```
EAST ANGLIAN BRIGADE        CROWBOROUGH.
EAST LANCASHIRE    "        SCARBOROUGH.
HIGHLAND           "        EDINBURGH.
HOME COUNTIES      "        TUNBRIDGE WELLS.
1st LONDON         "        BLACKDOWN.
2nd    "           "        CHISELDON CAMP.
3rd    "           "        WIMBLEDON.
LOWLAND            "        DUNFERMLINE.
NORTH MIDLAND      "        ALFORD (LINCS).
NORTHUMBRIAN       "        HORNSEA (YORKS).
SOUTH MIDLAND      "        BLYTH (NORTHUMBERLAND).
WELSH              "        KINMEL PARK, RHYL.
WEST LANCASHIRE    "        OSWESTRY, for WESTWICK PARK, NORTH WALSHAM.
WEST RIDING        "        RUGELEY CAMP, CANNOCK CHASE, for MILTON,
                                                              SUFFOLK
```

　　　　　　　　sd R.D. CROSBY, Capt. for M.G. G.S. Second Army.

O.B./2272.

Second Army.

1. It has been represented by the Home Authorities that it would be of great advantage if Corps and Divisional Commanders, would, while on leave in England, visit the Cambridge Staff School, and, when possible, a recruit training centre. The Field Marshal, Commander-in-Chief, considers that closer touch should be maintained between Commanders in the field and training establishments at Home, and approves of the leave of these Commanders being extended for this purpose at the discretion of Army Commanders.

2. The following extensions of leave may be granted :-

(a) 2 days for a visit to the Cambridge Staff School or to a recruit training centre.

(b) 2 additional days extension when visits are made both to the Staff School and to a recruit training centre (total 4 days)-

3. A Corps or Divisional Commander who is desirous of visiting the training establishment and has obtained the authority of the Army Commander should communicate direct with the Director of Staff Duties, War Office.

4. For these visits railway expenses and railway warrants to and from the Cambridge Staff School or the Recruit Training Centre will be granted, and allowances in accordance with G.R.O. 4346 will be admissible.

5. It is pointed out that the grant of the two days or four days extension of leave, travelling expenses, railway warrants and detention allowance will not be made unless the visit is made on the authority of the Army Commander.

     sd. G. DAWNAY, M.G.
     for Lieut-General,
     C. G. S.

General Headquarters,
1st August 1918.

S 174

S E C R E T.   40th Division No. S/146/A/4.

ADMINISTRATIVE INSTRUCTIONS.

1.   2nd Echelon 40th Divisional Headquarters will move to WINK COTTAGE (36.N.W/A.20.b.23.40) on 2nd October, 1918, under arrangements to be made by the Camp Commandant, 40th Division.

2.   The A.D.M.S. will arrange for LA MOTTE CHATEAU to be taken over and used as a Divisional Rest Station.   LA MOTTE CHATEAU will not be used for any purpose except this.

1st October, 1918.
WB.
      Major,
      D. A. A. G.,
      40th Division.

Distribution :- All Units 40th Divn.
              All Branches of 40th Div.Hd.Qrs.
              Area Commandant, Right Division.
              H.Qrs., XV Corps.

O/C 11th Bn. Cameron Highlanders

For information

T. Vernon Shaw
Captain
Staff Captain,
120th Infantry Bde.

S 178.

40th Div. No.10/77(G).

GAS ZONES.

(To all recipients of 40th Div. No. 10/76(G)
dated 3/10/18.)

Reference XV Corps Anti-Gas Instructions, forwarded under 40th Div. No. 10/69(G) dated 23/9/18, and to amendment thereto forwarded under 40th Div. No. 10/76(G) of this date. -

From midnight 3/4th October the boundary of the ALERT ZONE will be advanced as follows :-

Cross Roads, H.9.b.5.9. - Road and River junction H.4.c. - Northwards along LYS to B.18.central - Northwest along road to B.11.central - T.29.central - WHITE GATES - WULVERGHEM (excl.) - Cross Roads N.36.b.2.9.

NOTE. The GAS ALERT Line will also be the line in front of which steel helmets will be worn by all ranks.

Lieut. Colonel,

3/10/18. General Staff, 40th Division.

****

CAPTAIN
BRIGADE MAJOR,
INFANTRY BRIGADE.

S 201.

SECRET.   1.   O.B./2147.

Second Army.

An increase has recently been noticed in the dissemination of reproductions of orders, messages and complimentary cards, containing information which would be of use to the enemy in compiling our Order of Battle.

Indiscretions in the preparation of programmes of sports and other entertainments are also increasing.

The above are dealt with by G.R.Os 2801, 2211 and 3043.

Such documents, especially when printed copies are issued, inevitably find their way into the enemy's hands, either through his agents or by publication in the public press, or by being found by the Germans on the person of dead or prisoners. It is, therefore, essential that they should contain no information which may be of use to the enemy.

            sd. G.T. DAWNAY, M.G. for Lieut-General,
                    Chief of the General Staff.
General Headquarters,
13-8-18.

================

Second Army.   2.   O.B./2147.

With reference to O.B./2147 of 13-8-18.
Several instances have recently been brought to notice of the issue of documents of a confidential or secret nature, such as War Diaries or Narratives of Operations, which are not marked "Confidential" or "Secret", and in the case of which, since such documents have been intercepted in letters written by soldiers, sufficient precaution does not seem to have been taken to limit the circulation in accordance with King's Regulations.

All documents, the contents of which are of a secret or confidential nature must be so marked, and their circulation must be strictly confined to those persons who are entitled to receive an issue. The marking of a covering letter as confidential or secret is not sufficient.

If it is desired to issue narratives of operations for the general information of men who have taken part in such operations, these documents must be carefully revised and all secret details excluded, in order that the document may be rendered valueless to the enemy in the event of capture.

            sd. G.T. DAWNAY, M.G. for Lieut-General,
General Headquarters,   Chief of the General Staff.
14-10-18.
================
                       3.   40th Div. No. 215 G.
119th Inf. Bde.   C.R.A.,
120th Inf. Bde.   39th Bn. M.G.C.,
121st Inf. Bde.   C.R.E.,
17th (P) Worc. Rgt. "Q".
================
        For your information and future guidance.

                                    Lieut-Colonel,
                            General Staff, 40th Division.
23-10-18.

S E C R E T.   H.Q., 40th Division No. S/146/Q/6.

40TH DIVISION.

ADMINISTRATIVE INSTRUCTIONS, No. 6.

1. SUPPLIES.

    Supply Railhead - ARMENTIERES, from 21st October, 1918, inclusive.

2. RAILWAY TIME TABLE.

    With reference to Time Table issued under this office No. 815(Q) dated 23rd September, 1918, and subsequent amendments.
    Busses or lorries are not available to carry personnel from ST.OMER to STEENWERCK and HAZEBROUCK. Arrangements have been made whereby personnel - both Officers and men - can obtain accommodation in ST.OMER overnight, on application to O.C. Details, ST.OMER. In the case of other ranks, and Town Major, ST.OMER in the case of Officers. Personnel arriving in ST.OMER in the afternoon will take advantage of these facilities and will report at ST.OMER Station the following day at 12.00. O's C. Schools are arranging for rations to be issued for the following day.

3. D.G.T. LINE.

    The D.G.T. Line was advanced as follows with effect from 00.01 hours on 18th October, 1918 :-

    HOUTHEM (P.20.a.0.4.) thence along Canal to COMINES (V.4.b.3.2.) V.4.d.9.5. thence along road to ST.MARGUERITE, LE GRAND PERNE, QUESNOY, D.10.d.0.0. LA CROIX AU BOIS, LA PREVOTA and PARENCHIES Road to Army boundary. All above inclusive to Transportation.

4. ORDNANCE WORKSHOPS.

    14th Ordnance Mobile Workshops (Light) are now located at Sheet 36/I.1.a.3.4.

5. BATHS.

    A Divisional Bath will be opened at WAMBRECHIES (near the Field Ambulance) on the 23rd October, 1918. Capacity - 80 men per hour.
    Application for use of Baths and supply of clean underclothing will be made to the Divnl. Baths Officer.
    The Baths at STEENWERCK and ERQUINGHEM will be closed down on 24th October, 1918.

H.Q., 40th Division.
21st October, 1918.

Major,
D.A.Q.M.G., 40th Divn.

Distribution :- All Units, 40th Division.
                All Branches, 40th Divnl. Hd.Qrs.

(RSJ)

S 197.

SECRET.
                                        40th Division No. S/136/G/5.

With reference to 40th Division Administrative Instructions
No. 4 dated 6th October, 1918, para 2 (c).

The Main Divisional Bomb Store will be moved to
36/B.27.a.9.5. on 14th October, 1918.

12th October, 1918.
WB.
        Distribution :-
                                        Major
                                        D.A.Q.M.G.,
                                        40th Division.

        All Units and Branches, 40th Division.

O/C
11th Bn Cameron Highlanders

For information.

Vivor Shaw
Captain
Staff Captain
120 Infantry Bde

13/10/18

S 181.

S E C R E T and
U R G E N T.   Hd.Qrs.40th Divn.No. S/145/Q.8.

Reference 40th Divn. 'G' Instructions No.6 dated 5.10.18.

119th Infy.Brigade will be located as follows :-

Brigade Head Qrs.	TOUQUET PARMENTIER.
1 Battalion.	ERQUINGHEM Area.
2 Battalions.	West of the NIEPPE System.

Accommodation in derelict Nissen Hut camps to be utilized to full, supplemented by tentage. The huts in Squares B.19 and B.20 are suggested for one Battalion.

120th Infy.Brigade will vacate Battalion Transport lines near TOUQUET PARMENTIER and move nearer to ERQUINGHEM.

Transport lines of 119th Infy.Brigade will be moved only as necessary to meet locations of Battalions and position of railhead which will be moved from BAILLEUL to STEENWERCK Station shortly.

5th October, 1918.

WB.

Lieut-Colonel,
A. A. & Q. M. G.,
40th Division.

Distribution, all Units and Branches, 40th Divn.

O.C.
1/1th Bn. Cameron Highlanders

For information.

T. Vivian Shaw
Captain
Staff Captain
120 Infantry Bde.

HEADQUARTERS,
120th INFANTRY BRIGADE.
No. ....
Date ....

S E C R E T.

Hd.Qrs.40th Divn.No. S/146/Q/5.

With reference to 40th Division Administrative Instruction No.4 dated 8th October,1918, para.2 (c).

An advanced Divisional Bomb Store will open at 36/B.21.b.3.9. at 12.00 hours on 11th October,1918.

Major,
D.A.Q.M.G.,
40th Division.

Distribution :--

All Units & Branches 40th Division.

O/C
11th Bn. Cameron Highlanders

For information

T. Van Statt
Captain
Staff Captain
120 Infantry Bde

10/10/9

S E C R E T.　　　　　　　H.Q., 40th Division No. S/146/Q/6.

40TH DIVISION.

AMENDMENT No. 1 to ADMINISTRATIVE INSTRUCTIONS No. 6.
　　　　　　　　　　　　　　　　　　　　dated 21/10/1918.

With reference to para. 3, the D.G.T. Line will be as follows from to-day inclusive:-

Along the BASSE DEULE River from the Southern boundary of the Corps to the railway at D.10.c.0.9. - thence along the railway to the COMINES - WERWICQ Road North of the LYS River - thence along this road to the Corps Northern boundary. COMINES - WERWICQ Road inclusive to Transportation.

SALVAGE.

The main Divisional Salvage Dump is now located at 36/E.26.d.6.3.

H.Q., 40th Division.
23rd October, 1918.

　　　　　　　　　　　　　　　　　　　　Major,
　　　　　　　　　　　　　　　　　D.A.Q.M.G., 40th Divn.

Distribution:- All Units, 40th Division.
　　　　　　　　All Branches, 40th Divnl. Hd.Qrs.
(RSJ)

O/C
11th Bn Cameron Highrs

For information.

MMcdren

23/10/18

Lieut
a/Staff Captain
120 Infantry Bde

SECRET.   XV Corps No. I.G.41a/10.

40th Division.
----

1. It is certain that the enemy will have left behind him the means of obtaining the fullest information about our troops, dispositions, strength, intentions, etc.

2. This will be transmitted to him by means of
   (a) Agents, posing as French civilians, passing through our lines.
   (b) Pigeons.
   (c) Telephone or buzzer.
      (i) Conversations by an agent.
      (ii) Intercepts.

3. With very few exceptions, all the civilians in the recaptured territory will do their utmost to assist us and the loyal French inhabitants will be the first to recognise that extreme reticence on our part does not amount to mistrust in our Allies, but rather to our desire to spare them and their homes from further suffering and damage.

4. A number, however, of pseudo French civilians, though not perhaps actually concerned with the transmission of information to the enemy, will be well paid by him for any information they may be able to collect and give to those who are charged with its despatch.

5. The means for preventing information reaching the enemy and thus, possibly, saving many casualties are perfectly clear.
   (a) Great reticence in conversation either with or within hearing of all civilians.
   (b) The detention of all civilians proceeding Eastwards through our lines.
   (c) Immediate detention of all suspicious individuals who may show undue interest in our movements and reporting at once any pigeons flying Eastwards or places from which pigeons are observed to have been released; in the latter case immediate investigation should be made by the observer.
   (d) Avoidance of existing cables and lines until these have been traced out and reported safe for use by the Signal Service. Care in conversation on the telephone and an intelligent recourse to cipher in all signal messages.
   (e) Enquiries as to the bona fides of civilians in whose houses headquarters are established.

                    sd. R.W. BROOKE Major, for Brig-General,

XV Corps "I"
19-10-18.   2.   40th Div. No. 19/69 G.
119th Inf. Bde.   39th Bn. M.G.C., Div. M.T. Coy.   Div. Claims Off.
120th Inf. Bde.   C.R.A.,   Div. Empl. Coy.   S.C. for DCGD.
121st Inf. Bde.   A.D.M.S.   Camp Cdt.   S.C. for PCD.
17th (P) Worc. R. Div. Train.   Div Receptn Cp.   French Missn.
C.R.E.,   D.A.P.M.   D.A.D.O.S.   "Q".
Div. Sig. Coy   D.A.D.V.S.   Div. Gas Officer.

The instructions in the above letter are forwarded for your information and necessary action.

20-10-18.
                                           Lieut-Colonel,
                                    General Staff, 40th Division.

OC
7th Camerons

For information & necessary action

[signature]
CAPTAIN,
BRIGADE MAJOR,
180th INFANTRY BRIGADE.

21/10/18

CONFIDENTIAL.   XV Corps No. A.C. 48/21
                40th Division No. 1004 (A)

40th Division.

The Corps Commander wishes the attention of all ranks should be drawn to the large number of cases of pilfering, looting and robbery, which have recently been on the increase.

1.   Food is being given away or sold by the troops to civilians.

2.   Supply lorries and wagons are looted of their contents, whilst on the road, and whilst standing outside billets or at Railheads.
A C.R.O. has been published forbidding all civilians to be allowed to ride on lorries and wagons but this order is not being observed.
A look out man is to be at the rear of every lorry, and will keep a sharp look out, when their lorries are filled.

3.   As far as possible wagons should move in convoys with a mounted N.C.O. on the lookout.

4.   The theft of horses and mules has become very serious, and every day several are reported as missing. Many ruses are attempted, with more or less success, and most careful precautions are necessary.
Stables should be in self contained billets, as far as is possible, with only one exit. If there is more than one exit, they should be closed at night. Most stables in the area are in factories, and this precaution should be possible. Odd horses, such as Officers' Chargers, Mess Cart Animals, etc., should not be kept in stables by themselves where guards are not posted. Guards should be doubled where necessary, and an Orderly Officer detailed to visit guards during the night.

One ruse to steal animals is to cut mules loose in one part of the stable, and steal horses from a neighbouring stable whilst the guard is trying to round up the mules. As soon as a horse or mule is found to be missing, the O.C. of the Unit should immediately do all he can to trace it, and also detail an Officer to visit the local slaughter houses. The guard will immediately waken the officer on duty, and he should call out extra personnel to patrol the main roads in the district.

5.   O.C., Units are held personally responsible for every possible precaution being taken to put a stop to this pilfering of Government property. Any case reported where it is definitely established that proper precautions were not taken, the O.C. Unit will be held liable for the full cost of the loss.

6.   The theft of motor bicycles and bicycles requires the same care and all ranks must be warned that it is not safe to leave them anywhere except under guard either by day or night.

7.   Motor Cars and R.A.F. Tenders have been stolen. Petrol, spare tyres and motor rugs are taken off lorries and cars whilst they are running or standing; Offers have been made to the drivers to sell Government property. Such cases should be reported at once and the name and address of the culprits noted.

8.   It is recognised that the civilians, who are carrying out these robberies, are careful to avoid detection, but thefts have recently become so prevalent that most stringent precautions are necessary and all ranks should make it a point of duty to try and catch the thieves.

Any case of collusion on the part of British Troops will be dealt with by Court Martial irrespective of the rank or previous conduct of the culprit.

/P.T.O.

- 2 -

9. The Corps Commander would like you to issue such orders as you deem necessary to prevent this present state of things, ensuring that proper precautions are taken to safeguard Government property.

15.1.19.

Sd/ J. Scott, Major,
D.A.A.G., XV Corps.

CONFIDENTIAL

- 2 -

1. Forwarded.

This matter is to receive your careful consideration and every effort is to be made to prevent this large loss of Government property.

2. D.R.O. 2678 dated 13.1.19 orders all Stable Guards to be doubled and for them to be visited twice nightly by an Officer.

D.R.O. 2579 dated 21.12.18 gives particulars of the Bicycle Stands which have been instituted.

An armed guard from the Division takes over the Divisional Pack Train at HAZEBROUCK daily and escorts it to FIVES (the Supply Railhead).

3. Any suggestions for further Divisional arrangements of a precautionary nature which you may wish to make will be appreciated and should be sent in without delay.

A. L. Gorton.
Major,
D.A.A.G., 40th Division.

16th January, 1919.

Distribution :-   All Units 40th Division.
                 All Branches 40th Divnl. Hd.Qrs.

---o---

120th Inf. Bde. No. 120/474/
(JM)
10th Bn. K.O.S.B.   11th Bn. Cam. Highrs.
13th Bn. K.O.Y.L.I.   Brigade O.R.Sergt.

For information.
The Brigadier wishes Commanding Officers to give this their personal attention. An amendment to B.R.O. 533 dated 14-1-19 will be published to-day.

16-1-19.

40th Division No. D/30/A.

CONFIDENTIAL.

1. During the period of Demobilization it is more than ever important for Seniors of all ranks to handle their subordinates with tact, care and justice.

    This doubtless is already fully realised by Commanders, but it is thought to be of such importance that I am directed to draw your particular attention to the matter and to request you to leave nothing undone to prevent the cause or spread of any dissatisfaction or bad feeling.

2. It is well appreciated that the general conduct of the whole Division has been exemplary since the signing of the Armistice.

    To maintain this fine standard of discipline and patient conduct will be the natural desire of all responsible officers and men, therefore, any agitators or disturbers of the peace will be rigourously dealt with.

3. The Divisional Commander wishes this matter brought confidentially to the notice of all Officers and through them to Warrant Officers and Non-Commissioned Officers.

A. S. Corotan.
Major,
D.A.A.G., 40th Division.

13th January, 1919.

Distribution :-   All Units,
                  All Branches 40th Divnl. Hd.Qrs.

(JM) 120th Inf. Bde. No. 120/480/77

10th Bn. K.O.S.B.
15th Bn. K.O.Y.L.I.
11th Bn. Cam. Highrs.

Forwarded.
The modifications suggested by the Brigadier this afternoon should be made to para 3.

Staff Captain,
120th Infantry Brigade.

15-1-19.

S/213

40th Division No. 1001 (A).

CONFIDENTIAL.

1. It has come to notice that some Officer's Messes are holding dances which last until 3 a.m. in the morning or even later.

While being entirely in favour of dances, in moderation, the Divisional Commander does not approve of their lasting until the early hours of the morning and he considers that it should not be necessary for any dances to continue after 12 midnight.

2. It is also observed that in some isolated cases Officers do not exercise much discrimination in the choice of their lady friends with whom they are seen in public.

3. Brigadiers and O's C. Units of Divisional Troops will take such action as they may consider advisable to give effect to the spirit of these observations.

4. It is well realised, as far as this Division is concerned, that up to the present no unpleasant incidents have been recorded but the matter is now brought to notice in the hope of avoiding anything in the future which may mar the fine reputation now existing in the Division.

The Divisional Commander hopes that all Officers will co-operate to this end.

R. S. Corotan.
Major,
D. A. A. G.,
40th Division.

12th January, 1919.
WB.

Distribution :- All Branches 40th Divl. Headquarters.
All Units, 40th Division.

120th Inf. Bde. No 120/474.

10th K.O.S.B.
15th K.O.Y.L.I.
11th Cam. Highrs.

CONFIDENTIAL.

HEADQUARTERS.
120TH
INFANTRY BRIGADE.
No..........
Date..........

For information.

Captain,
Staff Captain,
120th Infantry Brigade.

13/1/19.

S219

[Stamp: HEADQUARTERS 120th INF. BDE. CONFIDENTIAL]

CONFIDENTIAL.

XV Corps No A.C.O 201/18.
40th Division No D /10/A

QD-6/50

    Investigation has proved almost conclusively that a large percentage of "lousiness" reported as occurring in cases of demobilized men, is due to private articles of clothing and necessaries authorised by General Routine Order 5958, being taken home undeloused, and in lousy packs.

    It is realised that the difficulties of arranging for the delousing of these articles in Army Areas is great, but it is pointed out that the time available at Base Ports does not admit of it being done there, and it is of the greatest importance that every possible measure should be taken to delouse packs and their contents before men leave their Unit for Demobilization.

Fifth Army
28th January, 1919.

(Sd) G.H.HICKS. Lieut-Col. GS.
for D.A.Q.M.G.

(ii)

[Stamp: HEADQUARTERS, 120TH INFANTRY BRIGADE. No. 120/480/3 Date........]

For information.

31st January, 1919.

(Sd) Samson
Major.
D.A.Q.M.G. 40th Division.

OC 11 Cam High for information

W.O.Mitcher
CAPT.,
STAFF CAPT., 120TH INF. BDE

31.1.19

To. O/c.
  A. Coy.
  B. Coy.

Will you please read out attached
to the men, then pass it on.
    O/c. D. Coy. will return same,
when finished, please.

                            JCWinson
                              2/Lt
                        for Capt & Adjut.
                          11th Cameroonians

22.1.19.

S 225

S E C R E T.

HEADQUARTERS XV CORPS.   Copy No.

Summary "Q" Branch. (442).
----

826. MOVES. (i) 2 Officers and all available O.R. 29th D.L.I. (14th Division) will move by rail from MOUSCRON to CALAIS, commencing March 1st, to join 2/6th D.L.I., 59th Division.

(ii) All available O.R. 14th A. & S. Hrs., 14th Division, by rail from MOUSCRON to HAVRE, commencing 1st March, to 2nd Battn. A. & S. Hrs., 33rd Division.

(iii) 2 Officers, and all available O.R. 20th Middx. Regt., 14th Division, by rail from MOUSCRON to HAVRE, commencing 2nd March, to 1st Battn. 33rd Division.

(iv) 2 Officers and 175 O.R. 1st & 2nd Bn. R. Innis Fus., 36th Division, by rail to BOULOGNE, commencing 3rd March, to join 7/8th Bn. R. Innis Fus., 30th Division.

(v) 5 Officers and 120 O.R. 23rd Bn. Cheshire Regt., 40th Division, by rail to DUNKIRK, commencing 4th March, to join 1/8th Bn. Ches. Rgt., 30th Division.

(vi) 4 Officers and 200 O.R. 8th Bn. R.I.R., 40th Division, by rail to BOULOGNE, commencing 5th March, to join 7th Bn. R.I.R., 30th Division.

(vii) 5 Officers and all available O.R. 17th Bn. Worc. Rgt., 40th Division, by rail to CHERBOURG, commencing 6th March, to join 1/8th Bn. Worc. Rgt., 61st Division.

(viii) 1 Officer and 40 O.R., together with equipment, Second Army Supply Details, located at LEDEGHEM Supply Depot, by rail as soon as possible to COLOGNE, for HEUMAR.

(ix) No. 53 Labour Company, located at CANTELEU, will move by rail forthwith to BOESINGHE. On completion of move Unit will be administered by Labour Commandant, STEENVOORDE, XIX Corps.

827. INFORMATION. (i) No. 3 O.M.W. (Medium) will carry out all XV Corps work as at present, but will become an Army Workshop from 1st March.

(ii) XV Corps Skin Centre, (136th Field Ambulance) will cease to take in patients after Saturday evening 1st March. All cases of skin complaints will be admitted to No. 11 C.C.S., or in case of COURTRAI Area, to No. 62 C.C.S.

(iii) Brig.-Genl., C.T. PALMER, C.M.G., D.S.O., Commanding 40th Divl. Arty., will temporarily carry out the duties of G.O.C., R.A., XV Corps, vice Brig.-Genl., C.W. COLLINGWOOD, C.M.G., D.S.O., who is reporting to the War Office, and Brig.-Genl., E. HARDING-NEWMAN, C.M.G., D.S.O., Commanding 14th Divl. Arty.,(who carried out the duties previously during Brig.Genl. COLLINGWOOD'S absence) is proceeding on 10 days leave.

(iv) Colonel Lord Hy. SCOTT, Labour Commandant, MENIN, who is proceeding on leave on the 28th inst., and who will be demobilized whilst on leave, will transfer the administration of Labour in the MENIN Area, to Labour Commandant, XV Corps.

(v) The Office of Traffic, ROUBAIX will close at ROUBAIX at 00-01 hours 1st March, and will reopen same hour at 80, Rue des Stations, LILLE.
Telegraphic, Postal and D.R.L.S. address will be :-
"TRAFFIC, FIFTH ARMY."

28/2/19.
ED.

Lieut-Colonel,
A.Q.M.G., XV Corps.

HEADQUARTERS, 120TH INFANTRY BRIGADE.
No. 120/46
Date......

S 221

CONFIDENTIAL.

XV Corps No.A.C. 47/159.

1. The following telegram has been received from the Adjutant General, General Headquarters.

"Leave had to be stopped recently and demobilization retarded owing to misconduct of men at CALAIS in which the leave men who left CALAIS last night to rejoin Units were involved. AAA The conduct of leave men was particularly bad and ringleaders have been arrested and are being tried for mutiny. AAA Requests of leave men were most unreasonable they asked to be returned to England and given ten days extension because trains were not running on Monday night AAA Base Commandant, CALAIS was prepared to enquire into the complaints of a few men who went on leave about 12th inst and have not been demobilized but these men refused to submit their grievances AAA Take steps to bring to notice of units to which these men are returning the misconduct of their men".

2. The men who were concerned in these disturbances are those who arrived at CALAIS on 26th and 27th January and who left CALAIS on night 31st/1st February to rejoin their units and as will be seen the ringleaders have been arrested.

3. It is realised that the above telegram does not give Commanding Officers sufficient information to enable them to take disciplinary action but it is forwarded for communication to all Commanding Officers so that they may realise what has been going on and be in a position to prevent further trouble on the return of the men concerned to their units.

A. L. Cowtan.
Major,
D.A.A.G., XV Corps.

Distribution:- To all recipients of Corps Routine Orders.

Major J. T. Gracie
Comdg
1st Bn Cameron Highrs.

For your information

CAPT.,
STAFF CAPT. 120TH INF. BDE

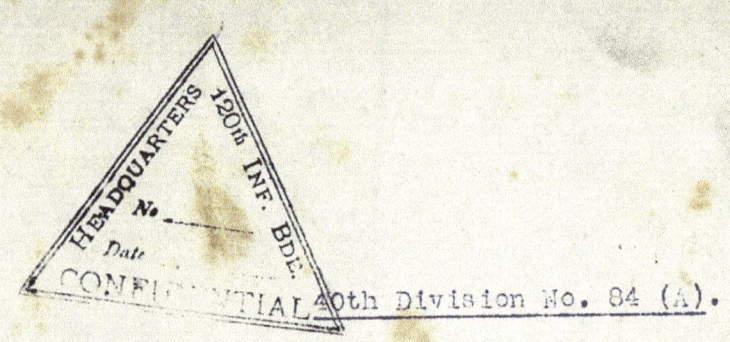

40th Division No. 84 (A).

C O N F I D E N T I A L.

It has been brought to the notice of the Divisional Commander that there is a tendency in the Division to relax some of the essential measures of discipline.

For instance Officers have been seen out walking in the streets with N.C.O's, and there is also a very evident slackness in some Units in regard to saluting.

The G.O.C. wishes this matter brought to the notice of all Commanding Officers with a view to instructions being issued to prevent complaints of this kind in future.

(signed)
Major,
D.A.Q.M.G.,
40th Division.

H.Q., 40th Division.
15th March, 1919.

Distribution :- All Units.

O.C. Cam. High

forwarded

(signed) Fletcher
STAFF CAPT.

18/3/19

All officers

The Commanding Officer recognises that the above does not necessarily apply to this Battalion, but hopes that all officers will do their utmost to maintain

HEADQUARTERS, 120TH INFANTRY BRIGADE.
No. 120/416
Date ....

and improve discipline

B&O Co. KM   [signature] Capt. agent

(asst.
  [illegible]
  H.y
  [illegible]
  G.S.Y.

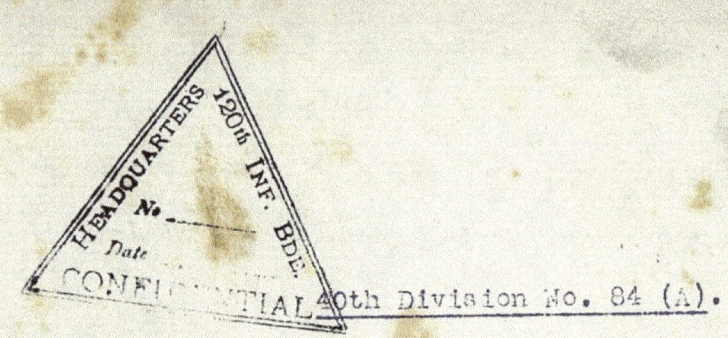

40th Division No. 84 (A).

C O N F I D E N T I A L.

It has been brought to the notice of the Divisional Commander that there is a tendency in the Division to relax some of the essential measures of discipline.

For instance Officers have been seen out walking in the streets with N.C.O's, and there is also a very evident slackness in some Units in regard to saluting.

The G.O.C. wishes this matter brought to the notice of all Commanding Officers with a view to instructions being issued to prevent complaints of this kind in future.

Major,
D.A.Q.M.G.,
40th Division.

H.Q., 40th Division.
15th March, 1919.

Distribution :- All Units.

OC, Camerons

Forwarded

Archer
CAPT
STAFF CAPT. 120

18/3/19
all officers.

The commanding Officer recognises that the above does not necessarily apply to this Battalion, but hopes that all Officers will do their utmost to maintain

HEADQUARTERS,
120TH
INFANTRY BRIGADE.
No. 120/416
Date

SECRET

```
Hd.Qrs.Staff.      Page 1.
Royal Artillery.   Page 2.
Royal Engineers.   Page 2.
119th Inf.Bde.     Pages 2 & 3.
120th Inf.Bde.     Page 3.
121st. Inf.Bde.    Page 4.
Divl.Troops.       Pages 4 & 5.
Attd.Unit.         Page 5.
```

27th January, 1919.

Page 2.

DIVISIONAL ARTILLERY.

Commander.	Brig-Genl.C.E.PALMER,C.M.G., D.S.O.,R.A.
Brigade Major.	Major W.W.Green,D.S.O.,M.C., R.A.
Staff Captain.	Capt.H.J.P.Oakley,M.C.,R.A.
Staff Lieut.	Lieut.W.D.Key,R.F.A.
178th Bde.R.F.A.	Lt-Col.R.M.Horsfield,D.S.O., R.F.A.,(T.F).
Adjutant.	Capt. W.D.Pile.
181st Bde.R.F.A.	Lt-Col.Hon.H.R.Scarlett,D.S.O. R.F.A.
Adjutant.	Capt.L.I.J.Sharkey.
40th Div.Ammn.Col.	Lt-Col.R.R.Stewart,R.F.A.,(T.F).
Adjutant.	Capt.W.G.Meacock.

DIVISIONAL ENGINEERS.

Commander.	Lt-Col.W.R.Wilson,M.C.,R.E.
Adjutant.	Capt.E.Wilburn,R.E.

R.E. UNITS.

224th Field Coy.RE.	Maj.E.L.Martin,M.C.,R.E.
229th Field Coy.RE.	Maj.F.W.Clark,M.C.,R.E.
231st Field Coy.RE.	Maj.J.E.Villa,M.C.,R.E.
40th Div.Sig.Coy.	Maj.G.E.Carpenter,M.C.,R.E.

119TH INFANTRY BRIGADE.

Commander.	Brig-Gen.F.P.Crozier,C.M.G., D.S.O.
Brigade Major.	Capt.A.J.Muirhead,M.C.Oxf.Yeo.
Staff Capt.	Capt.R.W.May,M.C,Welsh Regt.
Bde.Intell.Offr.	2/Lt.A.Peterkin,Sher.For.
Bde.Tpt.Offr.	Capt.C.R.Knowles,Lon.Yeo.

------oOo------

ORDER OF BATTLE.

40TH DIVISIONAL HEADQUARTERS.

Commander.	Maj.-Gen.Sir.W.E.Peyton,K.C.B., K.C.V.O.,D.S.O.
A.D.C.	Capt.J.S.D.Gage,Hants Yeo.
A.D.C. & Camp Commandant.	Capt.G.P.Lempriere, Royal East Kent Yeomanry.
A/Camp Commandant.	Major S.Tabor,M.C., 13th E.Lancs.Regt.
G.S.O. (1).	Lt.-Col.C.H.G.Black,D.S.O., 12th Lancers.
D.A.A.G.	Major A.L.Cowtan,M.C.(detached as Lond.Regt.(T.F) D.A.A.G. XV Corps).
D.A.Q.M.G.	Major S.Dewson,M.C,R.A.
Attd. A & Q.	Lt. B.L.Heighway, R.F.A.
A.D.M.S.	Col.L.Humphry,C.M.G,A.M.S.
D.A.D.M.S.	Major A.C.Jebb,R.A.M.C.
D.A.D.V.S.	Major W.N.Rowston,R.A.V.C.
D.A.P.M.	Capt.C.L.B.Powell,Gen.List.
D.A.D.O.S.	Major H.C.Patrick, R.A.O.C.
Div.Educ.Offr.	Major A.E.S.Curtis.
Div.Claims Offr.	Lieut.J.W.Bowler, The Buffs.
Div.Gas Offr.	Capt. J.Brett,R.E.
Div.Salvage & Burial Offr.	2nd Lt. F.Sherples,M.C., 13th E.Lancs Regt.
S.C.F(DCG's.Dept).	Rev. S.E.R.Fenning,M.C.,C.F.
S.C.F(P.C's.Dept).	Rev.E.Mathias,C.F.
Liaison Officer.	M.le sous Lieut. Desmazes.

-------oOo-------

Page. 4.

121st INFANTRY BRIGADE.

Commander.   Brig.-Gen.G.C.Stubbs,D.S.O.
Brigade Major.   Capt.H.McL.Chapman,M.C.,G.List.
Staff Capt.   Capt.D.B.Warren,Gen.List.
Bde.Intell.Offr. 2/Lt.T.F.Evans,M.C.,North.Fus.
Bde.Trspt.Offr.   Capt.G.Nickalls,Special List.

U N I T S.

8th Bn.R.Irish R. Lt.-Col.T.McCarthy O'Leary.
2nd in Command.   Major C.Cradock.
Adjutant.   Capt.W.J.Correll.

23rd Bn.Lancs.Fus. Lt.-Col.G.Hesketh,D.S.O.
2nd in Command.   Major J.P.M.Ingham,D.S.O.
Adjutant.   Captain J.Brown.

23rd Bn.Cheshire R. Lt.-Col.A.E.Churcher.
2nd in Command.   Major R.E.Druitt.
Adjutant.   Capt.W.A.Garratt,M.C.

121st T.M.Battery. Capt.A.A.H.Jones.

PIONEER BATTALION.

17th Bn.Worc.Reg.(P). Lt-Col.R.W.Becher,D.S.O.
2nd in Command.   Major H.F.Shepperd,M.C.
Adjutant.   Capt.T.K.G.Ridley.

ROYAL ARMY SERVICE CORPS.

40th Divisional Train.

Commander. Lt.-Col.H.McDougall,R.A.S.C.
A/S.S.O.   2/Lt.C.Woodward R.A.S.C.
Adjutant.   Capt.C.F.Flake,O.B.E.,RASC.

40th M.T.Coy. Maj.E.H.Hody,R.A.S.C.

-----oOo-----

Page 3.

UNITS - 119TH INFANTRY BRIGADE.

13th Bn.R.Innis.Fus.	Lt-Col.J.F.Plunkett,D.S.O., M.C.,D.C.M.
2nd in Command.	Major T.C.H.Dickson.
A/Adjutant.	2nd Lt. J.Mann.
13th Bn.E.Lancs.Regt.	Major H.W.D.Cox.
A/2nd in Command.	Major.Hon.V.H.Littleton.
Adjutant.	Capt.E.M.Stafford.
12th Bn.N.Staffs.Regt.	Lt-Col.E.R.O'Connor,M.C.
A/2nd in Command.	Major F.J.Pearson.
Adjutant.	Capt.J.H.Squire.
119th T.M.Battery.	Lieut.H.Morton.

120TH INFANTRY BRIGADE.

Commander.	Brig-Genl.Hon.W.P.Hore-Ruthven,C.M.G.,D.S.O.
A/Brigade Major.	Lieut.J.B.Third,11th Cam.Hdrs.
A/Staff Captain.	Capt.T.W.Rucker.
Bde.Intell.Offr.	Capt.D.McL.Oman,H.L.I.
Bde.Transport Offr.	Capt.L.J.Tritton, Som.Yeomanry.

UNITS.

10th Bn.K.O.S.Bdrs.	Lt-Col.S.Boyle,M.C.
2nd in Command.	Major T.J.Gough,M.C.
A/Adjutant.	Lieut.W.M.Clarke.
15th Bn.K.O.Y.L.I.	Lt-Col.T.W.T.Isaac.
2nd in Command.	Major T.L.Webb.
A/Adjutant.	Capt.J.W.Swanson.
11th Bn.Cameron.Hdrs.	Lt-Col.Hon.O.R.Vivian, M.V.O.,D.S.O.
2nd in Command.	Major J.T.Gracie.
Adjutant.	Capt. J.Neilson.
120th T.M.Battery.	Capt.Sir T.C.Eden,Bart.

-------oOo-------

Page 5.

MEDICAL UNITS.

135th Field Amblce.	Lt-Col.H.Harding.
136th Field Amblce.	Lt-Col.I.R.Hudleston.
137th Field Amblce.	Lt-Col.F.McK.H.McCullagh, D.S.O.,M.C.

VETERINARY UNIT.

51st Mob.Vet.Section.   Capt.S.Hunter,R.A.V.C.

LABOUR CORPS.

237th (Div) Empyt.Coy)   Capt.F.L.Parsons.
& O. 1/c Div.Canteens)

40th DIVL.RECEPTION CAMP.

Commandent.   Major J.Virgo,General List.
Asst.Commandant.   Capt.A.H.Baker,General List.

ATTACHED UNIT.

39TH BN. MACHINE GUN CORPS.

Commander.   Lt-Col.A.Fleetwood Wilson.
2nd in Command. Major A.N.Richardson,M.C.
A/Adjutant.   2nd Lieut.R.E.Burnett.

-------oOo-------